TO BE CONTINUED

Calvin and Elle series
two

November 20, 2016

Elle,

I'm not going to ask for anything. I'm not going to expect anything. I'm not going to label anything.

I cannot allow you to love me and then love you back when I feel like it. Part of me wants to love someone and you are so very lovable.

...but it is toxic. I will protect myself and hurt you over and over. I don't like being that person.

If this means you hate me and I never hear from you again it will hurt and I will feel the great loss that will be. But I know I am no longer being a jerk and hurting you.

I was trying to have everything. I see that now.

It is time for me to be a man and either allow myself to be in love completely and not hold back or stop hurting someone I care very much about by allowing myself to enjoy being in love and I don't know if I am selfish enough that I am enjoying you being in love.

I can't safely let go with one hand or just a few fingers while holding on strongly with the other hand to something else. The fantasy thing makes more sense now in that light. It was my way of holding on.

I am through hurting you. I am going to be a man. I am going to face the consequences, whatever they be of my not allowing myself to love again and be in a complete relationship. It's not about commitments to the future or anyone's plans. It is my heart being that closed door. I wish it was open and you are someone I wish I could let in. But I seem to be hiding inside still and that is selfish and hurting you.

Don't go. Asking is all I deserve to say. I can't justify why I deserve more.

Calvin

*

November 20, 2016

Hello Calvin,

Thank you for being mature about all this and handling the drama so well.

Thank you for trying. I really appreciate it. I feel much better but it's only been a day…

I'll try to wait and not jump to a conclusion yet. Oh, that's not me.

You made me laugh with your lame joke. I've been constantly smiling since I read your message. Thank you.

I just read an article about people with a special connection. I would have sent it to you, but it was in Hungarian. It's mostly bullshit. But there was something in it that I found helpful for me.

It said if two people are connected on a deep level they can lift up, help and teach each other. Their connection doesn't mean that they have to be together. Them being in a love relationship can actually be very dangerous and destructive. Because everything is intensified and their energy level goes way too high. It's very difficult to manage. It really sounds like bullshit. But I have to admit that it gives me a piece of mind and helps me let go.

I just kept being surprised of how similar we think and feel and it all put a huge pressure on me and made me freak out that I will obviously never ever find someone who can get this close to me. And my heart or mind automatically jumped to the conclusion that your happiness is now my responsibility.That's stupid but I guess I watched and read too many romantic stuff. So, what I'm trying to say is… I'm letting you go.

Yesterday night my stomach hurt from my inner pain because I just couldn't let you go. The emotional turning into physical pain just opened my eyes that I'm hurting myself so it's probably a sign that it's the wrong direction. I have to change something. I allowed myself to get lost in the pain. It makes me feel insane but the only thing that relieves me a bit is to scream while muting it with the blanket on my mouth. How did I come to speak about this? This sounds sick. I'm not insane. I understand that I'm not responsible for you. All I can do is to support you and be there, and watch you live whether you decide to die lonely and alone or meet someone. I'm lucky enough to follow your journey and enjoy our connection. It would be easy to be passionate, obsessed and just step in and out when I emptied you, focus on taking not giving. But it's the easy and the hurtful way. I'm so fed up being like that. I would like to give something more steady and safe and pleasant to you, so that you can rely on me and have a focal point and feel loved, but real love, not in a romantic, passionate way.

Even if it sounds like bullshit I somehow feel like you do intensify my already very intense feelings and it's almost impossible to not let them break me. I think if I am not this careful this could destroy me.

Us being us, there is no way to stop the deep stuff coming up again and again. I have something dark to share.

I'm still struggling with my mental health every day. It was always under the surface. I'm the black sheep of the family, the one who got the wrong genes. I can learn to live with it and handle it better and better but I'll never be a "healthy, normal person". People don't understand. They tell me to shake it off, just be happy, enjoy life. It's not something I can just get rid of. If anything these comments just make me feel more like an inadequate person, incapable, defective product. But I learnt to go on with my life even if it feels wrong and I want to not be here sometimes. I allow myself to be sad and listen to sad music and try to keep exercising, eating enough and doing things that make me grow as a person. I just have to keep in mind that it will be over and I will be so happy that my body is still healthy and sexy and that I kept learning things. I'm lucky in a way, because my mood changes are quite quick. One phase only lasts a couple of hours or days, very rarely weeks. So I know from experience that I can power through and there is a reward afterward.

I see the beautiful and am very grateful for having so much real value in my life. But I only put my seat belt on because my daughter needs me. I wasn't very careful with my life before having her. I knew I couldn't actually kill myself, but most of the time I was hoping for a fatal accident to happen. I'm still craving to leave my body behind and become part of the whole universe again. Most of the time I feel like other souls deserve to live more than me, because I can't appreciate and enjoy it as much as they would do.

That being sad, I love who I am. I love that being me is being someone who never gets bored. My life is everything but boring. I experienced so much in such a short amount of time. It's very overwhelming to be me though, very exhausting.

I'd love to use my dark side to create something, something shocking. Something that makes people go "What??? Why???" Just throw in their face something different that doesn't fit in their conception of things. It helps me to see my "sickness/craziness" as a blessing.

I have many plans and ideas but they are not ready in my head yet. Ahhhhhh... I miss the webcam so much. That's a place where I can fully live out my weirdness, just dive into it and let it take control and not be worried about losing the reality and doing something that I might regret later.

I'm so so so holding back all the time, thinking not twice but 12 times before I let words come out of my mouth. Trying to suppress and manage that huge force inside of me. Trying to act responsible and normal all the time. It washes me out. People have no idea how much effort it takes for me to do normal things and have normal conversations. When I'm worried I didn't hide something well, they usually say I seem ok, I seem normal. I speak like someone who is normal, I take care of my daughter well, I'm a good employee, a good wife... And I just can't understand how on earth don't they notice what's happening under the surface? I guess years of practice made me really good at hiding and being good at life. I am considered as good at things I do. But I'm such a mess inside.

I have car anxiety. Every time I get in a car, I'm convinced that, that's it, I will die during this car ride. My body gets all tense, everything hurts, my brain is covered in a fog. I often have to close my eyes, put on headphones with music and tell myself I'm somewhere else. The car accelerating to pass another car stresses me out, it's hell, and it's ridiculous because even if there are no cars coming in front of us, passing another car is horrible for me. But not just that. I'm almost fine when there are no other cars on the road, just checking nervously all the intersections and bikers and peoples to try to foresee who will do something stupid and step in front of the car. But if I see other cars around I'm in a full panic mood. So many things to watch and keep in control and try to foresee which one will go insane and cause an accident. Until recently I never told anyone and just panicked quietly but my brother noticed I'm holding on to the seat like crazy and he was very nice about it. Now I can make fun of myself and warn the driver that I have to close my eyes and phase off because driving as fast as 40 km/h is reckless.

I feel awful. My head wants to explode. This is what happens when I let my dark side come up. It's so powerful, it kills me. I have to go and take back control.

Send,delete?

This is me too, so I will send but try to come up with something more light and fun soon.
This is just my adjustment phase. I don't know why I always feel like sharing my thought process with you. Trying to be transparent, I guessed you would like to know where I am at.

I'm so sorry, I'm rarely like this. Maybe I shouldn't dig so deep. It doesn't seem healthy for me.

Elle

*

November 21, 2016

Elle,

You make me smile.

I am sorry I haven't said that for a while but you do. I am smiling and I feel much the same as you so well described.

But I am me and I am going to talk anyway. If the next short paragraph breaks the rules don't read it. I mean it within the bounds of friends... and I am still interested in sex! Definitely.

So don't read the next paragraph if you feel it might upset you. Then you can read the rest after you skip it.

Read this as an honest friend saying something I felt needed to be said. It wasn't a compliment when I said I held on with one hand tightly and only let go with a couple fingers. I want you to know I did let go with a couple fingers. Thank you for that. What little I was able to give, thank you for allowing me to give and feel. You were not reading things that didn't exist. Ok. That is all I will say about that. Not romantic!

If I was ever on a boat that sank in the ocean I would swim until I physically fainted. I would never give up. I am a winner and I always believe I will fight and will never give up. I would never hurt the people I love by allowing myself to die. I have a purpose here. I have people who love me and I am doing good things. Life is good. I look forward to tomorrow and appreciate how wonderful my life is and I love all the beauty around me and all the senses and love I get to experience. But the fantasy I gave up wasn't you. I lifted the veil and admitted part of me, and I have always known this, but part of me is still where I was. I will never stop enjoying every day. Don't misunderstand this statement. But when I look honestly I know I would be happier if I was dead. I am happy now. I can fantasize about having another marriage that lasts 30 years. But in reality, based on what I believe about heaven and being with my loved ones, I still feel I would be happier if I was dead. I don't like that. I would never stop fighting to live. I am here for a purpose and I am enjoying every day I get the gift of life. Life is good. But part of me doesn't want the life I could build. Part of me pretends that I am a new man and no longer have those feelings. I want to enjoy this life. Life is good. Thank you for giving me someone to admit this to.

Ok, happy thoughts, I totally get what you say. We are fun and funny and joking and sexy and clever people. I think we can get that back. There is nothing wrong with the fact we are both deep and think. I love that you are smart. but we seem to have gotten so serious about emotions we lost part of us.

I was cutting some firewood with my stupid friend. We cut down a tree 50 meters from the road. So we had to drag it to the road so we could chop it up. After 20 meters we realized that we were dragging it by the tree trunk and the top of the tree with all the limbs was catching on everything we drugged it past. So we decided to pull it from the other end. After a while we noticed it was much easier to pull the tree from the limb side and drag the trunk, but we were now 60 meters from the road. That was a joke. Lame but a joke.

If I can't hug you yet, let me send you a smile.

I am still Calvin. I still admire you. I still think you are strong, kind and capable. Still Calvin.

Sexy note... The spot in the creek by the waterfall in this picture is where the little fish are and where I swim naked.

Calvin

*

November 21, 2016

Calvinl!!

I have a French girlfriend!!! I met her in a special context a bit before I started livejasmin. A couple invited us to spend the women's birthday with them. We were one of her "surprise gifts" for the weekend. We pretended to be hitchhikers (the idea of his husband) and got into their car, Stéphanie seemed to be all about her job, a bit cold and distant. She is an amazingly beautiful mom of two kids and she has no idea how beautiful she is. Talking with her was amazing, we were crazy about each other, looking in the eyes and shyly touching the arm quickly, putting a hand on a leg...while drinking champagne. We talked about deep and personal stuff and laughed and without really mentioning sex there was an obvious attraction between us. The sex was amazing with her. Our swinger club experiences were always couple with couple, the women making out and then everyone just with his/her companion side by side. With her it wasn't awkward like it usually is. It didn't even feel like being with a woman. It just felt like having sex with someone amazing. Her personality and behavior was so sexy. She was shy in the car, that's why she seemed cold but she became so playful and open and cute and nice once she had some alcohol.

Her husband gave me her number through the boss a few weeks after meeting her. But I just started livejasmin and wasn't sure how to get close to someone, keep this a secret or speak about it? I didn't text her. Then I met you, things got complicated. I was focusing on trying to understand what's going on with me and feeling guilty about everything. I didn't want to tell anyone but I didn't want to hide either. I became very lonely.

At some point her husband wrote to the boss saying she is disappointed I didn't contact her. I felt terrible, I really liked her. I texted her something like "Sorry I didn't do this sooner, it's not because I'm not interested in you. Could we meet?" She didn't answer and I thought that's fair, it was too late.

But the boss just told me they contacted us again and wanted to meet us. Fortunately the boss already told them that we have problems...I texted her right away and asked her out. She cannot come this weekend but we exchanged a few messages about my current situation and she said she doesn't want to meet 4 of us, because she is afraid to lose her friend (me!) so we could just stay in contact, only both of us! I have a friend in France!

I'm so happy. It will be nice to get to know someone and think less of my life. It's such a blessing and such perfect timing, today I'm an emotional rack. I'm terrified to go back to the boss. He changed. He really changed. He speaks nicely, he acts differently. But I'm still terrified. I'm so angry at him and hate to be angry. The biggest problem is still that I don't love him. I feel like I'm a horrible person. There is a clock ticking and I know it's just a matter of time and I have to break up. Again. Unfortunately I'm not 17 anymore, and saying "I fell out of love" is not enough of a reason to give. But the more I think the more sure I am that it all comes down to that at the end. It's as simple as that. maybe I should stop feeling guilty about not feeling something and focus on being nice, the guilt and anger makes me hurt him. And that makes me hate myself even more. Pfff.. Elle, stop dramatizing and over complicating things, try to love him the way you can. He is a human being, I love human beings.

Calvin, I hope you are good. You don't have to write every day. You might have too much work to do or having fun with something or just being too exhausted or not having your thoughts together yet or not feeling like dealing with me.

I just became aware that if it's neither of these and there is something wrong I might not be informed about it. Does someone know I exist and care about you? Could you give my email address to a friend or someone trustful just in case?

I'm being weird... I probably shouldn't be worried.

Until I get an answer from you I always wonder whether I hurt you or upset you with something or made you leave. So there is a little bit of that too.

But it should be definitely ok to skip a day or more. I know I can be overwhelming. I will try to phase out my messages a bit. I'm used to getting a daily dose of you. Sorry.

Take care, sleep well

Next time I'll write to you from France.

Elle

*

November 22, 2016

Elle,

I'm alive!!!! Hee, hee hee. You make me smile.

If I am upset with you or don't like you or don't want to talk anymore I promise I will tell you. I promise, even if it is a short email saying I need some time. I will send something. Otherwise assume I still like you, I am still interested in all about you. I still find you extremely sexy. I enjoyed my English lesson.

I didn't get home until late. I read your email but didn't reply. I will write more tonight.

I have had internet problems so don't get excited just because I am offline someday, and next week I might visit my friend one night. He, yes it's a dude I am spending the night with, I probably will tell you more than you want to know if I meet a woman and even consider letting go with a finger again. But HE wants my help doing some handyman repairs on his house. Thursday is a US Holiday I had yesterday and today off. I will go out with my mom and her friend for lunch, then I will have a party with friends on Friday. But I'll be home eventually each night. I don't have much to say and I mostly don't want to think about anything too deep. Also I'm trying to be good and be close and deep and personal, and sexual without it being a personal romantic. Or drifting that way.

How do I go back to showing you my XXX when I know you appreciate looking into my eyes? See what I mean? Shut Up Calvin! SUC

I still want to know about you. My life is kind of boring right now but I will tell you about me and the boring things.

Ok I'll break the rules again. You once asked how I smell. Pretty darned good! I used to wear a deodorant called English Leather. When I couldn't find it anymore I switched brands. I am a mountain man in the fresh air. I tend to have scrapes on my hands and arms. But I also have scented soaps. I am a kaleidoscope of contradictions. My wife had them and I liked to mix them into my soap. I tend to have a little warm vanilla and juniper. Also not that it smells, but I find aloe vera really heals my scratches and sunburns. so I always mix a lot of that in. I also eat healthy and drink lots of water. In wrestling we had to make weight so I spent many hours sweating in dry saunas or while exercising. So I tend to sweat water and not smell. I do think I have a manly outdoors smell but a bookish math geek lumberjack.

Ok i'll write more later and eventually you'll get a video of some kind. I enjoy that. Both giving and receiving them. Right now I am trying to do work around the house. I need to clean the rain gutters and have been doing work outside. but it has rained and I have been away so at night I have moved things. Not so much cleaning anything, just moving junk from one pile to another. But my computer room is a mess.

Big smile and I think you are wonderful.

Unless I die I promise to say goodbye. So I am either alive and going to write and still think the world of you and want to stay in touch, or I have written to tell you otherwise. Right now you turn me on like crazy and I need to re-watch your videos and relieve some stress, and I love hearing about your life. My life is full but a bit boring to write about.

Can't I just give a small hug?

Still Calvin

*

November 23, 2016

Hi Calvin,

Easy, just show your XXX and/or your cute XXX.

Your smell... I have to find out how English leather smells. Although I'd prefer to find out how Calvin smells. The other day I was surprised how nice my smell was. I eat so much fruit that my XXX smells like clementine on some days. I don't like to use perfumes, it disturbs me to have my clothes smell like roses or whatever when I take them off. It smells so unnatural. Plus, this might seem ridiculous but only having my natural smell on me gives me more of a chance to find out who is sexually, chemically driven to me. And the pervert I am always wants to know and enjoy if a man is going crazy from frustration next to me. I'm really mean but I tremendously enjoy teasing strangers just a little bit so that they are not sure about being teased and watch them want me and try to hide it. Hehe. I know I'm mean.

Thank you so much, for the sun in your pictures and in your words. I have half an hour to run around in the house and get everything together, then "Up for adventure!" It's a traveling day. Car, flight, train, subway, bus...in this order.

Ok, I have to go. Quick kiss. Very friendly. Friends kiss on the cheek in my country. If I don't mistake your mouth for your cheek.

Elle

*

November 23, 2016

Elle,

Ok I'll do as you said. Easy, just show it.
Enjoy France.

Calvin

*

November 24, 2016

Hey Elle,

I was tired so I went to sleep. It's morning now. The days are getting short, Dark all morning and it gets dark sooner each day.

Everything is dark green now though instead of dry after the rains. The deer are out in force also.

I think you know me pretty well but let's see what you don't know about me.... I think I told you I fence. I read a lot of Alexandre Dumas as a kid. The Three Musketeers and The Count of Monte Christo and fantasized about sword fights.. Never won a tournament but I enjoy it. I studied Judo. I liked wrestling more but the philosophy, the gentle path and using your opponent's force against him was interesting. Water moves the rock and wears it down to sand without really crashing sometimes. It just chips away as it goes around the rock. Here I mostly hike and lately I seem to be doing more for my guests. Instead of exploring, and walking alone is not good to do, I tend to stick to trails I have already made. I tend to pack a chainsaw and clear the path of fallen trees so others can enjoy it more than just walking for pleasure. But I do enjoy showing off my trails and the land around me.

My dad was a genius and was offered a scholarship to have his college paid for at Cal Poly San Luis Obisbo. He was going to make nuclear bombs. Our family had served in wars and he was interested in Nuclear Physics. But after one year of college he started wondering what was right and wrong and decided to finish his undergraduate classes at a Bible college. He met my mom there and ended up graduating from there. So he was a genius with a degree in Math and Theology with Physics and philosophy minors. He loved learning. But he wasn't into money. He felt great at the end of the day seeing what he had accomplished. He was a carpenter and mostly built houses. He was always in great shape. He could run faster than me and farther than me even when I was a college athlete. I was bigger than him but he would swing a hammer all day and I always believed he could beat me up. but he was very gentle. I am more outgoing. He was always overly polite and gentle. He would never hug people but had a sweet smile and was very loving. ok I have been avoiding talking about him. I think that is all for now. He was a great dad.

I'm not sure where my pantyhose fetish came from. My wife was a bit of a Tomboy. She could get dirty and work beside me. She was cute. She used to explain why I would compliment her makeup. She loved knowing what I thought, but didn't change who she was to please me. She wore different make up for a fancy night out than during the day. I still don't know what she did, but she would explain that I liked her lighter colors of the day but that wasn't what she wore at night. She said I didn't like her pink lipstick but complimented it because I liked the eye shadow she wore with it. The eye shadow was subtle and she wore lipstick I noticed so I complimented that I liked her look but never understood what I liked just what I noticed. Does this make sense? I still don't get it. My point was she wore what she felt looked good and just enjoyed that I liked it or didn't. Sometimes she wore white stockings or something sexy because she knew it worked for me sexually. But I was trying to say, I liked her in black nylons and all dressed up but I preferred her in a more casual, cute and relaxed look. Formal wear wasn't a fetish for me. She looked good, but I don't think she had anything to do with my fetish. I like the feel of nylons. I do tend to like lighter colored nylons.Tan colored nylon looks amazing on you. But I have no idea where this feetish came from. It started when I was a teen.

I do like my life. I am not shocked or disapproving of your swinger lifestyle or your attraction for women. Not sure it would be for me, but I would probably enjoy watching you with another woman. Maybe I would be jealous if a woman knew the female body and how to get a reaction better than I do. The email before that one I am going to digest more before I comment on. Plus it is deep and serious and I want to be light and sexy and fun a little more. I love that I am sensitive and soft and gentle. But I felt the need to try to sound more rough. I know you know me too well to change your view of me. But it helps me avoid the deep emotional stuff. That's all.

Today is our national Day of Thanksgiving. I am thankful you didn't leave me. I am thankful you know me on a level many people who see me everyday don't. I am thankful we have a connection. Another thing on my list regarding you has to be SEX!!! I am thankful we are really in each other's lives. Thank you for understanding me and for all you know you have done for me.

Always Calvin

Always Calvin and Elle

*

November 24, 2016

Calvin,

Happy Thanksgiving, wonderful kaleidoscope of contradictions. I miss you.

Elle

*

November 24, 2016

Calvin,

I'm sitting on the couch and I just cannot make myself do all the setting up and I don't want anyone to see me. I thought I would have a session this morning. But even sitting here is hard. And I would probably just get from them "you are very calm today", "why can't you be smiling?" comments. I don't need that. I don't understand how anybody can make my body feel sexual while I don't want them. Inside I'm dying not wanting anything but... Is this my body? It feels like I'm not in it anymore.

I don't want to be here. I don't want to feel or think. I don't want to speak about it. I can't just speak about what's happening and how I feel about it, especially not to you.

I already know what I need to know. I just can't do anything about it.

So many things to be grateful for. I just feel like crying for help. Leaving the little left of me.

I put away all the inconvenient stuff in that box because I really can't deal with it and don't see the point in dealing with it. I adjusted well. But is there anything left of me? I can barely function, I'm censoring out 80% of my thoughts automatically before they could become words in my head. It was functioning until now but I should now build up a life from the little left. What is left? I look but I don't see. I touch but I don't feel. My body wants to shrink and disappear. I don't recognize my voice and the words coming out of my mouth don't feel like mine. This is not right. What is happening? It's like I lost all of my memories and my identity with it and I was told to go live that life there because that's mine and there is a place for me there. So I fell into it but it didn't fit. It doesn't feel right. Everyone telling me the opposite and what they say seems logical. They are telling me that they know me, this is what I would want, this is what I always wanted. What's wrong with me? I couldn't be more sure that this is not my place. I have no idea where it is. I don't want to think about it. But this is not ok.

Please don't answer. I know there is nothing you could say anyways. Just don't feel like you should. Don't.

Elle

*

November 24, 2016

Calvin,

Sorry for the previous email. I might have to title every second email I write like this. Just kidding. I want to stop crying. I can learn to control my emotional life better in this situation. I don't want to just give you up completely because it's too hard. I don't want you to go to make my life easier. I don't want to lose you. I will find a way to stop myself from sending disturbing emails. I'm pretty angry at myself now.

My mom is obsessed with aloe vera. Every time we have some injury, whatever kind, she goes "put some aloe vera on it". We mocked her for a long time but I have to admit that now I'm convinced too that it works magically on wounds. I used to have aloe vera plants. But I suck taking care of plants. May they rest in peace.

I loved running and cycling. I don't run anymore but cycling still makes me feel free and very happy.

I'm very bad at all kinds of team sports, especially at ball games. If a ball is coming toward me my first reaction is to run away protecting my head. My second reaction...is the same.

My swinger feelings: I'm not that into it anymore. It was exciting at the beginning because I didn't know anything about it, it was like having a secret second life I could share with my love. The boss is all about it. For like a year or two all our dates were about this. He always had to organize them by himself and convince me to go. Once there I had fun but I don't like that it became a habit. I don't like that when you meet those new people it's obvious and expected to get naked and have sex with them and gets awkward if you won't. It kills all the excitement for me. Too predictable. I like less explicit things. The boss noticed that I'm not that interested anymore. He just told me that when we got separated and I left for Hungary he went on two swinger dates. And that's when his mindset changed and he decided he wants to get me back. He just felt like I'm the one he wanted to tell about his new experiences and the one he wanted to share similar experiences with. But he added that he knows I'm less into it and that's ok.

By the way women usually suck with female bodies. Men have plenty of practice and know what they are doing. We have no idea what's happening to us during sex, because we are too busy enjoying it. So we never really get to learn the techniques or practice.

The boss seems to be determined to keep his calm and patience and a loving tone. We want a normal Christmas, we are trying at least until next year. I'm really trying. I respect the efforts he makes and I have all kinds of strategies to make myself make efforts too. If for myself I don't feel like trying, I feel strong enough to try for the small one and for my cousin who was the flower girl at the wedding and my childhood best friend, who is a cynical artist and doesn't believe in love but she does believe in my marriage. The first step is the most difficult but if things work out it won't matter why I made that first step back and how hard it was.

I hope you understand that if the boss and I seriously consider at one point to stay together I will tell him about this. I think a relationship is based on transparency. I unconsciously left him the moment I felt like keeping you for myself and not sharing it with him, when I was sharing absolutely everything with him until then. When you feel like keeping something just for yourself because it's so precious and you feel like it concerns you and only you, that's the end of a relationship. I still don't trust him and want to keep you for myself. And if at that point I still want to keep our connection and contact I will tell him what I want and he can either live with it or not.

I stopped reading the book about the prostitute. It's not that well written. I'm sad about it, because it was in German and I was happy that I was reading in German again and that I still understood it. I have a better one about book writing. This book is amazing. It explains step by step everything you need to know to write. There are writing exercises in it that I can make while I'm reading. I know it sounds boring but it is fascinating. So well written! I already know I love writing. I used to write poems but outgrew that skill somehow. I had blogs and got some good comments on my style from people who publish. I think it's because I have absolutely no holding back. I just write down my actual thoughts without caring about who will read it. I guess it's not just my body that I love to exhibit. I know it's in me. It has been a really long time that I have stories in my head I save up for writing whenever I feel ready for it. But I have no idea how to get it out so that it would become pleasant to read. Maybe this book will make me ready. I think it will at least make me start writing even if my writing will be very bad at the beginning. I'm excited about this. This is important for me.

How was your Thanksgiving? I love the idea of Thanksgiving. Can you tell me more about it?

Our next special Hungarian day is the 6th December when Santa Claus puts chocolate and clementines in the clean boots of children, so when they wake up this is the first thing they run to see. They have to clean their boots the night before. The bad children only get a rod.

In Europe it's all about Christmas already. We have all the Christmas holidays planned out. And I will soon start to decorate and look up Christmas waiting activities to do. I want to have traditions with the small one, she is big enough now to enjoy everything. The last two years the boss convinced me to not do anything. He is not a getting excited about holidays type of guy. I think this year he will make an effort though. He pretty much just brought me down, complained about everything, hated the Christmas songs, the decorations, the activities, slept through the family dinners. Like a Grinch. Last year was particularly bad, we celebrated it in Hungary and he was missing out on all the "yummy french holiday food" and never got over it. This year we are staying here so he'll get the "foie gras", the salmon, the snails and oyster (he doesn't even like it). And he gets to complain about having to buy too many gifts for the too many children in his family. I know he is trying but he is so used to being a bitter person. You know the kind of "adult" adult who hates snow and complains about how much work it is to clean the alley. (We don't even have an alley to clean so he complains about how cold it is and how disgusting it looks in a city) Stop complaining Elle. Really I shouldn't, he is much better at getting excited about life now. He stopped the mean comments while watching tv, and seems to have an overall nicer approach to people. He will never be you but it's not his fault. Shut up Elle.

I feel thankful. I hope you had a wonderful day.

Sleep well Calvin.

Elle

*

November 25, 2016

Calvin,

I am standing by the door. You are resting on the bed, with your mind far away, lost in some personal thoughts. Maybe in some deep and dark and lonely place or just thinking about the donkeys or what you should do with that student who calculated everything right, right until the result, what he didn't give, he did do an obscene drawing instead. This thought makes me smile. I'm smiling while I'm tip toeing toward the bed you are laying on.

You only notice me when I lay down next to you. The bed becomes harder under you as I put my weight on the other side of it and it makes you look at where I am and notice my presence. You arise from your thinking and smile at me tenderly. Before you could open your mouth or even start to overthink and overanalyze in your brain I put a finger on your mouth as if I would silently ask you to shut up. You are glad I do because you feel speechless. You don't really want to think right now.

I'm laying next to you, in a floral printed ruffled shirt, a gray pencil skirt and nylon stockings. This is my outfit for later that day when I will leave for a quick professional meeting. But I got ready super early as usual just to enjoy being dressed up all professional and have now time to check on you.

You can feel my breast against your side as you took me in your arms. And my nylon covered legs are really close to your legs. I'm craving you but you are holding me tightly and I cannot even move my hands. I'm so close to you and it makes my breasts get swollen and my nipples be hard against your side, my body is all tense and having you all around me is making me go insane. My body feels electric. (Wow. What a nice reference. High five Elle)

There is no way I could get out of your hug. I try to fight against it but without any result. You feel me moving and you figure out what I want to do. You are laughing and I can enjoy that playful look on your face, that playful look when there is that sparkle in your eyes and you raise your eyebrows. We smile at each other with a knowing smile. It makes me want to get silly with you.

I whisper something very quietly so that you can not understand and you turn your ears toward my lips waiting for me to repeat. Still whispering but you can now hear me. I start describing what I want to do to you. It turns you on enough to let my hands free.

I put my left hand on your cheek and gently take off your glasses with my right hand. You are still holding me in a tight hug but you let me slide up a little bit so that my lips are now almost touching your ears. I'm holding one hand on your cheek and your chin and caressing your face with the other hand as if I'm trying to grave in my memory the lines of your forehead, your eyebrows... You close your eyes while I slowly run my fingers down your face, barely touching it. I get to your lips and my fingers slow down even more. You can feel that I am dying to have them touch my lips and that I am dying to let your warm breath make me shiver as you run them through my body.

You unconsciously lose your hold. You are breathing slower and deeper as I take my lips from your ears to your neck, your shoulders... I keep getting down with my hands caressing and grabbing you according to the waves my passion flows. Your hard 22 folded is pressed against my chest. I feel comfortable. It feels right to be in that position but my lips are craving something.

I start to caress your dick still in touch with my boobs just because I like the feeling of it against them. I'm biting my lips to hold myself back but can't do it anymore. I want to taste you. As I am running my tongue on your 22 folded I notice that we are both naked and I have no idea how those clothes came off and when.

I still have the stockings on, it seems like we "forgot" to get rid of them. I'm almost naked. You are completely naked and completely mine. You are lost in the pleasure as my mouth moves around your hardness and my hand helps too, because it's freaking long.

You stop me at some point because you don't want to cum yet. You try to get your head to cool down a bit and push me on my back, your hands on my wrists. You don't want me to touch you now. You are having fun observing my reactions, what I try to hide but can not,

Your big hands are massaging my not tiny, not ample breast. A moan leaves my lips as you kiss my neck under my ear and my body is trying to get out of your hold because you just found out that your kisses on the side of my waist make me go insane and you enjoy torturing me. I'm all wet down there and only want one thing. I ask you to stop.

You lean toward me to be sure to understand what I say (strong accent) and I beg you:

"Fuck me now Calvin"

My eyes don't leave yours while we both think about your sentence in your bikini fantasy. I cannot believe how easy and evident it is to trust you. I'm in that pleasure with you, holding on to you. I'm getting louder as we move together. It feels too wonderful to be true. But I'm having so much pleasure that my mind can fortunately not start to worry about reality or whether I deserve this. I take it all in and when I feel like I can not take it any more I say to you still looking into your eyes:

"Do it now, CALVIN"

You say my name and your trembling body finds a support in my arms, we feel serene and safe and comfortable. We are both out of breath and don't need words to understand each other.

You make me drink and eat. I end up falling asleep naked, still smiling. You cover my naked body with a blanket and slip out of the bed, to come back an hour later and wake me up for the meeting. I can't stop smiling while taking my shower. I am still smiling while putting back my gray pencil skirt, the stockings and the floral shirt.

Elle

*

November 25, 2016

Elle,

Well done!
WOW!! Thank you and WOW!!!
When I can find words again I'll write back.
Thank you. and Wow!

Wow

Calvin

*

November 25, 2016

Elle,

wow and thank you, but I can talk again.

Today was a nice day. I slept in and sat by the fire. It is trying to snow and the storm and cold is here but not enough to really make snow. Maybe in the morning we will have gotten dusting. It was just a quiet warm day by the fire. After dark I left the lights off and opened the stove. I read a little. Then read a great story in an email. masturbated, then came back down and enjoyed the fire. I watched some sports too. Never really made it out of the house or to put on shoes. I guess I did go out to get firewood. There's a pump for the well inside of a little room outside my front door by where I keep my wood. Two corners of the shed are trees but I had to cut them down after they died. It is just logs just big enough for someone to lay down now that I have shelves on the walls. The opening has a tarp hanging over it. When I went out today I actually looked at it as though I was expecting my dog to peek out at me. When he got older he stayed in there when it was cold but he loved me and always came out when I chopped up some kindling or got wood. He loved being loved and felt even when he was old he had some kind of job to protect me. It was a sweet thought not sad.

The grass is turning green under the old brown grass. Kind of a pretty site. I like this time of year. Christmas. I have a rule I don't buy anything the girls that I tutor are selling to make money for their school or church. Also that I don't play favorites or exchange gifts for the holidays. But this year I am giving them each a gift I think. They live down the hill and seldom make a fire in their fireplace. It is a special thing for them and usually only when Calvin is there. So that makes it extra special. They have these paper wrapped packets and left over wood from when they had their tree trimmed. So this year I taught the oldest how to chop kindling and start a fire with a match, a newspaper and some wood. Not a big thing but she feels like she's some strong independent woman now because she can make a fire. We did it with just oak leaves and pine needles I'd brought once but strangely they smelled like someone had soaked them in gas. Hmmm. I bring them down some wood before they get low. We have more dead wood laying on the ground rotting than we can get to and cut up. Everyone on the road watches for a big tree, like an Oak, to fall close to the road easily. I sometimes help the older people on the road or sometimes I pretend we will work together and split the wood between us. Usually I do most of the work and give them all the wood, but they work hard and it isn't charity. Everyone on the road helps each other in different ways. The point is I have plenty of wood to share and could have more if I wanted to drag it.

So this year I am going to give the oldest her very own hatchet to cut the wood. I don't feel too bad because I am not going out and buying them gifts and they make me bracelets and draw me pictures and even make me cookies all the time for holidays. Because she is who she is and she loves me so much, instead of buying her a hatchet I am giving her one of my old ones. She will love it more because it is mine and looks used and not like she is a newbie. I already "accidently" left a sharpening stone there and told them to keep it because I have more. Her little sister wants a pocket knife and I talked to her mom and she wants me to give it to her because she will listen to me more when I give her a safety talk about it than she would to her mom or dad. Again I am giving her one of my old ones I used to carry when I was young. Younger! I am still young. I don't know what to do for the twins.

When my great grandmother was young her sister got an old box and decorated it by burning pictures on it. It was her wedding present for her older sister. I have shown it to them and told them the story behind it. So for the whole family the gift from Santa will be a wood burning kit. I spent $3 because I want to keep mine if I find it again. I know these are princesses who change outfits because their mood changes and have me paint their fingernails. But I also like strong independent confident women. They can do wood work and be a princess both.

Thank you for the story. I loved it. as per the masturbated part of the day today. I might send you back one someday but I just don't know if I will cross the line in my story. I do love the fact it was tender and a lot of touching, you crawling into bed with me softly being intimate, not just sex. Thank you for bringing back my story with the "Fuck Me Calvin" That got me really hard!

Tomorrow I have church and will go over to friends after. I am in a sweet mood and life is good. Monday I will be back to being busy but this was a short vacation and a chance to catch my breath. Also a time I needed. I am glad the Thanksgiving holiday vacation is when it is. I am too busy before to think of other things and I have a week after to not stress and reset.

I hope things are going well in France. I read your "Sorry don't read that last email" message so I am not trying to read anything into you having a down moment. Feel free to have me there and feel a hug from me if you need me. Write to me. Funny, but I think you know what a hug from me when you are down feels like even though we've never touched. (that's friends talk) What I didn't understand was if you were talking about going back online, or if you were not feeling sexy with the woman, or what you meant. I understood your feelings and I also got that you didn't feel like me being sexy or intimate with you at that moment, and that's ok. I was just curious about what's going on in your life. Did the ice cream shop close? Are you considering Hungary or France to live in? Are you going back to the office? If so I won't sign in or say too much. It's less about your safety and more about unfairly hurting someone.

But feel free to record yourself in whatever sexy outfit you wear.

Life is good. I hope you are well and will tell me if I can help. I can always listen and care and want to. When you do that for me it helps. Even reading this rambling about nothing I just wrote makes me feel important enough to have someone read it. You are good for my ego. Thank you... and WOW!!!!!

Still and Always Calvin

*

November 26, 2016

Elle

I was a pretty good baseball player as a kid. We had a small town and each age group had 4 teams. So if you were one of the top 8 players in town you were one of the best players on your team. I have a friend who is now a high school math teacher and coaches and we are still good friends. But we both played the same position and so we were always on different teams. We were team captains always and got into a lot of fights and got sent home from school. But we would trade a few punches and then be friends again. I grew my last year in baseball and while I was growing my coordination changed and I wasn't very good my last year at the top level. My dad held a track record at his college and encouraged me to run track instead of playing baseball. I think I did it for him. I didn't like to run. I did it to lose weight for wrestling and for football but I liked to knock people down. I never won in track and wasn't very good. but it was great because I learned to be a good teammate and understand how the players in the sports I was the star in felt. I think I was thought better of because I kept trying and was supportive and tried something I wasn't good at. It is easy to be happy when you are the star getting all the praise. Plus track had girls. Maybe that was why I wasn't focused and good at it. I was in band also and many of the prettiest girls in the school were my friends from band and some of the prettiest and most popular were quiet, shy and not very pretty when they were young and I was their friend back then. It is good to grow up in a small town.

Running was good for me. In college I could run a long way before I noticed or got out of breath at all. I was able to think and appreciate sites around town or in the early morning when life looked different. I was never fast. But my dad got me into marathons. I still hate running but I walk, hike and run because it is good for me and mentally it is still an escape. I sometimes daydream when running. I solved math problems in college because somehow running outside when I could fall actually cleared my head from distractions. I know that doesn't make sense but that's me.

When I started at college one of the ways they helped me pay for college was they gave me a job. Supposedly I was supposed to go into every wrestler's locker and take out their smelly dirty clothes and wash them, then dry them then put them back in their locker for tomorrow's practice. What really happened was the wrestlers would put their clothes in a barrel on a hook after practice. I would roll the barrel across the locker room to the washing machine and dump them in and turn the machine on. Another guy from another sport would take the clothes out and put them in the dryer for me. Then the next day I would roll the barrel back out before practice and everyone would get their stuff out. I did have the keys to all the lockers though.

The next year another freshman had my job. When I got dressed one day I noticed the shirt I thought I had hanging in my locker was gone. When I got to practice, the freshman with the key to my locker was wearing it. It was from a marathon I had run and was obviously mine. I asked him what he was doing. He said it looked like a cool shirt and would impress a girl he was trying to get to know so he wore it to school because she was in his class with him and she was a runner. So my running never got me a date, but at least it helped someone.

I think the fact you have a love for books will affect your daughter. You can't pretend to like books and value learning, kids see through it. but you honestly do love books and learning. That's a great example.

Usually Thanksgiving is a day with a big meal with the family. We eat Turkey and potatoes and pumpkin pie and too much food. Before we ate in my family we all went around and named what we were thankful for that year. It is a family holiday and the dinner is big because as many families as possible can get together. It is more intimate than a big reunion. It starts with your parents and siblings and maybe grandparents that are still alive. later your brothers and sisters come back from college and then after they bring their families. You remember the times when your grandparents were there with you but slowly you start having Thanksgiving with your wife's family or just start your own family with your parents coming over. My mother in law and her mom used to come with my parents to our place.

We had a war in our country when the southern states tried to start a new country. After the war the president named the third Thursday in November a day for the entire country to thank God for the peace and the unity of the country and for the fact we were prosperous and to recognize a greater power for the things we have. It was also to remind us how good things are and how bad the war was when brothers fought against each other.

Ok, I was just writing to you and didn't feel like stopping. I am feeling refreshed and back to my old self.

You make me smile, even when you don't think you are being that bright and sunshiny. You really make me smile when you write wow and make me go re-watch your video again for the millionth time. I might be exaggerating a bit on the number but I am glad you sent them.

Still Calvin

*

November 26, 2016

Calvin,

About the fantasy story from yesterday.. This is what your video did to me. I still cannot react with normal words to the video. It made me feel so much more than I expected it would. Funny, right? This is the kind of video that is meant and received in a sexual dirty mindset. But it was very special to me. And really messed me up. Writing down the fantasy helped with the sexual frustration.

I watched your videos and listened to some painfully sad music (pathetic, and weird, I know, but facing my feelings is actually the fastest way to let them go, if I learnt something practical about how I function this must be it), had about 6-7 orgasms and bits of that story kept coming up in my head but really just flashes of images and feelings. I still couldn't sleep so I started to put words on what kept me awake. Thinking that I can clear my mind once it's out of it. It felt liberating to write it down. It wasn't a writing exercise, I do them in Hungarian for obvious reasons. This was just for me, and for you. Ok, that's it, a fantasy. Your reaction was priceless :D Anyways, thank you for the video.

Your fantasy still turns me on, sometimes I remember whole sentences of it and get really embarrassed and can hardly get myself together to continue what I was doing.

Did I cross the line? I think I didn't, although you might be able to read me between the lines, but for my peace of mind I'll ignore this possibility. I held back some of the words, hence the rushing at the end, I also went fast on some parts because it was sexually unbearable for me to spend more time on them and detail it more. I love the details in yours. Let's change the topic, I am now constantly having the image of you getting hard in my mind but I want to speak about other things too and answer some of your questions.

"Wow and thank you but I can talk again"

Haahaa, yes. As if me or anything else could make you stop speaking. Two long emails to give me some reason to smile. Thank you Calvin!

I never had pets. I love December, Christmas is about family for me not gifts. My parents sucked at giving gifts anyway. My mom just kept buying us Tupperware boxes and shower gel and clementines... The food wasn't that exciting either. My mom is not the best cook, I think we always ate fried fish sticks with potato puree and some soup. (my grandmothers cook well though) But she knew how to make the whole thing feel magical. She made Christmas characters out of hard paper and glued them on the doors and curtains. The 4 Sundays before Christmas we had candles burning and the day I got to decorate the tree with my dad. That was our thing. And we always sang Christmas songs, everyone could choose his/her favorite and it was fun, our parents didn't expect us to be all perfectly dressed and behaved. Christmas morning was the only morning they let us play with a video game. We took turns. It was Tarzan. I sucked at it. I am still very bad at video games. In the evening we went to my grandmother and ate non stop and played games. Next day we took the train and went to my other grandparents where we were many in a tiny flat. That is something I love. Many beloved people in a tiny place. It's like a family pyjama party.

You are so kind and generous. I love that I can tell that from your stories, you don't hide the positive things about you or act like it's nothing. It's just always so natural and innocent, I think you know your own value, but also admit your defaults and limits. It's pretty rare. I like people who don't take themselves too seriously. I like you.

Yes you are still young! I am super-booper young, but yes you are still pretty young ! You were already 15 when I was born. And 33 when I became legally fuckable for you. (it's 18 in Europe). Wow. Let's not think about this again!

Speaking about busy stressful times. I know you must have stress in your life but you never pass that stress onto me. You know how amazing it is that it doesn't make you an awful person? For me you are just this always caring and kind man who releases his stress with me and relaxes with me. Someone I can joke around with and forget about my problems. Also someone who really listens to me when I am sad or upset or stressed and feels with me. And you are also a kaleidoscope of contradiction trusting me with your stories. Not perfect. But your qualities are so amazing that they outshine your defaults. Nobody has to be always kind and caring and amazing. But I think this is what you are most of the time. I'm sure you mess up every now and then but I also know you enough to know that you get up and try again to be the man you want to be. This is pretty awesome.

Isn't this the first time you are asking me (as many) questions? I think it is. I don't know why you asked now and these but they deserve an answer, you don't ask often.

Yes, I think I know what a hug from you feels like. Comfortable?
^^

The message was not about going online, well except the sentences where I mentioned that. No it wasn't about not feeling sexual with a woman. I'm trying to reread it to see what I left out because I didn't dare to put in but it's hard to even reread it. I won't. But I remember the context. I will tell you a bit about it. I got back to France on Thursday at about noon. There were flowers waiting for me at home, beautiful yellow ones, and the flat was clean. I had a nap in the afternoon. Then he had a nap. We put her in bed. And he ordered sushi for us and we watched "No tomorrow", "Big Bang Theory" and "Two Broke Girls". It was nice. He looked at me questioning me how I feel about all this. I answered "It's all very nice, you know I love to look at yellow flowers and I love to eat, so I am in a good mood but I wouldn't want to speak for my feelings because they are being corrupted with sushi and flowers. Let's take things gradually, see how everyday life goes, how we handle the little one's meltdowns and the next fight..." I went to bed alone. He came about an hour before my alarm would ring. It woke me up. I felt lonely and sad. He was tossing and turning around so I couldn't get back to sleep. He asked whether he could take me in his arms. I took a deep breath and moved there thinking if I'm trying I have to actually try and do uncomfortable things. Worst idea ever. I didn't have sex for like 3 weeks, a big change to adjust to after being in a relationship and I was craving to be touched. Being in touch with another body just made me lose it. He was very respectful and kind of just assisted me while I touched myself. Now, thinking back, that was very clever of him. Honestly his strategy is not bad. He is still respectful and not overwhelming, just trying to always move a tiny bit closer with his words or moves. He is careful and avoids the topics that might lead to us fighting, and always takes back his hand when I automatically step back or get frozen when it touches me "by mistake".

Anyways. I hated myself so much that morning. I spent the whole morning, and afternoon crying at songs. Oh, I can't believe that I just told you. I'm still feeling like shit. It destroyed me and I just can't forgive myself for hurting myself so much to just get some warmth. I wish I could forget the mix of physical pleasure and excruciating emotional pain. I think it felt a lot like cutting myself and it's not good for me to remember that. That, you do to get a relief from the emotional pain, because the physical pain takes over for a while. This was kind of the opposite, but the guilt is the same and the relief that is only a short term relief. It hurts like hell to separate the physical from the emotional so brutally, it's very unnatural. When we saw each other again, he told me he understands that I didn't have sex for a while and I don't have to worry we can step back and just build up things from scratch. So this is where we are at. Not confusing. Just uncomfortable. And painful. But it's peaceful at home and we do good teamwork with the little one. Let's see, it's Sunday now, so it took him 3 days to get verbally abusive with me again. He said several hurtful things today with no intention of hurting me I guess. He made fun of one of my "bikini pictures" on facebook, saw my tissues from yesterday night's crying and made fun of me, and had a sexist joke about me doing the dishes. I like inappropriate jokes and don't mind being hurt but I feel very lonely and can't even consider him as a friend. What friend would not care about your feelings? I told him about my writing book and he didn't even listen to me just went right away to give me advice about what to do and not to do, and started to enumerate mistakes beginner writers make. This is what happens every time I want to share something exciting with him. He is "helping" me with a bitter warning of how he thinks I will fail. At the same time he is being patient with me, helping a lot with Lily, giving me time. He is doing good compared to himself. Mom would say I should explain to him how I feel and ask him to react the way I'd like him to. The problem is, this is exactly what I do but it only works for a few days and even when he speaks and acts the way I asked him, it's not what I wanted. It doesn't come from him, he didn't feel the need to pronounce those words to me or treat me that way, so he is just pleasing me. There are things you cannot ask or beg for. Like love. or trust. or respect. These are either given with pleasure willingly or they are not. If he'd feel like giving those to me, maybe I could fall in love with him one day again. Maybe. But I don't trust or respect him or love him. So he is having these problems with me too.

What's going on in my life? It's hard to tell yet. We don't speak about the future yet. I am considering living and working in France. Spend some summer weeks or months in Hungary when the ice cream shop is open. It's open from May to September. I think I will go back to "the office" (office? really?) from tomorrow. I'm still keeping an eye on job offers.

As far as moving goes, we both want to leave this flat. This year, a car in our street was put on fire and burnt down completely, the windows of the butcher got broken every 2 weeks, until it closed and changed its owner, no broken windows now and a man was shot with a kalasnyikov 3 bus stations from our house, and guys are hanging out in our street nonstop just speaking. Whenever we go out they are there in groups. This definitely does not feel like a place we feel safe to walk around with a toddler.

I want to get a job first and have that conversation with the boss, the one that will be difficult and honest. And then we can decide to move, probably staying in the same town but in another district. I think we will end up in separate flats.
Things seem to go in this direction.

I have a doctor's appointment next week, just a check up for my "let's not get a second baby" device I got quickly after getting Lily. I didn't have the best birth or motherhood experience so that was my priority although the boss was and is clear about wanting more. I don't.

And I'll get an appointment at an association to discuss our legal/financial rights and options if we separate/divorce.

This is going on in my life. I guess things are going in a good direction and it will all work out, it's just not progressing fast enough to my taste. It pretty much feels like wasting time and energy on a dead relationship instead of putting all that into starting over our lives.

Thank you for not visiting my room!! I understand why and appreciate it.

Wow, it's impressive at how many sports you were the best or one of the bests. It's even more impressive that you still tried other sports, even if you weren't the best at them.

That story with the marathon T-shirt is so funny and so are you! At least your T-shirt helped someone else to get a date. :D That sentence is so adorable, it makes me want to kiss you. Friendly.

I think it's huge that you run a marathon. Wow. I got to know you as a math guy, funny and sweet. I can't believe you could resist so long to tell me your achievements and brought it up casually with only me listening to it. Who are you? Batman? These facts are powerful.
I mean, I like you just as much as before you told me about them. But I am a woman who admires strong men and loves to watch your photos and listen to your sports stories. It's a bit intimidating. very impressive. Marathon runners are not even human for me. My dad did it once. But he is so crazy. He loves to suffer. Go biking when it rains, running when it's over 40 degrees, hiking in snowy mountains and sleeping in tents. Maybe it doesn't feel like suffering for him. I stopped running because I did it for him and it felt like suffering for me both physically and psychologically. My mind wandered in bad directions.

I'm re-reading your messages, smiling at your words. This is the smile I would wear while chit chatting with you by a fireplace alternating between you and an exciting book or sitting on a bench, next to the lucky fishes who saw you naked.. or laying on my stomach, hugging a pillow while listening to you and feeling with you, for you.

Ups, it's already midnight. Time flies when speaking to you.

Take care Calvin

Elle

*

November 26, 2016

Elle,

I honestly understand what you mean about appreciating the effort and the things the boss is doing and saying, but wanting them to be what he feels and not what he feels he must do. I overthink everything. You know that. But I sometimes am suspicious of people's motives and can't appreciate the kind things when it isn't from their heart. Also a simple word or deed can mean so much when it is from the heart. In my car I have a small container in one of my cup holders to hold coins. I don't know how long ago but at least the summer before last, One of the little girls picked a dandelion, a weed flower, and gave it to me. It gave her joy to see it growing in a crack in the sidewalk and she wanted to share it with me. I remember how much love she gave to me. Every now and then when she is in my car I see her check and see if I still have the dead flower in my car. It is a dead weed, but it means a lot to her and to me.

I also had noticed, because you have/had no filter with me, you told me you were hurt when I offered advice. You just want me to care and listen and not try to "fix' your pain and problems. Just listen. This is difficult for me and I fail and offer my thoughts when you don't really need the advice of someone who knows nothing about the issues. But I understand and try to listen with my heart and recognize you can take care of yourself and just need me to be an ear and a heart. You know I have other body parts too though!

So I completely expected your response to him helping you with your writing. I am old and women seem to be honest with me when I mess up. So I learn. Although I am a math teacher and my instinct is to solve and teach, I am also wise enough to recognize when I don't have a clue about a resolution and that people need love more than to be told they need fixed.

I love your response to my video. It is so us! So not what anyone else would think of it. But I love it. Also I am just as weird because I have watched your video talking about your set up many more times than your orgasm. I love your voice and your accent. Most guys don't want to hear that a video of themselves made a woman listen to depressing music and write. But we are not most people and I get it.

About my accomplishments. I lived in a very small town. Around 150 kids in my class, 500 in my 4 grade high school. My class was very close. The fat band kid and the math nerd and the computer loner and the pot smoking drug kid all played sports. Everyone partied together and felt welcome. We all knew each other, mostly we had known each other all our lives. So being one of the best athletes or math geeks of the 60 or so boys wasn't anything great. I wasn't the best in most sports, just one or two and not always the most popular. I was looking for a picture of me running marathons. I couldn't find one because I am not proud of it. I survived but I was passed by little old ladies that run everyday. I finished and I am proud of myself, but I was never good at it. Here we have small races. Some have free soup at the end or keep track of the winner in each age group or by weight. I never was in the top half no matter how you made the category. I ran for fun and have a few T-shirts because I have fond memories. But it wasn't because I was good.

I sent some pictures of me growing up. I was normal height growing up. Then I grew very fast. I was stretched and very skinny, I was taller than most adults by 14 years old and was expected to be mature and act like an adult and not a 14 year old boy. I dated a girl who was years older than me and she loved me and was gentle but even though she didn't push me I felt bad because I wasn't ready to be as sexually active as she had been. She saw me as taller and so somehow older and I acted mature. But inside I was still a little boy. I didn't know anything and my first girlfriend and I still got excited holding hands or just when our hands brushed each other's. At 14 I really wasn't looking to make out. Just a sweet peck on the lips and maybe touch her leg or have her lift her skirt so I could see her knee. This girl was different from the girls my age that had been my girlfriend. She had been driving for two years and dating guys who were 18. Luckily she really did love me, but I think it affected who I am. Ok how did I go down that path? I was talking about sports. You have an effect on me.

Having long arms and legs and being taller than anyone my weight made me difficult to compete with in wrestling. I really didn't compete much in Judo, I just liked to study it. but my wrestling allowed me to beat people who were better at Judo than me but hadn't had the experience of combat I had from wrestling. I beat them with wrestling moves, not Judo. I think I won one fencing tournament but it was just fun later in life. I didn't compete at a high level at anything but wrestling. I also coached a little and feel good about the impact I had on the guys lives more than winning as a coach.

I don't like labels. I am probably a math nerd and the biggest compliment I could be given is to be described as gentle. But gentle and sweet and nerdy don't mean the person is effeminate or weak. I think I am friendly and I love that you joke about the fact I talk too much. I do. But I am also a man who lives alone in the mountains away from everyone and lives his life independent of others. I think I have few friends but really great friends. Maybe 12 friends is a lot of people to feel close to and have a deep love for. I have people I work with and students and people who admire me. But the few true friends I have are deep friendships. I'm not sure where to list you. but you are my friend.

I am a college professor, but I think my service is in encouraging kids, and they are kids still, to keep learning and keep trying and not settle for less than their best. I don't teach difficult math and even my master's thesis was blown out of the water by a man one year older than me. I examined one solution and he proved that my one interesting solution was useless because he proved there are an infinite number of solutions. What is worse, when I read his paper on the topic I had just written a master's thesis on, I had trouble understanding it. Terry Tao is smarter than me. I can live with that. I like who I am and what I do. But the label of college math professor doesn't sum me up. I am more and refuse to be put in a small box. So thank you for the compliments but I didn't mention my accomplishments because of modesty but because they weren't great accomplishments and they don't describe me well. I think you know me and runner is not the first word you would use to describe me. I love the way you think of me.

Ok this was all about me. I'll try to write about other things in another message.

Tuesday night I will be at my friend's. He is getting a new refrigerator and needs me to help move it plus do some handyman work. Oh and tonight my roof started dripping so I got to climb up and try to clean the leaves. We will see if I solved the problem. Your flat in the city sounds better than having to dig ditches so the water doesn't run down my road and wash it out so I am trapped and can't drive out, or cutting firewood to keep myself warm, or being alone when I feel afraid or sick. In college I had a sweet old widow lady who lived across the street. We had flowers in the front of our house she could see from her house. She would always thank us for giving her such a nice view. I would cut them and put them in a used bottle or just lay them on her step. She would make me soup or buy vegetables for me because she thought I looked tired. It was just nice to live by people and have them watch my place for strangers and care about me. I think I could live in the city for a while but I would miss this place.

Never feel you have to answer a question just because I asked it. I am not an invader or an obligation.

Still Calvin and I still love your messages. Thank you.

*

November 27, 2016

Elle,

I know you are busy and time to check your mail and enjoy videos is less with others around. I just wanted you to know I was thinking about you.

Life is good here. Everyone is refreshed after a vacation and my students are trying hard to learn before grades come out and the final exams. Everyone is happy and Christmas joy is out.

I am sorry you feel empty. I will not visit again. I am making your life difficult there. It is just difficult having you there to see and not being able to.

I will be gone until Wednesday night.

Get some rest.

Big friends can wrap their arms around you friendly and touch your forehead against their cheek and say comforting words as you fall asleep. Just lean against me and let me support your weight and worries and know you are safe. Nothing bad can get to you while you are in my arms. No sad thoughts, not concerns, no decisions, no responsibilities. You can just relax and feel my soft caress as you fade away into sleep. Life is good and things will be better. You're ok and you can deal with whatever comes. Just relax and let go until you wake up. I am holding you tenderly and you know you have greatness inside you. Just be you, Don't try to fit anyone else's mold. not even mine. Just be you in my arms and keep the rest of the world out. You are enough for you. I am just a place to lay.

Sleep well

Calvin

When you wake up you can watch a short video.
Life is good. Thinking of you.

Cum is running down my shaft.

*

November 27, 2016

Calvin,

This is what I can give.

I just want to give up. This is not how I pictured my life to be. Whatever I do, whether I stay in this marriage or leave it, it will never be what I thought my life would be like. Not a marriage without hope and love, not a divorce and a broken family!

My gynecologist is the sweetest person I know in France. She cares about my life, I'm not just a body for her. We didn't see each other for a very long time but she remembered my situation and asked me how things go with being lonely in France and not being helped by my boyfriend in the things I'm going through after the birth. She was so nice and honestly wanted to know what's going on with me. I told her about the situation and used the word "psychological abuse" for the first time in French. I don't even know why, but it felt right, and she asked whether he hit me and I said no. And she still understood me. I feel like she lived something that makes her able to understand what I am going through. She is trying to convince me to go to a psychologist. I might go this time. I feel so lost.

Big discussion yesterday night. I'm supposed to not write or answer you. To ban you from the website. Get over my "crush" and try harder to have feelings toward him. And I feel like begging whoever is in charge. "Please not this, anything else but not this" he convinced me that i own him to do this. He was bashing me pretty bad yesterday and got me all confused about what was and is real. He was doing this in a "loving" way of course. His words were the worst, I just wanted to get up and go hurt myself, and he also took my head in his hands and repeated me all over "I love you, let me help, let me make you happy, I love you, just stay with me and I will love you" Probably nobody would get why, but it was like a thriller movie, I just wanted to wake up from this hell where I only have bad options or maybe only one option.

I need you. But I might disappear to please him. I don't know.

I will try to find a professional to help me through this.

Elle

*

November 27, 2016

Thank you Calvin,

Wow, this is really helping. You keep surprising me. I'm not speaking about the video, it always wants me to have more of you. I enjoy them A LOT and will make good use of it.^^ Thank you.But they also make me miss you like hell.

Your words are really really helping. Thank you. Just perfect.

Elle

*

November 27, 2016

Calvin,

My mental health was always a taboo between him and me. I told him everything he needed to know at the beginning and we never spoke about it again. If I tried it got him really upset, so I avoided it because I didn't want it to become an excuse I could use in fights. But I think it's not healthy for me to pretend it does not exist.
He let me speak about the dark feelings his words trigger in me. It's a huge huge step. He didn't try to stop me. He might still think

it's stupid and I should just not feel this way but him saying nothing was awsome.

He even ended up admitting that he is aggressive when arguing. This is just something I thought would never happen. I know I am super sensitive and fragile. He knows it and reproaches it to me very often. But he always claimed to be nice and kind and perfect and it made me feel crazy. Why do I feel like he mistreats me when he says he is being nice to me? Someone must be right and the other one wrong. I thought I was wrong. Or that we will never agree and are living in 2 different realities.That his truth will never be mine.

Elle

*

November 27, 2016

Calvin,

It's crazy how much happens in just one day. The boss and I didn't really manage to ignore things and just enjoy being a family and good moments. The problems just keep coming back and up, disguised as a joke or a "nice" comment. And that eventually leads us to sit down whenever we can and also when we should sleep or do something else, and we share. It's hard and not nice things are being said and feelings being shared. We finally, finally agreed on being stuck and not being able to move forward. Now he thinks too that we need therapy, someone unpartial to give us a little push or help us approach things differently. Although it was an ugly discussion it wasn't a fight but a real discussion. It's good. And I feel like I might forgive him one day. I'm happy about that. I felt miserable hating him, and being so disgusted by him, I would love to be able to respect him at least enough to be able to enjoy the family moments without negative feelings.
I am working on not going in a bad direction with you. I don't want to ignore our connection. I do think it is a blessing and

something that is wonderful and for me a once in a lifetime thing. But I'm convinced that it's my choice how I interpret it and in which direction I let it flow. And yours too of course.

That's it. I have many phone calls to make appointments, psychologists, some marriage counselors, and that association for the divorce thing.

Things are better. I have hope again. I hope the boss and I can work out things, because whatever we decide to do we still have a child to take care of.

Elle

*

November 28, 2016

Elle,

I don't think this needs to be said, but if I have to I'll say it; I want you to keep writing to me, Please don't leave my life. I don't want you to stop and I enjoy and look forward to your emails.. I thought that was obvious but I'll repeat it.

I do trust your wisdom and you are not a child. If you think about this and decide it is best for you to stop emailing me for a while, to see if this is a crush, a fantasy or a connection, I will understand and keep sending you videos to encourage you to write to me back. I will not die or be crushed that you did something you think is best for your life, (For a short while). I am confident you will find this is healthy and we both enjoy it. But I don't like the fact we are hiding it and someone thinks it is a crush that is hurting your life and your chance at something. So I am trying to get you to keep writing. I am going to send videos or whatever you think I can do to sway you my way. But I trust your judgment.

If you say you think you need to stop me for a while. I have faith in you. This is a gift. You decided in the beginning to give me the gift of writing to me. I did not earn it. I have no right to it or deserve it. I want it. But I won't be hurt that you choose to put a pause in parenthesis in the middle of our story. I am confident this is not the last chapter.

In the end it is your decision. You know I want you to keep writing. But I understand and trust you.

I don't want you to feel you can't take a break... a small break, because I will make you feel guilty or be mad at you. I do hear your feelings. I do understand. If only for your boss and to prove him wrong, I understand.

I want to see you naked. DUH! I love your videos. Duh. I enjoy your messages. Duh. ( ) I look forward to having someone tell me I am someone special. Duh. Obviously what I want is clear. Don't stop.

But I have confidence in you and I understand. I am trying to ban myself from "the office." But you understand it is you, dressed sexy, being fun and happy and entertaining. being sexy and seductive, there to talk to live and it is just a click away. I am not that strong a man. But if you ask I will not let you know it is me writing to you, or if you ask I will not write, or if you ask I will try not to peek in on you.

To be clear I am in no way encouraging you to let go of me or stop caring about me or making me feel important. If you need some time to repair your family and get your feelings straight and be independent of everyone, even me. I will not be angry. I will understand. I appreciate the gift you gave me. Also I am confident you want me in your life in some form.

Ok, I'll write more later. I spent an extra night with my friend because he had car troubles.

Calvin

*

November 29, 2016

Calvin,

Just don't let me know you are there. For me it's very frustrating to know that you are watching and I CAN'T see you or tell you things I want to. We shared so many intimate and personal things in the emails, where it's just us. In the office, when I notice it's you, it makes me want more. And it feels unfair that you see me and I don't see you :(I can't see the expressions on your face or your sparkling eyes or tell whether you are bored or tired or stressed or happy.

Elle

*

November 29, 2016

Calvin

I want you so bad. I had to stop streaming for a quick temporary release. I want you so bad. You are the only one who could satisfy my complex needs. I want you.

Elle

*

November 30, 2016

Elle,

You are unfair.

I was good. I didn't say anything I would say. And after my second sentence you wrote. Good morning and a line of kisses. I thought she knew it was me! But I re-read what I wrote and decided, "There is no way she could know." I even threw in a line I would never say when the guy kept asking you to be his girlfriend and you said you didn't like the way it was going. I said I thought sex was better when you didn't care about the person and didn't have a relationship. So not me. like I have had so many women and the few I have were just women I fuck. I seldom even use the word "fuck". but still you knew it was me.

That's not my fault!

I tried to be good.

Calvin

But you already know this is Calvin!!!!!

*

November 30, 2016

Calvin,

Oops my bad, I thought you meant it with that sentence. Because you told me once that sex was amazijng with the big boobs woman. I don't know how is sex when you love someone without being afraid of him or even terrified. I really thought you think it can be more erotic and wild without feelings.

This might support your theory: I think of you when I have wild and erotic privates and also when I fantasize about doing things I never wanted to do to any other man. (no not kissing, dirty stuff) And I definitely have some kind of feelings for you. I don't know, it's new and weird.
I have a few videos made for you, I'll send them when I have time
friendly hug

You were good. it's funny that you can not mislead me. Heehee.

Elle

*

December 1, 2016

Elle,

Ok when you say, "I want you." That is like "Fuck me now Calvin." I enjoyed your pantyhose video already after I left so your video will have to wait until another night. but I will owe you one sexy video. and maybe one nice one too.

My friend was very appreciative. I stayed and helped him. We got a lot done. I am tired but I am glad I am me. I was reminded again today that the people who are getting ahead are people I am so glad I am not. I am glad I am the one being stepped on and taken advantage of. Not the one who is the user.

There is an old 1940's Black and White John Wayne movie called, "The Angel and the Bad Man." He plays a cowboy gunfighter and there is a quote that helps change him, "Each human being has an integrity that can be hurt only by the act of that same human being and not by the act of another human being."

The people who cut me off in traffic and drive on the side of the road to get 12 cars ahead of me, get 12 cars ahead and that's it. I still am proud of myself 12 cars back. I like myself and don't feel like a jerk who just cut everyone off because I thought I was more important.

So I worked hard and didn't get paid and stayed longer to help a friend. But I like myself and he likes me and what did I lose? I gained pride.

I am still not going to send you a story about two characters named Elle Electric and Calvin who visit places in California and have sex and tender moments watching sunsets. You still won't see it as two imaginary characters... and probably when I write it I won't either. But that is how I want to thank you for your "I want you." message. It would help you relieve some stress. but it is off limits for friends. I understand.

But thank you. You are very good for my ego.

As I said I came hard watching your video after I left.

Life is good.

I used to coach and I was thinking today; Educators are arrogant fools. They think a College Professor who teaches Mathematics is a better person to coach kids on how to fight and knock people down because he has a degree from a prestigious college. BS. I was head coach but my assistant coaches under me were good men and better coaches.

The thought I am sharing with you is that I think everyone has a part of them they are afraid to share because they fear people will judge them unfairly. The Physics students I knew and had classes with at this prestigious college, everyone I knew, had some plan on how they could create an earthquake by sending sound waves into the fault or some other super villain plan of destruction. They are all good people and they never would, but it always bothered me that they had put so much time and planning into their theories.

My secrets and the things you beat yourself up over don't make us crazy or bad or unable to make decisions for ourselves. I don't live with you. I only know the person I met recently. I judge you on who you are not who you were. I hear all the baggage from your past that you share with me. But I like the person I hear now. I think people forget that Physicists have a secret side that if that was all you saw you would lock them up. Yet they are respected for reasons that don't have anything to do with how respect worthy they are.

Thank you for still liking me after you hear what I see as less than perfect in myself. I like me. I wish I could allow others to see "me' and give them a chance to maybe like the real me too. I'm not there yet. I have a hair brush I use to brush my hair.

Also I want to remind you I gave you the code as an option. I tried not to force you to use it. I am not an invader. If you hadn't used it or figured it out I still would be visiting you. Yes I am getting basically free privates and videos of them. But I am also banned from buying privates or tipping you. So I don't feel guilty that I am getting a great thing.

I am not going to keep reminding you that you can leave for a while, because I don't want you to. But I don't like that the boss blames me for making you write to me. Seducing you. Tricking you. Forcing you to do this. I will survive and I will treat you kindly and care about you and would never try to make your life worse because you stopped writing and your life changed directions. Also I am confident in you. I know you will still care about me and feel good about us and think fondly of me no matter what the future holds. So don't think I am pushing you to do anything. Maybe I am sending you sexy videos to get sexy videos back and clearly I am trying to get you to write to me. But I don't like the word seducing.

Have a great day.

Maybe next week I'll send you pictures of Santa Calvin.

December Calvin wants you too.

*

December 1, 2016

Calvin,

I'm ok. Really. I'm very grateful and appreciative of my real life. Your messages definitely helped but the boss' critical words too. I enjoy what I have now and keep as an amazing fantasy what I don't have. You are right. Life is good. More than good because I'm getting a fantasy, something I can think about whenever I want. I'm happy when I'm falling asleep. And the boss is right that I should see my real life as a glass half full not half empty. I enjoy cooking for the family, having a family life, being on webcam, reading, working out, the warm and comfortable flat in the city, having love in me. Life is very good now. And if I hurt sometimes from missing you it hurts less and less and it's more of an I'm alive and I have someone to miss feeling. It's a happy little pain. Like when you have a wonderful family in another country and you miss them. Or when you found a job you love and you miss it when you are asleep or doing something else. I'm happy. I love to know that you exist. I love to know that we understand each other. And I love to have you messing me up sometimes and being always there for me and making me feel like you are something stable in my life. I need that.

My marriage is still as bad, ok a bit less now, but I let myself enjoy it anyway and not be so obsessed about just getting over it. I don't have to make a decision now. There will be therapy sessions and real life happening and I can make a decision when I am financially ready. And I will try not to blame myself for enjoying this financial security and comfort for now. Maybe me enjoying it is better for the boss too, than me feeling guilty and holding myself back to show any appreciation from fear of giving him hope.
Don't feel guilty. I wish we could have privates. I know you would make a budget for me. But I should ban you before going private. And I would prefer skype (or videos and emails)

anyways. Even if you are a fantasy, I feel uncomfortable with money being involved in this. I'm working on a website. Whatever they make me do or say I'm not even thinking about them. A whole part of me is switched off. They are strangers and I feel like it's fair to take their money for the show. But you, you are the one I usually imagine watching me while doing those shows. I wish I could show you the things I do there.

You are a friend. You make me feel like we are equals. Playing with you a domination game would be a fun game, not a bloody serious painful experience, after which I feel broken and am craving a hug. Uhmmm... where am I going with this? I was speaking about something else. You are priceless. I don't want your money. Why should YOU pay when I get so much from you too? Should I pay?

I wanted to hug you so much when you spoke about your older girlfriend. And I wanted to make you soup and be your neighbor when I read about how it is to be sick or afraid when alone. I would love to just live not far away from you, and visit you whenever you feel sick or afraid. I would be a nice old lady and visiting you would be all right. Oh, no. That means no sex. In that case I would be a normal aged woman you met while grocery shopping and helping me to reach a can of beans too high. Then we could have sex and nothing else randomly when we feel like to.

Whatever the boss thinks I know is just what he wants to think. I know you and I feel the connection. I trust your words because I feel like I can. If it were the same words but from someone else, I wouldn't trust these same words, they would seem just too perfect and calculated maybe. But I can feel that you mean them. Thank you for reminding me. I know but it felt good to hear this from you right now. I don't think you are seducing me, why would you be honest with me then and tell me about the three fingers knowing that I might stop sending videos and emails?

Your thoughts about not being the user and being stepped on and taken advantage of, they are so helpful for me. I sometimes am angry at myself for letting people use me. Most of the time it doesn't upset me though, because what they get from me is just so not worth the anger. As you said. I give it willingly because I like to feel helpful and nice. I don't feel like I'll be less because they took something from me. I'm still the same. They feel like they got ahead. Everyone's a winner. Ok, I might do this to an extent where I even feel like I could stand up for myself just a bit more. But I want to do that in a loving and nice and respectful way, not angry. So if I can't I just shut up and avoid the confrontation.

You don't owe me anything. But yes please I would love that.

The sunset is too much, don't make me want something we don't want. I want to be happy. I want you to be happy. I'd prefer to feel happy and not think about how impossible it is to go in that direction for like a million reasons. Not made up reasons, real reasons. It doesn't have to be complicated, said a very wise man once, right?
Santa Calvin, your message made me smile and laugh and smile and have tender feelings. Thank you.

Elle

*

December 1, 2016

Calvin,

You know how I like your personality and that I get easily excited and often exaggerate with my words. It resulted in this:

"You still won't see it as two imaginary characters... and probably when I write it I won't either"

Could you stop worrying about me seeing more into this, than you?? I will try to be more reasonable and choose my words better when I write to you. Just stop repeating what your position is. I already know that. I don't need to be remembered. I know about your other hand. I know there is no future for us. I know neither of us will leave his her life. We will probably never even meet. Fantasy. I like that it is all just a fantasy. It is a very nice fantasy.

I appreciate your honesty about it but I don't want to read something from you that is only meant while you are writing it. I love fantasy, but please try to limit it to something you would feel comfortable with and something you mean.
Aaaaa.. I am a little bit upset. I was ok but that sentence made me want to keep punching you in the chest and ask "How can you like me and not at the same time??".

I'm sorry. I know I write as confusing things as you do. I hate to feel lost about us. Because apparently there is an us, you mentioned something like "I like us". (??) This is definitely sexual. But not romantic. But tender. Loving, but not I love you. No future, but we don't want to lose each other. Sometimes I feel safe and comfortable. And sometimes just confused and lost and upset. And what was this ( ) in your "trust" message?? And why can't we just label it friends and move on?

I feel like I don't understand you anymore.

Oh no, I should probably shut up and go to sleep. I'd like to think about your friendly hug when I do so but I'm too upset that you think I am considering that hug different from how you do. I'm not! I just really like who you are and I could also need a friendly hug sometimes. I like having you as a fantasy. It gives me hope that I could be lovable to someone and not make him angry with my thoughts or feelings.

I had a great skype call with an old school friend tonight. Tomorrow I'll be visiting the french family and spending the evening with the boss watching the new Gilmore Girls episodes, eating tacos and popcorn. I think I will work Sunday morning.

I had a nightmare the other night. The boss was chasing after me in a huge house. I tried to hide but the floor cracked under my feet and he found me. He let me escape, I didn't understand why. But I could only get a few rooms away and he was very close again. I understood that he let me go because he knew I can't go far enough. I woke up feeling like this.

I also had a dream about you. Wasn't that good either. I met you and you were completely different from what I thought you were. And it felt stupid to ever see you differently from that man who stood in front of me. You seemed to be so cold and hostile. I remember feeling like I just imagined everything and men are all how I used to know them, at least with me they are like that. When they really see my faults and how I am they have no choice but behave like that.

I had these dreams the night after the discussion with the boss where he tried to make me come back to the earth and realize you don't know me, you never saw me living and failing and being difficult. That it is easy to like me from a distance and through the screen. that it is easy to write things to me that I want to hear based on the things I write before. That whatever you say you are not here and when he met me he came after me. Action not words. That I can find friends elsewhere, there are plenty of trustworthy people ready to listen and understand me. He doesn't mind me having friends. But this is just a perfect little fantasy in my head and he can of course not compete with a fantasy in my head.

I'm so tired I don't even know what I'm writing anymore. But it all made me feel so heavy. I'll be back and nice tmr or Sunday. I hope I didn't hurt your feelings. I didn't want to. It's all very unclear in my head, huge fog. Ok, Elle, sleep... fading into

Elle

*

December 2, 2016

Elle,

I love the polka dot stockings. I love the skirt. I love floral print blouses. I love the sexy body under them and the seductive way you show it off!

I agree I don't want money exchanged and Skype is an option.

Life is good.

Thank you again for the sexy video!

Santa Calvin

*

December 2, 2016

Calvin,

Thank you. For the pictures and the words and being there.

I am all caught up in this trying/separation process, it takes all of me, my energy, time and efforts and feelings and thoughts. Things are evolving. It is definitely progressing. I don't really know at what stage we are at. At some moments it is definitely denying, we get nostalgic, or make each other laugh with a joke, and appreciate something good in the other. There is no anger anymore. He is nice, just sad and hurt sometimes. I stopped feeling anger too. There is some bargaining where I make a list of the positive things about us and focus on the family and tell myself that it is not such a bad life, we could carry on like this, with time and a lot of silence it could be viable maybe. He is trying to bring back the mysterious man I met and could see how I wanted to see him. But eventually I end up remembering that it's not him. I know now his personality and desires and .... Depression is a constant for me. He says he accepted all this and is content with what is happening now. He found peace because he knows we are in this, both curious to find out for ourselves whether we can be together or not. We think now that whatever conclusion we get to, it will probably be together and to the same conclusion. He is not stupid. He notices that my eyes can not support meeting his eyes. That I push back his face with my arm very gently. He doesn't know I feel a desire to push him back violently. But his ego is still hurt. I don't feel peace. My brain hurts constantly from overthinking. And I don't even want to think but I just can't stop. For me it feels like it is my responsibility and I'll have to take the decision because I'm afraid he will refuse to admit how unhappy and un-understood and lonely we make each other feel. I am devastated to see my life fall apart and the ground being taken off under my feet. This was the only thing that was sure, a focal point, There was no me. Just us. We had a nickname for our couple that I used everywhere, mail account, blog, youtube channel, it became a brand. We spent all our time together from early on. We did everything together. And after every hysterical cry and bathroom bloody episode we went back, "as if nothing had happened" to the happiness. I apologized for everything I said and felt. He took my apologies and gave me another chance again and again. We can now talk about the beginnings and smile about it. See how unrealistic it was and still find it cute and think that we were so hopeful and innocent and just exchanged our hearts without any caution, without even knowing each other. We were sitting on the couch yesterday and sad but smiling we agreed that it was adorable how we built up something against the whole world, how dedicated we were and passionate, yes we skipped the basics and had no secure foundation but we experienced happiness and hope and gave life to a human being that we both wanted and I remember wanting him to be the dad of my child. It finally starts to feel like it wasn't a mistake. Even if it's not what we wanted, we lived. We did everything to the best of our knowledge. I didn't have these experiences yet, that allow me now to advance toward something that feels right. I'm so happy that he found peace. He seems happier than he ever was with me during these 5 years. I feel like we are both letting go, we let go of the expectations and we are open to find out who we are separately and together, whether there is/could be an us.

It could be worse. He is good at this. I think I couldn't wish for a better divorcing partner. Haaha. I am proud of us. I was delicate and nice with him when I started to feel like there is no us anymore and I didn't shock him but let him time to digest every bit of information I gave him. He only had a short phase of anger and denial but given that it just all felt out of the sky for him, his reaction is completely understandable. I was angry too at him, not that I have the right to, but I blamed him for being how he is and making me fall out of love and making me have to make hard decisions. We figured out how to make the ambiance better at home for the little one. And we managed to open up to someone we didn't trust and respect anymore. That was brave. And currently we manage to speak about uncomfortable feelings and hurtful ones without hurting each other. And I'm proud of myself to not give in when all I want is to numb myself with alcohol or self punishment. I'm proud that I choose to try things with him instead even if it feels horrible, or go get some rest to be able to carry on instead of wasting my time on youtube to exhaust my brain.

It's all gonna work out. Things will be better. Life will be good again. I might feel awful now all the time. But nothing lasts forever. We have an appointment on the 12th December at the association who can help us with the separation and divorce.

I'm sorry. I know I'm not very entertaining or a good listener. I am listening. I hear everything you say and also what you don't. I'm just useful now, I feel like I have nothing to offer.

Elle

*

December 3, 2016

Elle,

I had a great day up at the Apple orchards looking through the Christmas trees. Fun day but I am exhausted. Will write more tomorrow night when I wake up.

Take care.

Still Calvin

*

December 3, 2016

Calvin,

NSFW
not safe for work

Elle

*

December 3, 2016

Elle,

Awww the end was beautiful!!!

You look like you have gotten some sun?
I have a friend who was an engineer. His wife was friends with my mother in law. I saw him today and we talked for a long time. He designed airplanes and he is always interesting. He stopped a few times and apologized because he had to get his thoughts

together so he could speak and he changed topics once while we were talking. He was talking about a plane he flew and then suddenly he was talking about the training machine on the ground. Still he smiled a lot and we had a nice talk. His wife is very sweet and she said I was the definition of compassion. When I heard she was having a hard time I came over to clean up their dog poop in the back yard and do the dusting and some of things she was too busy to do at her age. He sleeps a lot and the doctors say that is ok just let him sleep. So I had a nice talk with his wife, then talked to him even longer than I thought we would. He has had troubles with his heart for years and has been in a hospital bed at his home for a couple years. Until recently he would let me help him into my car and go out to eat or something, but always something close and for a short while. Now he doesn't leave the house.

This was my day but I am sharing it with you because your words always help me talk to myself when I talk to you.

Compassion: when you can care about the boss and not want to hurt him and not matter what your feelings have compassion not to want to see someone suffer. You want to be selfish but you have compassion.

Monday the doctors have decided to stop the medicines that are supposed to help him and just give him medicines for his pain. My friend will be dead by the end of the month. His wife hasn't told him yet and she needed a friend to just care about her and be compassionate.

He knows he has been dying for years and he might know more than she thinks he does. He talked about when he gave up his driver's license and about not giving up, but his valve is calcified and the blood just doesn't flow through and they can't do anything because he is too weak to do surgery. It was hard not to tell him or let on, but he is a fighter and would just be sad. I have not given up all hope, but I am prepared if this was my last time to talk to him. Selfishly I mourn for my loss and I am happy his wife will be healthier because she doesn't eat or have a life because all she does is take care of him. I just don't know if I am selfish enough to allow this happy day and warm conversation with my friend while he was thinking clear and warm and happy to see me be my memory of him, or be compassionate to visit again for he and his wife's sake instead of my own selfish reasons to want to hold onto today's memory only.

I know this really doesn't have much to do with your message, but because of the mood I am in now When you were describing your relationship with your boss the word compassion came to mind. maybe not in love, maybe not hopeful for what was, but compassionate for another human and wanting the other to be happy and being willing to try to make things work out, even if apart, being unselfish enough and compassionate enough to not hurt the other.

Your message was very sweet, encouraging and happy. Thank you. But don't think you can only write when you have nice things like that to tell. I am smiling. Life is good.

Have I told you I like polka dots and skirts and that ending went straight to my heart. Not crossing the line. just sweet and even sexy. I loved it. Thank you.

Still Calvin

*

December 4, 2016

Calvin,

I'm still interested in everything you might write to me. Do you have a very busy week-end? Did I seem too off or far away? I'm here. Please write to me. You look very young Santa Calvin, that white hair and eyebrows and everything looks very funny. I'll go out this afternoon to buy stuff in the boots for tomorrow when "télapo" comes. I think I'll have a date with myself. Spend some quality time in town, wandering around. Lily is a bit sick so she will just watch cars and Peppa pig and who knows what or sleep. I think I can leave her with her dad.

I cried off my makeup this morning on the way back from school, and had to touch it up for the cam. I'm sorry, I know I seem off. The happy details of my relationship are coming back and I feel like I only let things go bit by bit, crying my eyes out for every little bit.

I just remembered how hopeful I was when I moved in here 9 months pregnant. The small wooden box I graved let's grow old together on it. He didn't even know the expression and we spent 5 min arguing about whether it really means what I think it does. How happy he was when I gave it to him with the ring on that bridge. I thought he would take it as a joke or say yes but never start to actually speak about a wedding. But he started to look for venues the next month and booked a wedding planner. Anyways, I always thought we'll have plenty of other moments in the future. But it all ended, we are only living from the past now.

Ahhhhh... you know I understand you don't want to confuse me now, or even be present in my life. I even appreciate that. But I miss you. being a friend I can speak with. We are just saying things now, not even to each other. It's not even a conversation. I feel so far away from you. I wonder what is going on in your mind.

Elle

*

December 4, 2016

Elle,

I think you are a Wizard or something!!!

There is no way you could tell that Texas guy was someone you knew. If I talk the same, you know, if I talk differently, you know. Whaaaat!!??? You are a Wizard! It is some magical power.

No fair.

You hear what I don't say, you know I want to hug you very badly. But that is not what is best for you. I am trying not to be selfish.
I love talking to you, even if you are talking to some guy from Texas!

I hear you and I do understand.

I am still Calvin.

I never shut up. Have faith I will talk again about deep stuff.

*

December 5, 2016

Elle,

For Christmas here people decorate with lights on their houses. It is nice driving home from work and seeing all the decorations.

I was blessed. We didn't have much money growing up and dad worked building houses outside all summer but sometimes in December he didn't have a job because it was too wet out to build in the rain. But I got many great presents. I remember Christmas as very magical but I don't remember many gifts that were memorable. I just remember my dad enjoyed watching me play with a toy even more than I enjoyed it. I think he saw something he wished he could have had as a little boy and bought it for me. This will be my second Christmas without him.

I am selfish, the thing I miss most about my wife and about my father is the way they looked at me. My dad was very proud. My grandfather always introduced me and talked with pride. But my dad just looked at me and I knew how proud he was of me. I miss that. He told me many times how proud he was, but I knew by his look. My dad lived 6 years longer than they expected and so he was getting his affairs in order. I knew this and it was hard. But he would continue to tell me not just that he was proud of the man I was but he would thank me for taking care of him and doing the things he couldn't do any more. I knew he meant taking care of mom and the family, taking care of the house, things like that. But also I think he was proud of who I was and that I was who he had hoped for me. I think anyone needs someone who thinks you turned out right and is proud of you. I was blessed to have people look at me with this admiration. I still have it. I told you about visiting my dying friend and helping his wife today... after I decided if I was going to do it or just be selfish and stay home and be lazy and not care about their hurt. So I still want people to be proud of me, but I admitted it to you because I know pride is something I have not something others give me. I like me even if people aren't proud of the real me and I don't have to do things or hide things to be worthy of my own pride. but I still miss seeing his eyes and his proud smile.

Sometimes my dad couldn't afford the gas to go to my wrestling but the team and coaches loved him so much they would let him ride up on the bus with the athletes. To a lot of the guys who didn't have good fathers he was also a father to them and proud of their accomplishments but also proud of them for being men.

Ok now don't read into the fact that my picture has the bridge in San Francisco and the Eiffel Tower both in it. Yes I thought of you when I saw it, but I didn't do the decoration the person decorating for Christmas did it.

You say good things about your sister who owns the ice cream shop. Did you want her proud of you, or was she trying to make you proud? Are you close enough that growing up you were best friends or did one of you follow the other around and were jealous of her friends?

Always Calvin

*

December 5, 2016

Calvin,

I'm watching a recent vlog of a youtuber in California, she just went to the Christmas parade with her kids. It made me think of your Christmas parade story. Did you go this year?

I didn't know you wanted to hug me. My wizard super powers don't go that far. ^^

Aww...that picture! Wonderful, that face. Let me just have a look at this when I need to be cheered up. How can you do a face like this?? I'm still laughing. You are adorable. You look cuter than the cutest stuffed animal in the shopping center every child begs its parents for. If you would be a stuffed animal even I would buy you. And I already have one to sleep with, a bear with red hair, a bit like mine. But I would still want you, that face. This is everything. If I ever wondered why I like you so much, this picture seems to have the answer with all the details I couldn't even verbalize. I don't even have to look at it, I just thought about looking at it and I am already laughing and feeling warm. Elle, relax. Stop. shut up. I got carried away. Great picture.

Do you know what city I am living in? I was wondering whether you think it's Paris. Did I say something you could figure it out from? I don't think I did. Ok, the person did it. But you still stopped and asked someone to take that photo from you, the Golden Gate bridge and the Eiffel tour... Busted! Hee hee. Thank you.

I like when you are selfish. You want innocent things. And you manage it well and try not to hurt people. Based on what you write you feel selfish rarely and act selfless a lot. I'm proud of you. And jealous... I want someone to be proud of me. I am proud of myself, but still... I'm only sharing this because you'll know it is not my way of begging you to say it.

What do you mean my message was encouraging and happy? That's funny. I thought it was sad and depressive.Oh, don't you worry, I am not only trusting you with the nice things, didn't you read my nightmares and me mentioning the alcohol... Uhh. I actually did drink a bit yesterday night. I couldn't sleep from everything I felt so I ended up drinking to numb my brain. And I drank some toward the end of the session. And if I start to confess I should also add that I got high with my siblings in Hungary, not just trying and not feeling anything but smoking until I really felt it. The next day my mental health was so bad I told them that's it, I didn't like to smile for no reason and laugh for no reason for a few hours and go down deep afterward. I wasn't in control of what I said. They said it was funny and I was adorable. They couldn't believe it but it seems like I am half pervert and half kind. That's it, this defines me. they loved my high and honest self and found the horny part slightly disturbing... I bonded with my brother whom I explained why I love and respect him while I was high. So that's good. Worth it. But it didn't feel right. I can't be cool. The boss loves it, my siblings love it, and many of my friends too... I feel more lost and lonely and not where I belong than ever. Ok, that's it. You make me feel guilty for so many things... You don't seem to have any bad habits and few get down from the right roads.

My sister... Oh, she is very special. We weren't best friends. She annoyed me. She was full of life and ideas to mess up things and behave bad and then make it seem like she didn't do anything. I was the boring one who just wanted to read in the corner. She found that I am strange and loved to make fun of me. I loved to go to school very early, arrive before anyone else did, put the chairs down on the floor and clean the chalkboard, daydream in the empty classroom. She started to get up early too and leave at the same time. I hated her for that and we were running and pushing each other in the trench all the way to the school building. At high school I started to become the perfect child of the family, with good grades and no problems. She was very good at sports. I think she started to envy me at that time. She wasn't studious and had only guy friends. She might have envied my friends too. At elementary school I had a close friend group and she wasn't allowed to hang out with us. At high school I had another close friend group but this time she was often with us, we all liked to have her with us. She was into partying and dragged me with her several times against my will. We always ended up fighting. I usually had a meltdown, kind of social anxiety, just wanted to go home, I didn't feel safe with her, she often left me at parties for a handsome guy or a girl. Then I had depression. She became my big sister. She is two years younger but saw me weaker and more vulnerable than she was and the dynamics changed. After my graduation I left to work in foreign countries. I became the pretentious one whom Hungary and her family is just not enough. Plus I met the love of my life, and went to university. Everything seemed to be perfect. She told me several times that this is what she wants. She envied me. I envied her. Because she was very popular. It was frustrating to go anywhere with her because men ignored me and were crazy about her. She complained and behaved badly with them, treated them badly and still they just all wanted her. She is extremely impertinent, to the point where it is almost mean and hurtful. And I just couldn't understand why men prefer this. I know her. I see at home how messy she is, she is not even that into sex, she throws tantrums, she gets always what she wants. But no matter how heartbroken she is, how much weight she puts on, how she behaves...there is always a line of men waiting for her to show some interest. She is currently dating 3. It is a constant that she has one guy in her life who is desperately in love with her, waiting for an occasion that never arrives. She uses this guy until she can take her here and there to entertain her, crying on his shoulder. She is honest and tells them that they have no chance to have more, but still it seems a bit cruel to me. There are 1-2 heartbroken guys because of her, each year.

She is considered an easy woman who likes to party. I know she is just desperately looking for love. And I think the excitement she throws herself in a new relationship each year is adorable. She is full of life. I love her.

She is also the one who loves family programs just as much as I do. The one who can cheer up anyone. She is very funny. She is like sunshine. Things are just more exciting and funny and worth living when she is there. She knows her importance and isn't generous with her presence, so it makes its value even higher.

So... I would say we envied each other taking turns and now we still envy each other. But also not. Because we are both considered attractive now. And I learnt a lot from her and she learnt from me. I'm more sexual and she is more impertinent. And we are now both letting go of a toxic person and it makes even more things we share. It's crazy. He had only nice guys until now, guys she could dominate and take advantage of. But this last one was like a gangster, psychopath. An aggressive guy who liked to crush people and throw money. He was charming.

Wow. I just wanted to say we weren't best friends and we envied each other and now we are called "family name" girls. At home we are now considered a public danger and we like it! I was learning from her this summer how to tease men and stay funny no matter what. She is awesome at this. I owe her a huge part of my current confidence.

We are rotten in a similar way.

Thank you again for that face. You are special.

I'll keep the little one home tmr. I don't think I will get up before her to make a session. By the way... were you watching me when

I had bikinis on? Is this why you say I look like someone who got some sun?

My date went well. My favorite decoration was a string of snowflakes, very delicate and elegant with only warm yellow lights. I didn't take my camera. I wanted to be alone, try not to think about anyone. I ended up going to the bridge where I thought of you last time when I discovered it with my friend. This is where I imagined your fantasy taking place. I didn't have time to wait for the darkness and the lights and it looked all gray, washed out colors. But it is a remarkably charming spot, if you turn around you see beautiful old buildings everywhere.

I feel happy. That picture…

Elle

attached : elf Calvin, new york paris Calvin

*

December 6, 2016

Calvin,

I'll have a job interview tomorrow. I will still go online from 9 a.m. but just to start my day on a good note. I will only be there for about half an hour before I leave for the interview. No, I won't change, same outfit. I can't wait. I'll probably be awkward and go to speak too much and seem like a too confident person whom nobody wants to work with. Always in the extremes.. Group interviews tend to make me act not like myself. I'll try to act like myself this time but if it goes wrong that's not too bad either. I need practice anyway, this will be just the first jump back in the pool. Let's hope there won't be any silence where I'll feel the need to fill it up by saying something funny. That tends to go wrong too.

It's a cashier at an office supply store job offer. Normal job, looking into people's eyes, speaking to their faces while they are wearing clothes on their bodies. Very exciting. It will feel like some role play. I can already see myself trying to not think about this tomorrow but not succeeding. Let's hope there will be no mind reader wizards there.

It will be fun.

It's a much needed happening, I'm so happy that I have something to think about. I cannot wait to have colleagues I can cheer up and entertain and turn work into fun with. I'll probably have to wait for that, but at least something is happening with this interview taking place tomorrow.
The little one loved the chocolate in the boots this morning. And I loved to watch her get excited and try to make a sentence with the few Christmas related words she knows. She is so adorable when sick, cuddling and sweet and calm. She is feeling better now. You know how I know? She took back the power in her hands. Told me very strictly to finish my plate and said well done when she was content with me. Such a dictator... She loves to be in charge. The preschool teacher told me she follows her everywhere and repeats the instructions to the children (they are all older than her) , ragging them for not doing it well enough. I think she will be the one who will finally teach me to stand up for myself while staying funny and nice. I'll have to otherwise she will subject me.

And now some less exciting stuff because I can share this with you.

I feel frustrated and angry and aggressive. Today we kept sending small hurtful things into each other's faces with a smile, disguising it as an innocent comment. I hate to pretend to play with him. Play the « let's try to fix things » game. One week down. 4 more weeks to go. I'm counting down the time. The more we try the more obvious it is for me that I already made up my mind about it and it won't change. The distance keeps growing. I have the list in my head with the pros and cons, the cons outweigh largely the pros. The cons are things I can have without him, living on my own... That's not good. I feel like I would do absolutely anything to get a fixed salary and be able to get away from him. He is smiling and hugs me and kisses me but somehow still manages to insult me all the time. I hate to be like this. I hate the person I am with him. I have very violent feelings toward him. I hate this.

Elle

*

December 6, 2016

Elle,

I love learning about you. Thank you. I hear you smiling when you talk about your sister. You are blessed.

You are very lovable, huggable and unique. Being you and not like anyone else is a good thing.

I don't know and don't need to know where you are. I love to learn. I am interested in cultures and different lands, but travel and geography has never been something important to me. I love meeting new people from around the world. I told you about being in Yosemite and just enjoying meeting people from all over the world that all shared the same awe for nature and had familiar smiles. But if you told me about France I wouldn't know what you were talking about. I barely know where Hungary is on a map and honestly that is more interesting to me. France seems like a tourist spot and European/American. I want to see the mountains and fields and waterfalls and meet people on a personal level. Real people not people trying to serve the rich customers. Good people who share their soup. French people have a reputation for being rude and judgmental. You are Elle, that is what I know and who I am interested in, I don't need to know more precise details.

In the town I grew up in.. I guess I have already told you the name of it. But they used to have the firemen drive through the streets with a trailer behind the fire truck. On the trailer was a big sleigh with Santa and the reins went from his sleigh up onto the fire truck where they had fake reindeer. They played loud music and the sirens and their lights flashing and the lights around Santa were colorful. It was an overwhelming sight for a child. They would stop on every street and all the kids would come out Christmas eve and they could talk to Santa Clause. I have a younger cousin and to this day he swears he never saw the fire truck and he remembers he saw Santa fly away and those deer flew up our street. The magic of being a child in awe of the magic.

In your video, thank you for the video, I have already planned out your next video but my room is a mess and school is taking so much of my energy and time. But I am going to explain math concepts to you. But in your last video I noticed your tan lines. Maybe it was the lighting. but you looked great and like you had gotten some sun. I like tan bodies. I like your body! I'm sorry I missed your bikinis.

I have many flaws. but I do like myself and I have pride in myself when I do something good and am not selfish or trying for instant gratification. I am cheap and like to get deals. I am not impressed by people with money and the people I know with a lot of money, have a lot of money because they don't spend it. My family used to raise horses and work cattle, and one saying I heard a lot was: "Big hat no cattle." I found it was true.

Ernie Caddel was a good friend of mine. He came to my wrestling matches from the time I was 13 until he died. He was always ignored because he was sweet and wore coveralls and dirty boots. He dressed poor and was quiet. When I was 13 he was the richest man in the room but he never let anyone know. He never bragged but I knew he was a real man. I later found out he broke 3 ribs playing at my college. He continued to play football the rest of the season but was kicked out of college because his injuries he got playing for the college kept him from playing baseball also for them. I asked him about it and he said, I was never bitter. Losing my scholarship allowed me to become a professional football player, good things come from bad, you just have to see it.

Sorry I loved him and got off topic. I tend to just write when I talk to you.

Big hat no cattle: The man with the $600 cowboy hat who brags about what he has is trying to impress you because he has no cattle. The man with the little hat and cheap clothes quietly standing in the corner laughing at the braggart spends his money buying cattle. Rich people have money because they don't spend it trying to make people think they are rich.

The message that my family was trying to get across to me was that if you know you have worth and value you don't have to brag and convince other people. The guy with the big hat is insecure, be content and know that YOU believe you have worth. What shows, like a big hat, doesn't make you who you are. Smile in the corner and know you are better even if they don't. I was blessed to grow up around simple people with pride in what they had who didn't care about what they didn't have. My great grandfather was happy to play his violin and see people smile. He loved his animals and family. He lived to be over 100 and was sharp and was loved and valued his entire life. I don't know if he ever wanted more than what he had.

Calvin talks too much. you are fun to talk to. Thank you for sharing about your sister that made me smile.

I have many flaws besides talking too much. I tend to see my flaws at the end of the day and review my mistakes. It hurts when I see my flaws repeated and my mistakes being more than mistakes. Sometimes it is good to be able to honestly see my faults and still love who you are. I guess one of my faults is I am too weak and it helps to be loved and having others love who I am and all of what I am even my shortcomings makes it easier to love myself. I am working on being more honest and not caring if others disapprove of things I approve of.

Ok, I'm going to try to look for you and leave before you recognize me. Wizard.

I think you understand I leave because I see it makes you change and work differently when you see me and uneasy about the boss. I don't leave because I don't love seeing you.

Yes, I have already masturbated to your last video.

Sweet friendly hug.

Calvin

*

December 7, 2016

Calvin,

Something went wrong yesterday night. I need to figure out what to do with myself. Please, someone tell me it was just a bad day and it doesn't mean that I can't function anymore. I'm scared. I will deal with this after the interview. I guess, I'm just surprised, I thought I'm in control. Anyways. I seem to be a different person this morning from my yesterday night self. This is scary too. Oh, shit. What if he is right about everything?

Elle

*

December 7, 2016

Elle

I am not an expert on you and I have not known you for long. But I think you are a good person. Don't be scared. trust yourself. Don't stress about things that haven't happened and might never happen. I don't know why you are upset but I think you are fine. You are better than fine, you are a good person. Relax. I don't know what you are talking about but trust yourself.

I trust you.

Maybe it was just a bad day.

How you feel and thoughts you have aren't who you are.

Please be ok. I care about you.

Always Calvin

*

December 10, 2016

Elle,

I understand you are dealing with a lot, but when you have a chance send me 3 words:

Either "I am alright"

or "Care about me"

I am worried but not because I don't believe in you, just because I don't know the problems.

Calvin

*

December 10, 2016

Calvin,

I'm afraid to tell what I did because it makes it more real. I kind of just want to forget that it happened and act like it didn't. I cut myself yesterday. I wanted to kill myself so bad that all I could think about was hurting myself somehow to make that stop. It only worked for a few min and I started to go insane again so I just did it again and again. At some point I realized it won't help me more than for a few minutes so I had some vodka. I still felt like the pain was unbearable. I was desperate. Went to the boss and asked him to come to the bed with me and hold me. I fell asleep like that. I just wanted to get a quick fix and get some sleep before the job interview. I really was thinking about the long term and I wanted to be ok mentally when I get to the interview, that could get me a job and get me out of hell.

I still have no idea how this happened. I was having a bad day, usually I realize it and can deal with it. I'm trying to remember more but it's like my brain doesn't want to. The little one was sick. We were home all day. I don't remember what we did. I don't remember when the boss joined us and how it went. The only thing I remember is that we decided to watch a movie that night. It was very disturbing for me. The mom in the movie committed suicide, she had bipolar disorder. I remember the boss commenting and me feeling hurt. Him trying to pull my face to kiss my cheek to make me forget the comment. But it was something about how lucky I was to have the dad I had and not the one in the movie and something about me being the problem and not others if I repeatedly find myself with people I don't like in my life. I pushed him away and curled up hugging my knees. We fought after the movie. I can't remember anything of that but hating myself so much that it became more powerful than anything else. ... And I ended up giving up my pride and crawling back to him to ask for help. I hate that I did that. I'm not there anymore. I don't want to keep that cycle alive. But I felt like I had no one I could speak to in the middle of the night and I couldn't afford to hurt myself all night before a job interview.

I took an appointment at a psychologist this Friday afternoon. I just want to speak to someone who doesn't hate me and could have a non judgmental but honest opinion of me. The boss is furious, he thinks I'm not behaving as an adult, he is hurt because I don't try the way he imagined I will, he mentioned that I don't sexually spoil him anymore like I used to and asks me what it makes of me that I sleep with him while not liking him. He thinks I exaggerate if I take these as an insult. He is super mad at me. I feel like he lost it, there must be a fog on his brain that makes him only want to hurt me. He told me to take my stuff and leave tmr. But also that he would love to speak to a psychologist about who I really am and how I cannot take it if people have a different opinion than me. He keeps saying that I will never be happy. Never find a man who makes me happy. That he never saw me happy. (Here I felt relief, because I know for sure it is not true, I am doing well for about 2 years now. I remember waking up enthusiastic about life during my 9 months internship, when the little one was 6-15 months old. I remember being well after it. I remember feeling happy and strong this summer. Genuinely happy about myself and life. And I still am now some days or moments. I don't even need you or your fantasy for that. I remember how I succeeded at things lately and how I overcame things and that's enough memories of the successful me to be confident about my current self) You know, I know that he must be right about me in the way that this is his perception of me, so I am like this for him. I am super sensitive and have a tendency for depression. I don't know... it is very scary to think that all I am is what he claims me to be. I'm afraid that he is right, because he has lived for me and knows my defaults and so he could be right. I don't think he will force me to leave. But it does make me feel unsafe that he felt like he needed to say that to get out his anger. I guess I can always ask his family for help, they like me. Although that would make him furious, his family has no idea about all of this. My friends are gone. My friend from Finland moved back to Finland. My Japanese friend left too. My Hungarian friend from here moved to Thailand with his boyfriend. But there is one Chinese mom friend from the playground and a french girl from the internship who was cool. And that swinger friend, who I only met once, yeah, not her. I will be ok. If there is an emergency situation I think I can reach out for help.

Today, I had a private last moment with a quick orgasm, a nice experience at the job interview, a nap in the afternoon and playtime with the little one while his dad was napping. A whole day without communicating with him, it was amazing and when we got to speak at the end of the day I was strong enough to put things in perspective. I started to feel like yesterday but I still remembered how nice that guy in the private spoke to me, how professional and kind the manager at the interview was (I just told him my honest life situation without going into details and we joked about it and he treated me like a person with a brain, a potential employee. I think it went well. He really gave me an opportunity to show who I am and what I want and how I like to work. I have a good feeling about that job. I like the actual work, it's not far away from here, the working hours are compatible with our life, it could be my happy place.), how amazing it was to play with Lily, we laughed so much and I felt like I managed to take very good care of her. We usually do bath time and cooking at the same time. I did both myself because he was still asleep. It went really well. All of this gave me enough self confidence to hold myself together when he started to fire at me again. He is just extremely cruel and aggressive now. I wish I could make him not be like this without having to crawl back to him and apologize for everything. I didn't. I called my Hungarian friend instead. I'm repeating to myself that he will eventually calm down. That it will stop feeling like hell here or I can get out of it. There are appointments scheduled. If I get the job, I will take it. It will allow me to rent a flat and eat and spend my days smiling, hopefully with nice colleagues. If I don't. I will get another one. And I will save up money to buy myself a pc that is powerful enough to stream jasmincam. I'm currently streaming from the boss' pc. I want to continue that. It makes me happy and it will also allow me to gain a bit of money if I need some more.

At worst I have to calm the boss down and squat at his place pretending until summer, then go to work at the ice cream shop in Hungary. Come back to France in autumn and get a flat.

I'm trying to tell myself that there is hope and this hell will end next year. I will learn and ask for help and information and figure out how to live on my own. I took the hardest steps, the first ones. I don't always feel like I'm progressing but today was a good day and I know I am.

See? Honest message. Not sunny and bright and encouraging. Well maybe the end, because I need to end it on a good note, for you to not worry and for me to keep hope.

Care about me? I don't know. Thank you for your help. I hate to use you. My automatic reaction when I'm hurt is to push away everyone and suffer alone until I find a solution myself. I don't want anyone to see me like I am now or even know that I am like this. My desperate reaction is to cry out for help to anyone available. And I hate myself for doing that. It's like admitting that I'm a failure and I was stupid enough to get in trouble and can't come out of it. I hate having such a fragile and unstable self image. It's like walking around in the world silly and hopeful with no emotional skin on to protect me. Why can't I just be strong?

Elle

*

December 10, 2016

Elle,

You are not your past.

Your struggles have happened, I hear you saying you "have a tendency for depression" that isn't a sin. You are sensitive.

Someone who has a tendency for alcoholism has to be careful at parties and clubs. You may have to be careful watching movies that imply people with a tendency for depression are horrible beasts and monsters. You are not. I hear you saying you know you are healthier and can be happy and can have a good life. Listen to you, not to me or to the boss. You have a tendency for depression and if you are not careful you can slip if you walk right up next to the cliff. You know that. You are doing good in a hard situation and feel strong enough to look over the edge. So you made a mistake. Life goes on.

I am not trying to downplay that you just said you wanted to die. That scares me big time. I am just saying that you also said; You know the solutions and are meeting with a psychologist Friday and finding a support group of people, (I volunteer to be part of your safety net). you are progressing toward a better life. Finding security in yourself. Believing in yourself as a parent and good person. and even willing to humble yourself in order to stop what you understand is destructive. I understand that you hate that you went to him to feel loved and secure and stop the crushing feelings. I don't understand. What you deal with is beyond my experience and understanding. I have anxiety and negative thoughts, but they are not what you are talking about. I approve of you seeing a psychologist. I think she will tell you that you "have a tendency for depression" and you are not crazy or a monster or a time bomb. That you are a sensitive deep thinking person. But don't listen to me. I am not a psychologist. But neither is the boss. I am proud you found or at least returned to a way you knew would stop the pain and the problem. Live to fight again tomorrow. Stop hating yourself. I think you are lovable and pretty great.

My world is nothing like yours but we all need to be held and loved and feel secure. My arms feel empty and you need to be held. Sad world.

Please use me. I'm not sure how you think you are using me. But thank you for telling me you know I do care. From anyone else this is just words. From you it means something. I accept that compliment. Thank you.

I know the answers to the following questions: Would you hate me if I failed? Would you think less of me if I told you when I was weak? If I had a bad day and regretted my actions would you encourage me for tomorrow? If I thought badly of myself would you do everything you could to build me? If I felt lost and alone would you comfort me and let me know you care? Does the fact you would do all those things make you a great person? Let me try to be half as wonderful as you and love you the way you love me.

Love yourself the way you love me. Show yourself the same forgiveness and make allowances for the faults you see in yourself like you do for others and their faults. I am far from perfect. but still you are generous and kind and wonderful to me.

More work around here this weekend. It is raining now and will rain again next week. I hope things are dry enough for me to clear brush and all the work I need done. One of my favorite jobs I might have to do this weekend. Even when it is wet here I live in the woods and fire is dangerous. All my neighbors are careful because one fire would burn forever through here and ruin many lives. So I pile the black berry bushes and the dead brush and pour gas on it and make a big fire. But I can't just leave it. No matter what else I need to be doing I allow myself to just sit and watch the fire and make sure the wind doesn't blow it and spread it. It is relaxing to listen to it crackle and watch the fire die down then stir it up and add more to it and have a big fire again. In this weather when it is still wet out and the air is damp and cool, it is nice to feel the heat on your face while the cold is against your back. I just curl up inside my coat and have peace. I am doing something important and don't feel guilty for just relaxing and enjoying the fire.

Life is good and you are good.

I wasn't trying to hide who I was yesterday. I was worried and I am still a little worried. Please don't think I am making light of this. I just don't think my talking about how concerned I was helps you. Obviously I knew you knew it was me asking about your interview. You even answered my not so cleverly disguised question and good luck wish. Please don't say, "good night C" be safe, I know.

If anything, say, "Good night you."

good night you

Still Calvin

If my thoughts or feelings or opinion of you changes I will tell you. Assume I think well of you and admire you and think you are a great person who treats me fantastic. Always

*

December 11, 2016

Calvin,

He is still furious. I feel strong today.

He didn't let me take the little one to pre-school. and started to fight with me in front of her. I have no respect for him. I stayed calm and explained to him it would be better for her to not experience this. That our couple is suffering. He hasn't slept yet at all. We could both need a break. It would be better for her in school. But no. He decides to keep her home. And hurt me. He says he would be ok to repeat anything he told me to anyone. I would like him to tell a therapist the things he says to me. He thinks being the responsible perfect person who is always nice and loving. I have to go.

I feel like I have to be better than superwoman to survive this. I don't know what will happen but I have to use all the strength I have and also what I don't and just keep surviving.

Elle

*

December 11, 2016

Elle,

Yes.
I am here.
You are superwoman.
You can do this.
Survive.

I care and believe in you

Calvin

*

December 12, 2016

Elle,

I hear good words in your bad words.
I remember you doubting if you could be a good mother. The boss told you that you are too selfish and think of yourself and not Lily.

Now I hear you saying you know you are being the better parent and he knows you care about her so much that he uses her to hurt you because he recognizes you are unselfish and puts her ahead of yourself. It hurts you if she hurts and he doesn't care. (and you still listen to his mean words of judgment?)

I hear you say you are stronger today and he is out of control of his emotions. You are the secure one and he is furious. You are not the needy one. You are honest about who you are and you are going out of your way to show a psychologist the truth about the real you. You think this is not who he is or that he is brave enough to do what you are doing.

I hear you say you don't know what will happen, but you either have enough within yourself to handle it. And even though you don't know what it is, or if it is greater than you, I hear you say even if it is too much for you, then you will become greater and find more in you and survive.

This doesn't sound like a weak scared unstable frightened victim. This sounds like the Elle I admire so much!

Do you hear what you write to me? That woman's pretty super!

Lucky Calvin to know someone like you.

*

December 12, 2016

Calvin,

WOW. You are overwhelming.

I have trouble finding the appropriate words. Yes, I am using you. Thank you for letting me use you. Your words are helping me. Always. Who is the wizard now? I don't know how you manage to give me what I need. Thank you. You think you know what I want but you prioritize what I need. Even if you would want more or less or different you still prioritize what I need. This is very generous. It feels good and it is helping and I want to be selfish and just take what I need and ignore everything else. I'm sorry if I don't let you express yourself without holding yourself back and always paying attention to not cross lines. Just know that it means a lot to me. Thank you also for understanding that me not saying it doesn't mean that I don't care about you a lot. You are right about the answer to your questions. Thank you for not taking the "I don't want to think about it" for "I don't feel anything for you". I am not thinking about you like that anymore. But if you'll want me to face my feelings and analyze them I will do it for you. Sometime, not now, not soon. You being worried and concerned made me feel like I probably owe you to do so. It's very selfish but I like to be in this safe place, where I get to use you keeping my heart to myself. Sorry.

Thank you for the "you can do it" messages! You are an amazing safety net piece.

I feel spoilt.

Elle

*

December 13, 2016

Elle,

I have multiple degrees in logic.

When you hear something good said about you it is a compliment and you feel humble and want to deny it.

But I know logic and you are logical enough to accept that what I say is facts. You are thinking of lily. You are more open and actively seeking counseling. All the good thoughts you have about yourself are undeniable. Even if it is hard for you to accept. You are pretty great. by your own standards too.

You don't deny that part of who you are, not a hard decision or choice but just deep within you is someone who cares about me and others and has and will overcome. You don't deny the laws of logic just to make yourself feel bad about yourself.

Forget if I am proud of you and admire you and think you are doing great. Admit that you are proud of you, you admire you and you know you are doing great. Even if you fail.

I like that person. I like hearing from you.

I like your body!

Still Calvin

*

December 13, 2016

Calvin,

I want a white Christmas now...It sounded like you.

That something with giving a hand made me think it might be you. You probably meant it in a sweet way, just something that describes you. But it sounded very dirty. :D I don't why but I was still confused when you kept writing.
Something went wrong with my super power :)

The other day after the job interview, taking public transport I took a bus in the wrong direction. I was thinking about what I want to share with you about my day. This is the third time that I got on the wrong bus or subway because I'm having a conversation with you in my head. This is how you are part of my real life. Heehe.

Yesterday was a good day. He slept through the whole day. I played with Lily, took her out (mental note to myself: remind him that he could not take care of a child alone, so he cannot get rid of me as her mom). She was running after the pigeons, complaining that they fly away :D And she laughed while playing football on her own. She was so damn cute. I had a moment of "this is happiness", that perfect beautiful moment that you want to stop and grave in your heart. Something that is so perfect that you can't believe it is real and not just part of a movie or book. I contacted that Chinese mom and met her in the afternoon. Sadly there is no connection between us, it is just not working. She was nice and we talked and the children like each other but it wasn't a close friend feeling, definitely not someone I can turn to when needing help. Now I remember why I let this friendship die. There were no words exchanged at all that night, I just went straight to bed, exhausted.

I'm a little bit anxious about my appointment. Also excited. It has been years that I kept pushing the thought of a psychologist away and not making that call.

I love watching the flames.

The boss actually told me that morning when he kept Lily at home that I only want her to go to school to have fun on camera. I didn't mention it because it is so horrible. I have difficulties speaking badly about him. I learnt to not do so because in a couple problems have to be discussed and solved inside, mentioning bad things to an outsider makes me feel very guilty. I am also afraid that just because we are angry now and hurt if we start, I can't stop. That I will complain about the things that don't even bother me, about the compromises we made and worked out well. I have to remind myself that the problem is not that he is on his pc playing video games when watching Calliopée because he always reacts when she asks him something and he takes care of her even if not giving his full attention and very little quality time to her. The problem is not that he hates to walk, take her outside or come with us. The problem is not that he never does the dishes or cooks, because he does cleaning and washing clothes and hanging them. The problem is not that he sometimes leaves his socks on the floor and cake packaging on the nightstand. It's hard to stay human and not to start hating him for everything he does or doesn't do. It's extremely hard to respect him and treat him well while he is ruled by anger and hate.

I understand now that I can doubt his judgment. He knows my weaknesses, things that hurt me the most. So this is how he can make me feel guilty for my sexual drive and liking to show myself, or for not being a perfect mom, or for having mental issues. He will find my insecurities and as long as I feel guilty about something he can use it against me. So I should accept those things and know he is using them because he knows that it affects me, if it doesn't it won't work anymore. Thank you Calvin. It helps me so much.

You must be exhausted by the time you open this email.

Sweet kisses, I wish I could be held by you, sleep well

Elle

*

December 13, 2016

Calvin

Wizard skills not working.

Ok, you have to tell me what you wrote today in free chat if you did.

Elle

*

December 13, 2016

Elle,

Your Harry Potter skills are working. I was dreaming of a White Christmas. Then I went to bed. I couldn't sleep so I came back later. I said good night and was singing along with the guitar (watch it) on 21 pilots. I was tired and wasn't making sense so decided to wish you a good night and go back to bed.

I didn't sleep well and I am starting my day early. But it is nice. Warm house, very quiet outside. It rained all night. At least while I was awake, I didn't listen while I was asleep. But the rain has stopped this morning and there is a sense of calm.

I am glad, and not surprised, that you see the beauty and blessings in your life. It is not having the coolest or the newest video game. It is not about having a fancy car or impressing others. You see the priceless beauty of a child playing. Also the priceless pride that it is your child and the priceless comfort in knowing that she is happy with and because of you. She has a joy beyond what they can show in movies or games. but also you know that she would feel less secure and less open and less free with that joy if you weren't there. She kind of wants to share that joy with you. that is so much better than anything on TV or computer.

I mean what I say. We have many layers. I love the sex layer. But there is more. I love that in your video, even though you have allowed me to watch you have an orgasm, you were still shy about what you showed. I love that. Your expression. I meant what I said from the first day I met you. I can see body parts or even have a doctor put them on me. What is priceless is seeing a REAL person. Seeing you smile when you are a wizard. Priceless. Seeing your joy. I see you cry. I know you never do, but still I see it and hear your emotions when you write. Your daughter in a pretty dress with her hair brushed perfectly is not priceless. Your daughter smiling because of you and smiling at you is what is beautiful, not what you bought her.

I have never been a father. But I think having someone you love run to you to be held because they are hurt is both the worst feeling in the world because you can't do anything to help, and the best feeling in the world because she believes you can and writing to you or having you hug her helps. There is magic all around and people choose to be blind. I am glad you see how blessed you are and how perfect that moment with your daughter and the pigeons was.

Remember that your appointment is for you. She is there to help you not judge. You want her to see all your ugliness and fears and who you are. No fear. You already suspect that I am right and you are awesome. If she can make your life better and help you cope and build you up, let her. You are not the woman you were when you broke down. You know this. Doubts are normal. Don't be normal, be super.

I love this paragraph; "I understand now that I can doubt his judgment. He knows my weaknesses, things that hurt me the most. So this is how he can make me feel guilty for my sexual drive and liking to show myself, or for not being a perfect mom, or for having mental issues. He will find my insecurities and as long as I feel guilty about something he can use it against me. So I should accept those things and know he is using them because he knows that it affects me, if it doesn't it won't work anymore."

You only left out the part about how everyone loves that you are sexy and have a sexy drive. Doesn't he complain you don't take care of him enough and have a bigger sex drive? Your weaknesses are that you love your daughter. What better and more important thing makes someone a perfect mother? Still not sure why it is your fault you have issues? It sounds like you are humbling yourself and sacrificing in order to deal with your issues. I mean you didn't choose the pain? You didn't want the issues or the breakdown? Why is it your fault you are a victim? But I still love your paragraph!

And I love your sex drive and my video! Thank you. you never disappoint! wow.

My college roommate had a signal. If the light was on in the kitchen oven his girlfriend was staying the night. I am not perfect. More than once she came over to make him a surprise romantic dinner and all the dishes I used to make my dinner the night before were dirty in the sink. She cried and I ruined his night. We were two of the most easy going and calm men you will ever meet. We loved each other and nothing bothered us. But neither of us was a great roommate. I am not neat and I am cheap. I bought a lot of meat and vegetables we shared. But his girlfriend, now his wife, invited me to eat what she made for him a lot, and I seldom remembered to put on my shopping list the small things like salt and mustard I used up. We had a cookbook in the kitchen and in it was the phone numbers of every restaurant that delivered food or that we could order ahead to. I definitely paid for my share of the junk food we ordered. Also I remember one year the little girls came by selling cookies. I bought 3 boxes for me and 3 boxes for him. They came back the next day and he bought another 6 boxes not knowing I had already. I miss him. He was a great guy. but men are hard to live with even when you love them.

Have a great day. I will be praying for you. I do that. I think your appointment will be something you will wonder why you were nervous about and feel great about after. But that's just the opinion of the horny guy you met on a sex site who gets sexy videos of you and you praise him when he masturbates. So what I know and my thoughts shouldn't matter.

I am Calvin

*

December 14, 2016

Calvin,

I feel miserable. The woman was adorable, like a big chicken mommy. I spoke non stop for about an hour. She teared up several times while I told you my life story .... Pfff... I'm laughing because it's so bad, I can't believe I'm a person who makes someone cry with her life story. She must hear all kinds of stories.

It was mostly me speaking because so much happened in my life and she was listening. She told me a few helpful things. Like for example, I'm not just BPD symptoms, I'm a person. "You didn't have great experiences with men, ha?" and she started to speak to me like one speaks to a child. I didn't like that. She told me that because of my childhood I never got a chance to grow and build myself up, because I wasn't given the healthy environment to do so. There is no point in doing marriage counseling.

I trust her, I spoke about everything. Even on the webcam, We didn't have time to speak more about my sexuality, but she said We will speak about what you think is your "perversion".
And of course she made me understand that I do most of the things because I want to be loved, and that since I was an investment for my dad but tried to get his love and how the boss saw potential in me, I was also an investment for him. We touched quickly on the men I had a chance to have in my life. She seemed to be surprised how on earth I only met those types of men, so I ended up thinking all of them are like that. I saw pity in her eyes.

She told me that legally the boss has no right to kick me out of our home, that's French law. And that legally half of the money we own is mine. (haha, I know who won't agree with this) And I apparently also have free layers from the french state for the divorce.

I don't like to be treated like a child. I went through a lot, I am nothing like a child. Maybe emotionally I am still one. I have a child in me like everyone else. But I feel like I am more. I definitely don't want to be seen as a child by my future partner, if there will be any. Nor like a charity case. She makes me pay less (it's still freaking expensive if you ask my opinion) because I'm poor.

I just felt like a total failure, who spent 25 years of her life not growing and letting people use me. It all feels like my fault. Everything seems to be a mistake.

Dating older men? Wrong decision. Having a child at 22, Wrong decision. Asking him to marry me? Wrong decision. Cutting myself, and still doing it? Obviously a terrible decision that just shows her that I am not capable of taking care of myself. Accepting this job to pay rent, giving up my career dreams? Wrong decision. And it all comes down to me being a faulty product, everything I touch is a failure. So it is because of me at the end that this divorce will take place. It's because of me that Lily will never experience how it is to grow up in a happy family, to have a good father like person in her life. Because I attracted all of this with my behavior and poor choices. Because I never knew there was different or that I deserved different.

It's so f* funny that I discover men can be nice and humane and sweet on a pervert website where I basically sell my body and soul. There was a foot fetish who was concerned in private when I was trying to get very flexible to do what he asked me to do, he told me to not hurt myself while trying. I almost started to cry. Why would he care about it? The man I was currently sleeping with never cared about me being comfortable during the action. I don't want to exaggerate that the boss is not a monster. He always asked me how I feel about things when trying something new, we only did things if I was willing to. And if I told him that something hurts he would stop. It's just that he would never feel my suffering or uncomfort and never even tried to. Not the kind of person who puts pillows behind your head before taking you against the wall. A person who gives you a hug counting the minutes to know when it is finally appropriate to touch the sexy parts. Not a person who just hugs you to hug you and definitely not a person who sees a point in just holding someone. Why would anyone do that?

Shut up Elle. I don't even dare to just go on and tell you about what I told that woman. if she looked at me like that, I can't even imagine how you would look at me.

I have an appointment for next Friday. I can't wait to finally start problem solving. Because the opening up part was very discouraging.

Let's change the topic.The other day Lily watched Nemo. I had to leave the room. I'm too sensitive for nemo!! WTF. The music was so dramatic, his mom died and his siblings too, and then his dad lost him. I couldn't take the feelings. There is not much I can watch without turning into an emotional mess.

I hope you will sleep better tonight. I'm so sorry to hear that you got up again because you couldn't sleep. That's not good. And I am not there to put you in bed.

I watched 500 shades of gray yesterday night, alone. I felt so miserable after the appointment and exhausted. But I didn't want to go to sleep with those thoughts. The movie... Heehee. The sex scenes were good, detailed and they showed (surprisingly) everything. It was like watching porn with a story. bad story. Bad lines. No suspense. These kind of movies who take you for a stupid and explain you obvious feelings over and over again instead of suggesting them, make me laugh. I laughed out loud multiple times and it felt good.

I checked my emails just in case before going to bed. And what a surprise, I had one. I could fall asleep thinking about its content. It was good for me but I was sad for you. Those last words....

What??? This is not what you are. Stop making it sound disgusting. It's not like that. Think a little bit, if you act and write like you are praised for masturbating, it's like saying I am someone who sends sexy videos to a horny guy and praises him for masturbating. This is not very flattering for me. Stop. I wouldn't do that. I do that because it's you. I do that because I don't want to get romantic with you. I can't touch you when I want to express something. I can't just look into your eyes and read yours and hope that you can read mine and there will be no need to use words. I can't do that. So I send sexy videos. Although sex is "just" (what?) one of the multiple ways I would want to take care about you. Shut up Elle. See, if we send sexy videos to each other it's because as you said it's easier for both of us to get naked than open up. I know my videos seem to be impersonal, just a body in outfits but I do make them for you and only you. I also know that you can read my messages to get something more personal so it doesn't help me to try harder to get personal in the videos. Calvin, I send the sexy videos because I trust you, because I would trust you with my body. I don't praise you for masturbating. Every time I send you something I imagine what could happen if I wasn't on the screen but next to you, and I secretly hope that you imagine something similar and that turns me on. See? Same thing but if you simplify it and look from a bad angle it sounds bad.

Take care, rest. Sleep well.

Good night Calvin...or morning.

Elle

*

December 14, 2016

Elle,

I should be asleep right now. I really wanted to read about your appointment but the internet was down.

I read and I will say only two things about it.
First, I love that you are so open with me. So tell her! tell her you feel like she is talking down to you and that you feel bad about it and you don't want to be treated like a child. if she says she isn't

just saying, "I feel like you are." She's there to help. Make her help. I tell my students it is their job to make me teach them. If they don't understand, make me explain it again. if I do it wrong make me do it again and again until I explain it well enough for them to understand. It is your job to make her help you. If you feel like she is blaming you or saying you are a bad person or like you are a child. Tell her.

Second... Did she say everything is your fault? or was that you?

I spoke wrongly. I was de-emphasizing my importance in your life and stressing that you shouldn't listen to the boss or me or anyone else. I was trying to make a point. No, I don't think of us that way. Yes I know we have something obviously deeper. In trying to make a point I lied and used words like "just". Our videos are beautiful and we both know it is not body parts.

Lastly, because I am tired and not thinking straight, I should stop and sleep.

Calvin

Thank you for writing. I don't need to know all the details. I just want to know if you like the psychologist and feel it is good and how your thinking changes or doesn't. I do care and still see this as a positive step. I don't blame you. I still adore you and see all the good things I always have. I am hopeful.

*

December 14, 2016

Calvin,

There was something positive in my appointment. It was tough to speak about my mistakes and dark side. But last time I was with a psychologist, he sent me right away to a psychiatrist and he sent me right away to a mental hospital. So now, I have confirmation that I am not dangerous to myself or others and that I can and want to handle my life. It made me be aware of how different everything is this time around. I have happy moments. Many of them. It's definitely not like when you give up deep inside and are hopeless even at the best moments in your life, you are not capable of enjoying them anymore and that makes you feel even worse... I don't have that now. I feel strong. I don't want to raise my arms and step out of my life and go do nothing in a hospital. I even feel excited and scared and brave about getting my life together. I have plans and hopes although I don't always believe in them. But still, I feel like trying and even if I fail again, I want to enjoy the ride.

The boss is still in that bad mindset. He tried to bring me down today. I'm getting better at not going down when he wants me to. I start to feel horrible but I also remember why I shouldn't believe everything he tells me. And I start to use logic and usually find something in his words that I know for sure is not correct and that helps me to feel human again. So I just smile and walk away. I listen to some hopeful music if I need to. I also started to try to answer him, stand up for myself and in a calm and confident voice correct him about how I behave and see things. He is convinced that I want to destroy his life and take his stuff and money. I have no idea why he expects me to behave like that. We always had separate bank accounts. I payed for everything we bought online (amazon stuff, flight tickets, sexual accessories or whatever). When we both had an income one of us paid the food the other the rent. When one of us stayed at home with the baby the other paid for food and rent. And we always separately paid for our own clothes. Everything I bought for only my use I did it with my card. I'm not materialistic. I don't have any feelings for the objects in our flat. We got some of the furniture from the "baby welcoming money from the state" but I still don't see myself taking any of those either. I thought he knew me after living together for so long. It's just stuff and money. I can slowly get money and stuff but if it would only depend on me we wouldn't have this much anyway. I wasn't kidding when I told you I am minimalist. I am almost maniac about it. I give to the charity everything non necessary, I only keep things that I need. If I buy something I instantly get rid of something I own. When he told me what he thinks I will do I just looked around and realized there is absolutely nothing in that living room I would need. The only things that matter to me are luckily mine, the colorful blankets, the pillowcases I made, my clothes, my make up, my laptop. I wouldn't even take the web camera because I'm not sure anymore who paid for it. I will stop the webcam thing when I move away and buy myself one when I can.

Do I have a bad influence on your life? You don't seem to sleep well or enough. And I'm afraid that you are more concerned about me than I am concerned about me. I am not your responsibility, you got that, right?

You already did so much for me. You can take time off and not worry and be confident that I can handle my own life.

Yes, your advice and comforting words make it easier and make it just an overall more pleasant experience. But I feel strong enough to do this on my own.

That is sad. I am going crazy now. I want to speak to you so bad. I know it's too early for a skype call. I know I'm supposed to feel alone and lonely and try to get over it by myself. But I can't. I just called that one normal ex I had. The boss is out tonight. He has no nice words for me anymore. because I'm not crawling back to him anymore and I'm being strong and not giving in. Daring to disagree with him, nice and calm but still disagree. But now that he is out I just feel so lost. There is no man in my life anymore to take care of me. I almost wrote to care about me but I know you care about me. Sorry. I know I should stay away from everyone. I know I should not contact that guy who finally got over me and bought a house with a woman. But I just did. Because I wanted to have an interaction with someone, a male, who likes me, so that I could love myself. This is so disgusting. I hate myself. Never doing that again. The worst is that I don't even like him. I just used him selfishly knowing that we won't ever get each other's jokes or references. I'm so pathetic. Ok. I don't like myself like this. I have to learn to love myself because I don't want to use you. You are not someone I want to use and empty and throw away. I'm sorry if I hurt you with my honesty. But this is what I am and this is what I did. I am so dependent on men. But I want to change that. It is toxic and hurtful. And I am done with this. I want to have something real and genuine and innocent.Someone I don't need to a point where I can't exist without him but someone I want and... I don't know.

If I don't progress I will never have that.

I'm sorry if I disappointed you. Turns out I am someone who uses a man I know has feelings for me just to cheer myself up. And I don't trust myself with you either. Maybe it is good that this can not be real. My very first boyfriend was a psychopath who told me one day that he wanted power to kill as many people as possible. I managed to fall out of love when I got to know that guy whom I just called. He was nice, just proof that I won't have to be alone and unloved if I leave him. It didn't work out with the nice guy because we had nothing in common. But I see how it became a pattern in my life. I didn't learn from the first lesson. I should do something differently this time and work on myself to get out of this pattern. I hate that I put you in this situation. I don't want you to be the nice guy who helps me to leave a toxic relationship and takes me over, while I just jump from being dependent on a man to being dependent on another.

I think I know inside you are not like that for me. But I still have those fears. And I still have that work to do on myself.

Tonight when you feel sleepy, just go to bed and sleep please. Otherwise you might do nonsense like singing along to twenty one pilots. Oh my God, I have a bad influence on you. I know it's an Elvis song, I prefer this cover. I like the feeling of the song.

Well, this is quite a challenge. I should go to sleep now and all I want is to speak with you in real time. It feels awful. I am strong. I'm strong. I'm strong, right? You wouldn't want me to obsess about it. And I wouldn't want to emotionally black mail you. So ... maybe see you tmr morning. I plan to go online at 6.30.

I also got a phone call about a job interview tonight and it is quite a dilemma. This is also why I felt like I needed you. I don't think I would be able to even admit that I thought about it. Shut up Elle.

I don't know who I am.

Elle

*

December 15, 2016

Elle,

You are not a bad influence. Seee! I even slept last night. It is now early Sunday morning now.
I am hearing your strength and optimism. Please use me. I am not being used. I am being talked to and shared with. That is not bad. If I care for you I am a big boy and can protect my heart. We are fine. Don't worry about me. Or worry and care but know I am fine and life is good.

You are so logical. My heart feels for you and I hate thinking of you suffering and stressed and needing me. But I also hear you saying that you always survive and feel better because you didn't Skype. You know it is you not me doing it. You are relying on you. I am sure we are going to have a time when we just talk. You will see me on Skype and see me looking at you and smiling and adoring you. Just from my smile you will be assured everything is fine. You are a pleasure for me.

I also know I am not on Skype often. If I am talking to my cousin or helping someone with their math and I don't see you, I know you will assume I don't care and be hurt. If you know I am available to you on Skype so you allow that to be the thing that will "save" you.. and I am not there. Also I am a big boy and I will say, " No Skype tonight." I know you are a big girl and will be fine with that. I just think a sweet conversation when you don't need it is good. A Skype conversation because you think I will help, my heart says yes but my head says that isn't helping it is just making me feel good and good for my ego that I am your superhero. You don't need a superhero and I don't think of you that way.

So that was a long way to say, I am still deciding about Skype. I did give in already. I am just clever.

You are not a disappointment. I write how much I enjoy you and ask you to not leave and show you how important you are to me.. and somehow you think that means I am disappointed with you? I like you. I have flaws. You have flaws. The most beautiful and wonderful woman in the world married me.. and she would fart in bed almost every night after she fell asleep. So no one is perfect. There is a point where farting becomes something I miss.

You are handling the boss well and everyone but you see that you are not materialistic. Says the man who was told not to send tips and given a way to send messages for free. You always used to miss out on privates because you were generous with me and let me steal all your time.

Then you wouldn't let me tip or go private just to be nice or talk and hug. DUH anyone, including the boss, knows you are not scheming to marry him so you can get his money and stuff. That's just stupid talk from the boss and you shouldn't have wasted your time explaining to me that you are not what he says. DUH you're not!

You are doing good and I love that you are doing it calmly and confidently. I love your honesty. You have plans and if they don't work out it is not the end of the world.

You talked to the nice guy... Why is that bad? Did you sleep with him without his new woman knowing or just talked? Did you ask him to leave his new woman for you? Do you allow someone who cares about you to be kind and share a soft word with you. Would you share a kind soft word with a stranger on the street you say was struggling. I'm not sure what your sin was. He's still with his new girl?

I enjoyed the crescendo from just him simple to the whole concert singing. I enjoy a cover that changes the original instead of just copying what the first artist did. I am glad I have both versions now.

You do not manipulate me... you say, "I am manipulating you now" whenever you are honest with your emotions but you know my reaction. Thinking/knowing I want to act out of emotions and caring is a compliment to me. Thank you for thinking I can be manipulated. But you really aren't manipulating me when you admit it.

You give me too much credit, I don't know what you are saying about considering the job interview. You compliment me by thinking I have the same wizard powers as you do. I am just a nerd.

Nerd reference: The other night I watched a rerun of Big Bang Theory. Leonard was giving a lecture on a discovery he and Sheldon had made. Sheldon complained that he had left out the anecdote of how Sheldon was inspired like Newton was with the apple. He said he noticed the pattern of kids playing in the playground. I mentioned to you before the mathematician that made my masters thesis obsolete. Well I think Sheldon lifted the kids on the playground from Terry Tao. He and another math professor were watching the kids at the daycare on campus and started a discussion that led to a joint publishing. I just thought it was nerdy that I had mentioned the guy recently and like the next night Big bang theory copied him

Ok, I better go.

You are doing fine. I am here. I want to hear. Life is good.

Calvin

*

December 15, 2016

Calvin,

Your message was like a hug.

I survived the night! It was very easy. I was enough for myself. It felt like a big step forward so I slept well and woke up happy and confident. I had an amazing session. Two long privates, both amazing. The first one was just very satisfying and the second one was a first for me. I was killing it today!

These last days really made me stronger. I felt like I can take anything from the boss too now. He didn't sleep at all and looked miserable. I was worried that he took something or is not going well. He looked sad and told me he wanted to speak to me. We sat down and I was expecting him to either ask me to leave as soon as possible because this situation is hurting him too much or letting me go and making peace with the separation and divorce. I felt crushed when he finally felt ready to tell me he wants to try but better. He was calm, peaceful and sad. I really thought he would pronounce the words "I'm letting you go."

I don't really know how to feel about this. I'm happy that he did research and opened up and managed to stop being angry. I even felt proud of him. I wish he wouldn't be so obsessed but I have some respect for him now because he knows what he wants and he is doing anything to get it. He realized we have to compare our views and expectations on relationships. He told me how he imagined it. He listened to me while I explained what is not my type of man anymore, what is, what kind of treatment I'm looking for, how I see teamwork, what love is for me. He listened, really listened and wanted to understand. He agreed to speak about his parent's divorce for the first time. Very brave. It made me seriously reconsider keeping the family together. But we agreed that whatever we do, she will have reasons to blame us and there is no sure way to avoid scaring her for life. So in the end it won't influence my decision. I will feel guilt if I break this family but I feel like it will be a compromise between what she deserves and I deserve. I'll do everything to make it the smoothest and less hurtful experience possible, knowing it will still be horrible for her, but I'm not a saint. I want to be happy. I had the childhood that I had, I cannot change it but I do have the choice to have a happy adulthood. As a child I will take care of her the best I can and I will support her to build herself up and have a happy adulthood. I can live with that guilt even if she will hate me for a long time. I know she will understand me later, much later when she will be confronted with a situation that helps her understand my position. I noticed that I happen to find myself in situations that help me to understand exes or parents or other people I had negative feelings toward. Strangely life makes me have to do the same thing to someone else, the same thing they did to me and that makes me be able to finally understand them and forgive. Back to the boss...and me. He absolutely wants to get a marriage counselor, he thinks the problem is the communication, we have to learn to do it more and better. I'm glad for him. He has the willingness to open up and change something very deep. I told him I need more affection. He hugged me.... yeah. This is never gonna work out. He is willing to try but again this is not his way of showing his love. It felt awkward. It wasn't a good feeling. He crushed my head, I told him, he told me to move it, it crushed the wall...

I am at a point where I wish I could make this work. I wish we wouldn't be what we are. He admitted that it is not his thing and he will never cry on my shoulders or take me in his arms for fun. But he will buy me food and download my favorite series. He thinks our love language is different and it is not a problem, we just have to ask the other when we want something different. The problem is I don't want something, I want someone different. I don't see my need for affection as a weakness anymore. I told him nicely that I can't live without it. He is very stubborn. He read online that even if things seem hopeless a marriage can be saved so now he is all hopeful. He made me read that stuff. What bullshit, it made me so angry. The usual, "you have to keep the spark alive by going on dates, doing sport, not neglecting yourself, having sexy time, communication is key, different love languages.."

Bullshit. We had all of this. Our relationship didn't become boring at any point. We went on dates, had an exciting sex life and took care of our appearance. The articles he showed me all suggested that wanting to divorce is actually a cry for help, just to scare the other to make him realize things are not evolving in the relationship. Our problem is so different.

The boss and I have completely different views on love. He thinks there is no such thing as two people being compatible. Nobody is compatible with no one. Things always get harder and worse with time. you have to work it out. Ok.... I believe in compromises, and that nothing is perfect. But I also believe in compatibility and same values and wanting the same things, and functioning in a similar way. I think some people get us better than others.

Anyways, I enjoy the change at home. Life is just more pleasant and easy with him now. I am hoping the marriage counselor will smoothly take us in a peaceful separation. I did tell the boss that he cannot keep me if he cannot let me go. He cannot only give me two choices, one being to leave him and he makes my life a hell and the other one being to stay with him and he does everything to make me happy. I should choose him from many good options, not like the only viable one. That he has to make peace with the idea of letting me go and having absolutely no influence on how things will end up with us. He doesn't get why I don't trust him now after he reacted so cruelly.

He doesn't want to kick me out anymore. He admitted it was just him being angry. And he is willing to stop saying bad things about me in front of the little one.

I'll tell you more about that job tomorrow after the interview.

I'm going online now.

Elle

*

December 16, 2016

Elle,

I am Smiling.

Those are good words. I think you are seeing that you are stronger and better than you thought and the boss is human and afraid and confused. He is emotional and doesn't have all the answers. Maybe he took care of you during a time when you needed someone to take care of you. But now you are definitely equals and maybe you are more in control and aware, less emotionally overwhelmed than he is now. I think you're doing good.

Things are going well here. I have a friend who plays piano who keeps inviting me over to listen to him play Christmas songs. He is older and alone. I think he sees me as alone but with many friends and I am his connection. He wants to throw a low key get together but he doesn't have people in his life he socializes with. His kids are grown and live far away. He has all his friends from when he was a pilot but none live close. I feel bad because he keeps asking and I keep telling him no. I am too busy before Christmas and I really am not lonely. Thank you.

And not just you I spend time with students all day and then my sweet Fridays and friends on Sundays. I really don't feel alone. For me Christmas is fun, it is November and I miss people. But I am sympathetic for him without pitying him because his life is good, he just feels alone at Christmas. My other friend, I have to decide if I am going to be selfish or not. He is a really good guy but doesn't have much money. His house has a leak and some problems he cannot fix. I usually help him. His house is nice, it is just old and he can't afford repairs easily. So he wants to hire me to fix it. I am not a carpenter but I also won't charge him much money. He has family coming for Christmas and really needs some things fixed. I could use the money. But he wants me to stay with him and work when I get off school each day.

First I am lazy and working all that time while final exams and school is stressful is something I am not looking forward to. Second he needs it done before Christmas, I have vacation after Christmas I could do it. If I am selfish I know it is his problem and so his schedule should be ruined not mine. But I might go next week. I don't want to.

Ok you are about to tell me I am not such a bad person. So let me tell you first. Elle you are not a bad person. I love that you care so much about your daughter, but also know that you love her and are going to try your best, and I think the boss will too, to make her life good no matter what happens to the family. I think a mom and dad both are what we hope for. But that isn't always best. You decide what is best. Don't let me influence that. I believe in love and marriage. But don't be so hard on yourself. Many people grow up fine even though their parents divorce.

You sound hopeful and positive and like things are better. The boss is trying to not make you feel bad. He is trying to understand. You are trying to do what is best for everyone. but you now include your best in that everyone. You are an important part of everyone. I hear confidence.

Have a great week. Don't get too high in the highs or too low in the lows. Life is good. Stay kind. it pays off indeed.

Big hug.

Still Calvin

I missed visiting you online. The girls were playing with candles outside and we took a couple cute pictures.

*

December 16, 2016

Calvin,

I'm all dressed up for my interview. It's tonight.

We had this morning our appointment to get all the information about the legal procedure four our divorce.

I'll tell you more about all this later.

I'm alright

Elle

*

December 16, 2016

Calvin…

So much is happening right now. I'm overwhelmed and have all kinds of emotions I didn't have time or energy to acknowledge. First, my account is suspended for 24 hours. A member thought that it is a good idea to give me his email address in private. He even offered flight tickets for Switzerland... pfff. I was busy doing my thing and had pleasure so I wrote him something like "I don't promise anything about writing to you" Which is my most confident way of saying definitely no, stop this. I know, I'm horrible at saying no. It was a good private I was in it and enjoying it and didn't want to think about how to react best to his stupid invitation. So this is why I'm not online this morning. And also because I need more sleep. I feel nauseous and weak.

Grrr...I don't have enough time to write down everything I want and explain things well enough. I'll try to be efficient.

The legal appointment ..upset me. I was almost crying there. She explained our options well. I hate the French administration. The most simple thing takes ages and is over complicated. I didn't expect a divorce to be simple. But I didn't expect it to feel so unfair either. It felt like the law was not on the side of the "victim". There is of course no way to prove that he abuses me verbally and how much of a hell he can make of my life when I'm living with him under his influence. Even if I could, the system doesn't care, it's not domestic violence or a double life or something serious that allows one to start a very very long procedure of asking for divorce because someone did something wrong. That procedure is not efficient. I find this scandalous.

Anyway, Our procedure would be the one where we decide together (I really don't have the vocabulary in English for law terms) . I'm not advised to move away without his consentment, legally it would be abandoning my family and my responsibilities as a wife and mother. And it could hit back in a divorce procedure. We have to sign a paper together, write down that we move in different households with mutual consentment.
This is the only good legal way to go. How could I explain how I feel about this? Legally weak and dependent on my "abuser"? Sorry, I will be ok, it is not that bad but I feel powerless and abandoned by the system. Good things: we have a low or non-existent income so we'll have one common free lawyer or one for each if needed. I can ask divorce , even just myself, although we

are advised to do it together. Together the procedure could take 6 months. If it's just one of us. We have to prove that we lived in different households, (out of mutual consentment) for 2 years and then a divorce is possible even if one of us is not willing to divorce.

My interview was awesome. It is a long story I don't have time to tell. It is my current dream job. It's a sexual environment but I'd be the barmaid/manager who is responsible for the money and the girls. Normally the activity of the club is less explicit than in Geneva. The job fits me and gives me adrenaline and makes me feel alive and happy and I just can't believe it. I was daydreaming about an opportunity where nobody touches my body, and I'm the untouchable desired taboo. The interview was very professional, I was spoken to like a business partner. We ordered things and managed the ice cream shop together with my sister so I already know how things work. I will only have to learn what's different. My Geneva experience was quite similar (minus serving alcohol), being 25 I am older than some of the girls and I already have experience managing people in this kind of environment. I still can't believe my luck. It's so freaking.... Calm down Elle.

Your photos messed me up too.

I have to sleep, too much happening in too little time, I cannot NOT get too high, too low right now. Elle, go sleep and eat now. Ok.

Tell me if you'll be away to help your friend. I guess we won't speak while you are there.

Bye

Elle

*

December 16, 2016

Elle,

You are so perfect.

You understand me so well. I don't want to dominate your life but I love being able to share it. I need to hear you write "I'm alright". especially when you have drama in your life. I hope someday you don't have drama in your life. I fear that will feel wrong to you.

I love writing you long emails, when things get eventful or I have drama you will, or when I am feeling nostalgic or sexy or lonely or.... my point being that It meant a lot to me that you took the time to send me a quick message to assure me you were ok, but I didn't feel like I was making you hide to write me or take time you should be doing other things with. I felt loved and special and important, but not an obligation.

The video was perfect too. Yes I would have loved to ravish you and gotten you naked, but as hot as the outfit looked and look that drives me crazy on you. It was perfect. the fingers crossed. It was nothing like a private. It was talking to your friend and sharing a special moment. Not a celebration, the more intimate moment of hope and excitement with the chance of disappointment. This is a moment not shared as often and felt much more personal. Thank you. I loved it.

Here I think divorces take about a year to be final.

I have compassion for what you are going through.

Not much excitement in my life. I have simple things. My mom had her toilet get clogged. I dropped by after work and unclogged it. Boring. forgetful but to an old woman who is crippled and uses that toilet 10 times a day I am a superhero!

Perspective.

I like me.

Thank you for liking me too and being so thoughtful and kind to me.

Calvin.

You look awesome!!!!

Sounds like you are doing pretty great too. Life is good!

*

December 17, 2016

Calvin…

I just finished my homemade pizza from yesterday: soy sauce base, barbecue chickpeas, mushrooms, red pepper, spring onions, pineapple, nutritional yeast... Better than sex. depends on whom. But Oh my god, this pizza.

Yes, I know. I fear my ability to live a drama free life too. I will touch on this with the psychologist. And on you too.

I will not write for a while, not even open the mailbox if I'm strong enough to avoid that too. You can write to me if you feel like it, And eventually I will read your messages.
We got to speak about my heart today and how it is not here and available at all. We decided to take off the pressure from our "trying" by acting as we are kind of dating but I don't have feelings for him yet but don't feel like I should either. This way we can have a few nice moments and take it easy and I will be more open and less wanting to push him away and run away.

I always knew that I had to stop talking to you at least for a while to be able to see clearly. I just couldn't do it. I am quite addicted to my daily dose of Calvin. But I also feel less needy and dependent and definitely more strong now. I actually want to be alone now. I want to stop writing, for myself. I want to find myself alone and not see pictures or words that mess up my thinking and emotional life.

So I am dating him to see whether my feelings will evolve for him. Now I feel tenderness and understanding. I might even be able to not see him as superior anymore and feel equal. I actually want to see how far I can feel for him. He shared something awful from his childhood today and I wanted to mother him. It's not fair. I wanted to fix him, to love him more than her mom did and does and give him what he so desperately needs. We joked about how he can let me go if I find a replacement, a pretty girl, that he could turn into a hot one, someone who loves him and never rejects him. Ouch, my heart hurts so much for him. He got very vulnerable with me and I am not the one who can appreciate it. I don't want to destroy this vulnerable loving being. Because of me he thinks he is not perfect, but should be. He thinks that him being hurt and hurtful made me reject him, because he had bad reactions. It hurts so much. It's not like that at all. A bad reaction or multiple ones don't kill love. I wish he would feel lovable. I wonder whether I can lift up his self confidence and build him up without sacrificing my whole life and future to him.

Once I cleaned up my heart and head I will come back and be your friend. Or .... But you can of course bring your part in the decision and it will count. I think I know where I am with you but I am so scared to face it. And I have doubts. You might have discovered by now that I don't fit your mold. I want to be me and feel the adrenaline rush in my blood, get excited about my life even if it means I don't fit your mold. That scares me. And I don't really trust my feelings because I don't know if they come from bad habits and bad choices or if they are sincere and real.

He knows how important you are to me and actually wants me to meet you and see how I feel about it then. This scares me like sh*it. We are not even ready to skype yet. And it's not like we can just take the subway to see each other. So it is not a "let's see, whatever" thing but kind of a big deal. Even writing it down gets me all stressed out, also because I fear your stress reading something like this. Sorry. you didn't see anything. Delete, delete. paragraph gone. You know, we don't have to.

You know how I see the world. Everything is waves in the ocean. It just all happens the way it is meant to happen.

« A river flows surely to the sea. »

Cheesy reference. So yeah...I don't know what is meant to be, but we will see when it happens.

You are my superhero. Don't have to be, but you can't stop me from seeing you like that. Blue shiny bulging..

I hate to make you feel like I leave or abandon you. I don't. You know I'm here.

Don't be lonely. You are not.

Elle

*

December 17, 2016

Elle,

I do understand.

I am going to keep writing to you even if you don't read because I need to write to you. But I understand.

I believe you are being brave and I applaud you sacrificing something I know you enjoy. I know you enjoy me and want to keep me. I understand and believe you. I will only be disappointed, because I know you would, if you fear I am writing less and seem busy so you are dropping me before I can hurt you. I believe you are doing the noble thing for the boss and yourself. I believe you know I am always here if you need me. but in case, let me assure you I still adore you and I'm not leaving. Even if my life is busy, you are still important.

Ok so no sweet stuff because you are reading this just because you were worried about me. I am being good and giving you a chance to get you feelings straight regarding us. That is ok. I'm here because I think somehow the river will flow back in some form.

You know my heart.

Always your Calvin. I understand.

Want a bite of my hamburger?

*

December 18, 2016

Calvin,

This is too hard. I'm worried. Are you busy? Are you ok?

Can you feel when I think of you?

Elle

*

December 18, 2016

Elle,

I'm here always,

If I can help calm things for you I will write. but I also believe in you. You don't "need' me. I am just blessed to have you look to lean on me or enjoy me.

I am fine. I am leaving Monday after work and staying Tuesday night. then coming home Wednesday after work and staying home Wednesday night. then going back Thursday after work and coming home after work Friday. or actually going to my sweet Friday after work then home. I have the next week off work. Vacation.

I was hoping being light and joking was helping at work. But I also noticed my presence was a distraction. So I asked.

I'll write you a story, any story just so you know I enjoy writing to you. I thought reading here was an issue for you. But I will write even if you don't read.

Life is good, don't worry about me. I hope you are fine.

Merry Christmas.

Still your Calvin

*

December 18, 2016

Calvin,

I'm spoiled.

We have a Christmas three! This is our first one.

I picked up six books at the library. The first two are very good so far.

The psychologist is great. At the second meeting she helped me to analyze my feelings toward you, and the boss with the help of the happenings of last week and my emotional reactions to it. It was great to dig deep and see clearly and not doubt my emotions. But it made things more difficult at home. The boss could feel it as soon as I came home from the appointment.

He was and is amazing. Entertaining me, taking care of me, complimenting me. He wants to know everything I feel and think. It's very hard on both of us. I still miss you even if he is perfect with me. He can feel it. He usually even makes me say it. He keeps doing everything he can to be perfect. But we always end up hugging and crying. Him being hurt for loving and not being loved and being compared to a not real perfect person. And I am heartbroken from his helping words. He is on a mission to make me fall out of love. I couldn't say if it is a good method or not. It's for sure a very nice method. He is there for me. But he is verbalizing my biggest fears about you. Then when he sees how much I am suffering he takes me in his arms and lets me cry on his shoulders. He starts to say that he doesn't want to be a friend I cry on.

He provoked me yesterday, he was very very sorry for neglecting me and mistreating me to a point where I "had no choice" but falling for the first nice guy. He is angry at himself and often begs me to "punish" him. He just kept repeating nonsense and I ended up punching him on the chest with all my frustration of being in love but not wanting to, trying and wanting it to work out but I just can't. Ridiculous, we are at a point where I beg him to take off my heart and make it change, fix it, whatever he wants. because I'm fed up and he is fed up. And nobody is happy. I hit him and burst out in tears for the first time in his arms. Today we had 3 discussions about the same topic, him trying to explain to me why and how you don't love me and then trying to demonstrate how real he is and determined.

I am exhausted, he made me cry three times today. Every time I feel like he doesn't deserve this whole situation.

It's hard having him say that I want someone to love me and when he does I push him away. It's very similar to what you said. He is suffering from my new potential job. He keeps repeating that I'm strong and beautiful and whatever and I don't need to please multiple men all the time to be able to love myself. Next topic for the psychologist. I am not stupid. I am aware of how I am going through life looking for people to love me, and when they do I am upset and don't let them do it. I don't contact them, or answer to them, always finding excuses how busy I am, then I feel unloved when they leave me alone as I asked them to do. A vicious circle, because feeling unloved makes me of course go and find anyone, but mostly men to appreciate me by being sexy. When I feel sexually desired I instantly turn them off and go away feeling unloved, and thinking there is no way that person loves me.

See, now for instance I am not taking well that you seem to be feeling absolutely fine without me. I want you to be fine, more than fine. But still.

I am very angry at myself for writing. Interacting with you helps. Writing to you is not the same as any other friend or psychologist. I can't replace you. I have people to talk to. But it's not talking that I need. it's talking to you.

There are so many moments in my days that I would share with you. All kinds of moments. It just all makes me want to turn to you and just smile at you or share my excitement or worries, just have you there to be a part of it.

I really needed to talk to you. Sorry and thank you. Tmr we'll call a marriage counselor to book an appointment.

I'm bad, and broken. And bad.

I have absolutely no right to ask you anything but please write to me of your busy days when you get a moment to do it. You don't need to prove that you are what I think you are. Just write me anything, your writings make me feel good.

I'm alright. My heart hurts, but I am doing a good job at surviving and functioning.

Elle

*

December 19, 2016

Elle,

I hope you enjoy talking and writing to me. I hope you feel comforted by me and comfortable with me.

I hope you are not in love with me. I am not in love with you. I care about you. I enjoy your company. I like you.

You are good for me. At my age I don't know if I ever want to fall in love again. The women here in my life I won't allow myself to fall in love with. We are fun sexy friends who care about each other but you should not be arguing with your husband over me. I do not plan to be in a relationship with anyone. I will say not yet or not now. but that is not for your benefit, it is to be honest. I had a time in life when I was young and excited about building a life together and growing and spending my life with someone. that is gone. I don't think I want to fall in love like that again. It isn't that I can't. I am the problem. I know that. I would have liked to grow old with her, But now I have memories of my life and I don't want to pretend to relive that time again. I want to live today and the future. I just don't think I'm at a point where I want to build a new life. It wouldn't be fair to someone else to have her in my old life. I am not that person anymore.

You helped me let go with almost one hand, but I never let go of what I have. You know that. I have no future. I have no future. I have no future. I am alive and living a good life. But I am alone. Yes I am lonely. Yes, I wish that I wasn't. But down deep I know I am to blame. I could find what I am looking for maybe. But I am not only not looking but I run when I feel it gets close.

If I am an example of the type of man you deserve I don't mind that. I believe you deserve someone better than I am. I think you are not broken. I think you are very sharp and very deep and very brave. I don't like the words I said in the first paragraph because I am not brave enough to want to see that truth. But I do care about you. I don't want to hurt your life by allowing myself to lead you on because I like your feelings for me. I would prefer to hurt your feelings instead of your life.

We have had this talk before.

I do understand part of what you say. I do admire you and I don't want to let you go. But somehow I need to be sexy friends. If you have to let me go, do it. Do what is best for you. Hate me even if you must. But don't be in love with me. Love men like me. Love being treated the way you deserve to be treated. love someone caring about you. love having someone in your life who wants to know what you think and what you feel and will patiently listen, really listen and read and reread everything you say. but please don't be in love with me.

I am going to end with something light and happy because I hate being the one who makes you angry or feel bad.

You are going to be fine. I am not leaving. I am never going to be upset or hurt by anything you say. I will always think fondly of you and have a little part of my heart be in France or Hungary. I say this in case you are angry or feel you must get rid of me. But I hope you understand what I am saying and still treasure what we have as much as I do. You are someone special to me and I am proud of the steps you are taking and that you are standing up for yourself and believing in yourself. Because you really do have value and worth and are a special person. I like who you are. Please don't go.

To add to this problem I am going to be gone until Wednesday night then gone again until Friday night. I will try to get onto his internet but I don't know. If I don't write back for a couple days please don't think it is because I don't want to. I want to continue to have you in my life.

Calvin

*

December 19, 2016

Calvin,

I needed to hear this. Thank you. It made me go for a run. It started to snow while I was running outside. I wish I could fly.

I am not a sexy friend. I don't want to be in that position. I just don't feel like I have to settle down for less than I want and suffer to have crumbs while dying from hunger. The thought of "only" being that for you makes me feel horrible, I can't do it.

"Not yet or not now" means "not with you". It is not the first time that I am being told "I'm not ready" only to watch him be ready with someone else not long after. If it is not the right person, time doesn't change that. If it is, I guess the right time, and being ready is not even a thing.

You are not to blame. Nobody is to blame for feeling or not feeling. I understand. I'm sorry I couldn't realize it by myself without you having to be brave and write down the truth. It was very brave. And generous. Thank you, Calvin.

While I am writing this I am also realizing what I wrote is not even me. You don't know me. This is not my first reaction, not even my second or third one. You might not even like me if you'd hear those. This is just the calmed down, thought through, trying to be a realistic version of me. This opens my eyes to how little I know you. And makes me wonder whether the psychologist will say that I am in love with someone I built up in my mind.

Why is your message so hard to believe? You did a great job turning me down, but.. this is not what I am reading between the lines. Part of me will never believe you when you say "I don't love you". But what I believe doesn't matter. You said it. Even if I don't want to believe it, you said it. You also said you don't want to fall in love at your age or allow yourself to fall in love. That should finally make me realize that you are not in love. Someone in love knows it is impossible to not fall only by wanting it to not happen, that it is impossible to not allow it to happen. It has nothing to do with age. If you can stop this from happening it wasn't happening.

What am I for you? Why didn't you stop this earlier? Why don't you still want to stop this? Why could you stop it with the big boobs woman who you didn't love?

Elle

*

December 20, 2016

Elle,

My friend didn't buy the materials so I am going down tomorrow and coming back Friday night.
I'm not sure what to do.

You are welcome to take a bite of my hamburger.

I am trying to be honest.

Calvin

We seem to have had this conversation before. November 21 and 22, 2016.

*

December 20, 2017

Calvin,

NO.

Yes, but last time we had this conversation I still had hope that with time it would all work out. Young, stupid and hopeful. I probably refused to hear what you were trying to say. You know that I keep trying to make the boss understand that I am not in love with him and at the same time I try not to destroy him. I just want him to be a friend and co-parent I can laugh and watch movies with. I think I see now that you and I are in the same situation. It is good for me to be able to feel what he feels. I definitely understand him better now. Thank you for that, this experience might help me turn him down. It also makes me realize that we cannot be friends. I cannot be friends with the boss if I break his dreams and heart. For him I will be a reminder of a failure and rejection. Forever.

By the way even if I said then that we can be special friends and I am ok with it... I have the right to change my mind. We tried it and it didn't work out with time. I kept feeling romantic and it kept bursting out of me more and more. I cannot just ignore my desires and satisfy yours. I was in love with the boss and let him use me however he wanted to, to get a little bit of affection in whatever form he felt comfortable giving it to me.

I won't play this game anymore. I want to keep my dignity and not sacrifice myself for a person I adore.

Thank you for making me feel like I'm worth being in fair human relationships. You changed me.

Now I have to stop loving you the way I do, and being friends would just keep the hope alive.

I don't want to be angry or hate you because I know you often did what was best for me, even now.
I will be grateful for it. When I'll feel better.

I feel strong and I'll be alright.

I am just disappointed because I thought I knew what this was. It felt so evident and good and I was so sure about your feelings. I don't know how I could be so wrong.

I'm hurt because I wanted to be what your wife was and is for you. I was so sure that you feel the same thing as me. It's really embarrassing. I know I shared many embarrassing thoughts with you. But this is something that will stop me from looking into your eyes forever. I don't want your pity and I don't want you to like me. And I prefer to show my naked body to strangers.

It is good to have myself as the only stable thing in my life. I guess this is exactly what I need now to build up myself.

I feel like I grew up now. And I don't want to grow up. I want to believe in magic and love that survives everything. Thanks to you I believe in kindness and don't feel anymore like it is a weakness.

Also thank you for doing this before Christmas. I read that these kinds of things are better to do before holidays when one is surrounded with loved ones and joy and everyone is busy. I'm very grateful that I have all the Christmas craziness around me to help recover.

I really really hope that this can be turned into something very positive, like loving you actually means that I started to love myself, because I loved things in you that I didn't love in myself. It's weird how hurt but at the same time very grateful I feel toward you. Everything is weird about us.

Please forgive me if I go cruel or hurtful, you obviously brought good things in my life and I am growing.

Elle

*

December 24, 2016

Calvin,

You must be exhausted by now. I hope your busy week went well and you feel relieved and are happy about being on vacation.

I'm sorry for all of this. I'm very bad at all kinds of human relationships. I think I understand what happened.

I am really not angry at you, not even hurt.

Merry Christmas you wonderful kaleidoscope of contradictions!

Take care

Elle

*

Decembre 25, 2016

Elle,

Thank you,

I don't want to cause you pain, but I also don't want to just let you go. if I don't make it difficult, you will think I let you go. I accept it is your choice. but I am not going to help you leave me.

Also don't think you imagined or read things into what I said. I said what I said. I tried and the thought that I wanted to not be lonely and to have someone replace what I had is a compliment to how great you are and what you did for me. So don't blame yourself for hearing what I was saying. But I also stand by the truth. I cannot let go of my past. I am not in love.

Have a merry Christmas and all the joy and fun that comes with it. I got to celebrate 3 times this year. Life is good. Be happy.

Be Elle, she's pretty great.

Always Calvin

*

December 31, 2016

Calvin,

I want you so bad!
Are you here?

Elle

*

January 1, 2017

Calvin,

Happy new year!

Elle

*

January 1, 2017

Elle,

Life is good.
Enjoy your family.
Smile... You have a beautiful smile.

Calvin

*

January 2, 2017

Elle,

I believe this year will be better for you. Maybe the best ever with you in charge and seeing who you are and how much worth and value you can see in yourself. We know you are special. I hope you see how special this year.

Big hug.

Always Calvin

*

January 8, 2017

Elle,

Your choice. Not trying to make things difficult for you.

I could sure enjoy masturbating to a video of you wearing pantyhose.

Calvin

*

January 10, 2017

You,

I just saw this... What are you doing?

I do respect myself more than that actually. And I am very happy to feel this way. You disappointed me by asking this. You are the reason I am suffering and you don't even respect my pain and still want to benefit my body. I guess you just described what I am for you. I have a heart. And it was my first time to feel so close to someone, my first time to genuinely love. Not abuse and let abuse out of being desperate for affection. But the same kind of love I have for windy weather and sunshine on my face and waves around my hips and even for the little munchkin. You cannot take that from me. I enjoy feeling this for you and I'm really sorry for making you feel uncomfortable feeling like this. It is just a feeling. It really changed me and I will always be grateful for making me discover that I am able to love and be loved.

My feelings won't change overnight. I understand that you are sexually frustrated. I
know it is not fair that we never got to go there and can't have after break up sex either.
I really don't feel like giving you some empty body with a broken heart to cum on. This is not what I deserve and not what you deserve either. This is not the you I want.

If I am not special enough for you to fall in love with, you will find someone who is or remember someone who was.

I would love to keep our special connection, divorce and be free to chat with you and share my days with you in messages, and skype and just enjoy this without feeling guilty but also without having any kind of pressure on us. Long distance sex friends with you would have been very special and exciting. You know I don't need a boyfriend, husband. You could have been there for me to have someone to come back to in my weak moments, watch me build up myself. What we had at some point was very satisfying for me in all the ways. I want that from life.

I am not stable yet, I am not strong yet, I am not independent yet. I am getting there. In the meanwhile I am just leaning on whoever is willing to be here for me.

I couldn't promise anything to anyone now, I am barely existing yet. I have no idea who I will be in two years and what I will desire.

I wanted you. I don't want anything now. But people here want me so I can give that to them and use them in my weak moments. Because I am human and I need support even if it is not the affection that, I know now, I would be able to take and give. At least I have something to keep me from falling apart and helping me to advance.

I still think highly of you for your honesty and letting me go. I am not happy, you know that right? But I do think this is all good for me. Thank you.

I wish I could brighten up your life but I guess what I am trying to say is I love you but I love myself more and I want to take care of me.

Take care

Elle

*

January 24, 2017

You,

Are you ok? I heard of the big storm this week-end. Did it mess up your road? I would love to hear from you.

How do you like my name? This is my favorite potential writer's name so far. I opened a new account again, just in case. The symbol of starting fresh I guess. One day I won't feel like I have to start all over again.

This would be my third name. When I had the opportunity to give back my father's family name, I was happy to do it. It meant that I'm not his thing anymore. My second name, and I realized this too late, only gave full ownership over me to another person. So silly of me to ignore that he is making me feel like my dad. That he abandoned me emotionally like my dad. The pain is less sharp but I am still processing. I don't feel like an open wound anymore though and it allows me to start to focus on what I want to be now and from blaming others to accept my faults and try to forgive myself. Huh. It is so much easier to forgive others. In order to forgive myself I have to go back to my baby years sometimes to be able to understand how I grew up to be like this. If you'd known it was such a blessing to hear from the therapist that the way I was treated as a baby was not ok! It was my first time hearing that. I was just telling her funny stories about my parents parenting skills in my first years, the way they tell them everywhere and everyone laughs about them. So I always thought it was ok. Hearing the opposite was a huge milestone in my recovery. It influenced absolutely everything, put all my life until today under a new light. It was like a missing puzzle piece. Add it to the incoherent other pieces and voila! It suddenly makes sense and shows you a clear image.

I also learnt why I can't remember things properly. I always felt so self conscious about it. But apparently traumatized children cannot develop a healthy memory function. They only have images and feelings and the details get lost. It is a sort of self protection they unconsciously use to be able to survive. They are left with those images and feelings and have to somehow make sense of their past and build their personality about it. That of course results in a very low self esteem and thinking that what they deserve is... well not much.

I feel different. I feel strong and good enough to recontact you. I guess the good thing about living an intense emotional life is to get to live the emotions fully out and recover in a relatively short amount of time. It was a huge loss for me to not be able to lose myself in a romantic love story with you. Well, somehow even writing this down makes me realize there is "losing myself" in it. How could that be good? I find myself being very happy alone. I Enjoy spending time with myself. I feel more relaxed and safe and confident.

I had to get here. It wasn't good to want to lean on you. I know now that I was constantly looking for substitutes... to fill up the need for affection in my life. It's normal for people who had a similar childhood to mine. Getting attached to whoever comes on our way, even if the person treats us badly or doesn't want us. And we stay and cannot let it go, out of fear of rejection. Rejection that traumatized the emotional body in childhood. How weird... realizing how I function and why it hurts so much, it is hard to accept but as time goes on it also helps to analyze what I did and feel in certain situations. And mostly, it helps to change the pattern and discover more pleasant and sustainable ways of feeling good.

I got a good deal from the boss. For him it was either a bad divorce or forcing them to stay together as if nothing happened. My therapist advised me to explain to him that the old me is gone and I am processing deep and hurtful things. It's a lot. I haven't built myself up yet, therefore I am unable yet to make decisions. It is impossible yet to know whether the relationship could work or not. So, this is what I told him. Our fights changed. I started to stand up for myself, talk back, use arguments, not freeze and feel terrified anymore. He ended up giving in to my desire of just being flatmates and parents, trying to slowly build up a friendship, keeping a distance, no romantic expectations, everyone focused on him/herself. It is amazing. I can finally be myself and just live, keep up the good vibes at home, we are ok as a family, Lily is happy. I promised him to not bring any other man in my life. It is a promise I make to myself too. I want to discover the whole happiness of being me and taking care of myself. I asked him to try to enjoy this by doing the same. I encourage him to go out and meet people and even go on dates and have adventures without me. This way he would be able to really know whether it's really worth it for him to stay with me for the long term. He needs to compare me, I think, to other women. I hope he'll discover that a relationship doesn't have to be like hell, fights and drama and anger and mistrust and fear. I couldn't give him much actually. He has his own shitty childhood and somehow being with me in this hell seemed normal to him. Even though I ignored him emotionally a lot, manipulated him with my meltdowns, used him sexually, and let him terrify me. Compared to her mom I was definitely more satisfying emotionally. How could he know it is still not healthy? Moving to Hungary so that I can do my studies is part of the deal too. Once I feel ready (might take a lot of time) and he can opt for a friendly divorce or a healthier relationship, we will reconsider getting romantic or separate further.

In the meanwhile I am eating a bit of raw onion every day to keep him away from wanting me, part of my malicious plan, how clever, right? Hehee.

Wanna have a review on La la Land? I watched it Sunday night on my new computer. This pc is like a Ferrari. For someone who buys expensive things like this: "Oh, wow! So cute, so tiny, such a lovely color! I'd take it, please." This is how I bought my last laptop. This one is so powerful it can run the lj cam. The screen is wider than my angle of sight. The letters are so far away from each other that when I'm typing my book I push in between more than on the buttons. And now I can strip everywhere: in my bedroom, in the living room, in Hungary! Haha!

I have issues with sex. Please avoid the topic, I have to work things out with the psychologist first. She is awesome. I am so lucky she managed to change my way of thinking and feeling. She is very subtle but effective. I love how easy she is to trust. The way she is giggling when I say nonsense. She is so sure about some things and it gives me something stable to build on. In my mind everything is so unsure. I cannot trust my memories or feelings. I don't know what's good or bad, She makes things simple. "Abuse is bad" "Tenderness is good" "Leaving a baby cry until it gives up and grows up never asking for help and not being able to accept and give affection is bad" "leaning on someone else is bad" "being with someone who makes you feel bad is bad no matter what he does to you" "being yourself is good" "feeling good about your life is good" Easy peasy!

Do you remember when I told you about a shitty day, many bad things in a row? What was the expression you answered? I am going mad not being able to remember. I know it seems unimportant but I hate half remembering a word or expression. It was to say "bad things in a row".

This is not the first email I wrote to you. I wrote some this last month but ended up deleting them because I could feel that the emotions attached to them were too intense. I didn't want to write to you feeling like I need you. This time I will push the send button knowing that I'll be ok whether you answer or not, no matter what you write. It is good for me to have friends, to talk to calm and sweet people while trying to figure out who I want to be. Will you be my friend? It would be an honor for me.

Take care

Elle

Attached : funny video

*

January 24, 2017

Elle,

You worded that perfectly.

You saw humor and you showed your brighter encouraged self. Eating an onion made me smile. I saw you were searching for the answers before you saw the psychologist. I am glad you found someone who can explain the things to you so you can find the answers. It sounds like she is guiding you but you are finding the truth and are confident in Your answers and Your truths, not just the words or guesses of a stranger. I give you the credit for being brave enough to lift the veil and for really wanting to find the answers and become who you want to be. I believe in you and I think you understand you better than anyone.

I will respect your wishes. I will say I will mourn the sexy part of our friendship but I was concerned I had lost you and honestly I am going to examine my thinking a little. I felt you ignored me and sent the signal you didn't want me in your life. Not out of anger or to be cruel, simply because it was what you needed to do and what was best for you. I tried to honor that even though I didn't want to have you disappear. So to protect myself I let you go emotionally. It will be difficult to watch you work and not find it sexually exciting so if you don't see me at work often, understand I am placed in a difficult situation by watching you turn me on then not being able to comment. But I am going to respect your wishes and I do see a strength in your asking. I like it very much. I also see a strength in your new view of strengthening yourself before you try to fly to another decision. I agree with your evaluations of yourself. And I love that my evaluation really doesn't matter anymore. Or at least if it matters it doesn't affect your evaluation.

The log by my creek washed away. I think I sent you pictures of the 4 girls sitting on it by me and it was by the well. I am fine and enjoyed the snow while it lasted.

I will try to be your friend, nothing sexy, not a replacement or someone to fix you, not someone to turn to because you don't think you are good enough to deal with things yourself. Just a friend who cares. We must decide if it is best for both of us just to be long lost friends who tell each other we are still alive and share events in our lives, or intense friends who write every day and share closeness and things we have difficulty sharing with others. Maybe the sex and lack of sex will be an issue. Maybe my trying to move on will be an issue. but thank you for writing to me. The fact I continually visited you should mean I am still ok with being friends under these conditions.

I don't want to lose you completely.

Still Calvin

"bad things in a row"? Did I use a phrase as a substitute for that phrase or did I have an encouraging response? Series? Avalanche? Something about fire strengthens metal? Bad things happen to good people?

If I can be your s... secretary again and help I will look it up if I wrote it in a message here.

Attached: photos of snow and rainbow

*

January 25, 2017

Calvin,

I want you to be happy. Not forced happiness, not shutting up about your worries. Please keep sharing those. Just "Life is good" happy and happy about us being happy and knowing what you want. I would still do anything I can to cheer you up. Almost anything. (I wouldn't feed Lily to werewolves but you get what I mean...)

If you don't feel good about this, yes we can definitely stay in touch and only share events and tell each other that we are still alive. I don't want to lose you. You could probably always find me on lj as long as I have a profile there. If I don't, that means I'm too old and ugly to strip. And to be your friend.

But I feel like I couldn't find you if I wanted to. It is scary. I am terrified to not have any answer from you anymore and I won't have anything, no more name than Calvin, no more of your living area than North California in the woods, and no more of your job than math teacher at some university. I can't imagine my life not having you in it at all.

If you decide to get rid of me I'd request personal information from you. I need to be able to find you even in 10 or 50 years. Even if you don't contact me anymore. I just have a feeling that I might want to or need to some day. Maybe for a business meeting for a book.

However what I would love is to have you be my close friend. Whenever you feel ready. My dream is to be free to write and call each other. Even being able to skype and I surely don't want to die without meeting you in person.

I let you go emotionally. I might feel more relaxed about us and not greedy but I still feel connected to you. I can feel your distress through that email and am concerned about it.
Part of me doesn't want you to move on. But I don't really have much to offer and I certainly cannot ask you to wait for me. So, I

support you moving on. It would be amazing to know you are not lonely.

We are on two different continents. You have a mom to take care of. I have a toddler to take care of. You have a job there. I have a dream master here. This is just a reminder for me why sticking to protecting ourselves was and is the best thing to do.

Take your time to decide.

Take your time to answer (weekend is fine, I won't freak out if there is no mail in my inbox tomorrow)

See you

Elle

p.s. Your homework: Watch La La Land. Alone is fine. With someone is better. Taking a lady is even better. We'll compare our reviews, ok?

*

January 26, 2017

Elle,

Your inbox is not empty.

I think we agree that we don't want to lose each other and enjoy a deeper connection than just superficial conversations about the weather and a new haircut. So let's not worry so much about us disappearing. This email address I use for many things and I am not going to stop checking it even if you disappear for five years. You can find me here. Skype is not a no, just a I am still figuring out what is best for me. I get you want to be strong and not feel you need me or that I am something you will lean on when you should lean on yourself.

Elle, I don't think you will ever need me, I believe you are stronger than you think and deal with your emotions and bad times. But I want you to know, and I have been annoyed before by things you have said, but I will always listen to you and be here for you Elle. If I am not online I will try to write you back as soon as I can if you need me. If you just need to write something to get it out of your head, I will read it and care. Always. If you don't write to me again for 5 years, then have a bad day and need someone to listen. please write and expect a kind word in reply. I would never say hurtful things, not care about you or not try to help. I think I have already shown this.

What you are insightful enough to read into my words is that I hesitate and wonder what is best for both of us. I definitely want to be friends. I want my heart to be free to love someone. But is it best for both of us for me to keep my heart a little.

We have a deep friendship. Let's see where it goes and not deal with the future until it is real. You let me go emotionally and I am trying to do the same.

Ok this is the stuff we weren't going to talk about.

Not fake happiness but maybe personal stuff that isn't so much about you and me. OK?
I will say even though I am not supposed to breach this topic either... You will never be too old or ugly to strip. Also I have many old ugly friends. Frame and picture remember? Once you are real you can never be ugly to that person, only to people who can't understand.

Still Calvin

I heard you and understand.

*

January 27, 2017

Calvin,

"I have been annoyed before by things you have said"... That's great, so this is where we are at. A whole new level of friendship. You dare to tell me that I am annoying sometimes? I'm feeling amused but now you have to explain. What is exactly annoying that I write? Time to wrestle.

The streets were covered with crispy whiteness this morning. I've never seen anything like this before. Walking on them had the same feeling as throwing small candy balls in your mouth, the ones that explode on your tongue. Fun!

My cute little toddler is fun too. Yesterday I got angry at her for throwing some crayons on the floor and told her "Calliopée /last name/" frowning and holding up a finger. She stops and goes with the exact same expression, holding up a finger "Mom /last name/". Haha. I was laughing so hard. Sorry. I guess this is not that funny to read but living it was funny as hell.

I love the word breach. What's the word for barely touching, just with the fingertips? Until I looked it up I thought this is what it means but I mistook it for a similar word maybe.

No livejasmin session this morning. I want to rest. Yesterday night's session was not bad. I ended it at around 11 p.m. And went to sleep at around midnight. But I don't sleep well. The other night I woke up to my own voice screaming, feeling all embarrassed. I didn't even remember what nightmare I had. Pff. When I sleep I feel only half asleep and my head just keeps looking for an answer I don't even know for what question.

The psychology session was not great yesterday. I usually go on Wednesdays. Unlike the other effective times where I managed to get out a lot and just spoke and spoke and felt like I progressed, I was shaky and could hardly word a sentence. I feel a bit like a monster these days. Like everything is my fault and I am a horrible person. It is not to complain. This is just a step I need to go through.

The psychologist thinks that emotionally I am in my teenage years now. In my "I don't need anyone, I just want to be alone, I can do it by myself. Let me alone" rebellious phase. Sounds right. I didn't have this as a child. Turns out skipping it was not the best way to grow up.

Otherwise everything is fine. I'll have a session on Saturday from early afternoon. Boss will be helping a friend to move. Lily at the grandparents'. I will be skype available but I am not mentioning this to say let's skype. Just saying that I can.

Oh, forgot to say. The boss is changing his mind. He doesn't want to get me back anymore. That was quick. Being flatmates with an ex is tricky. There are calm days and not that good days. On the good days Lily is enough of a joy to just smile and be polite and just feel proud of what we made.

Is this annoying?

Sleep tight, have nice dreams!

Thight hug

Elle

*

January 28, 2017

Elle,

You do not annoy me, the things you have said didn't always make me feel good. "I don't agree. I'm angry and I hate you. But this feeling will pass and I'll come back to apologize for it."

wasn't one of my favorite emails.. But I understood. I never stopped liking you.

If you know the person's heart and you believe they are a good person then forgive them when they don't act like themselves. They can do wrong but the person they are inside doesn't want to hurt you and isn't selfish, they are acting against who they are. If you think they are mean and hurtful and they make you feel bad about yourself and you are not happy around them. Then ignore the gifts they give you and when they apologize because they don't mean their words. I always say I like seeing the real you. You do not guard what you say to me. If you feel it you share it. If the emotions are bad or even spiteful, I know you are telling me your feelings and you are still a good person inside. I like you even if your words can annoy me. I also understand you are not playing with my heart. I don't like when you say I can't go private, no more sexy videos, you can't say my name or have me let you know when I am there. Even though you are a wizard. But I am not annoyed at you because I know who you are. You do these things to protect my feelings and also to protect your feelings and also to protect his feelings. So I love your heart and motives and who you are. Even if I am disappointed or annoyed by the things you have to say sometimes.

Ok did I explain?

To win a wrestling match you must hold your opponents back flat on the mat for 3 seconds. I once beat an opponent in 2 seconds. I don't know if the timekeeper started the clock late or the referee counted the fall a fast 3 seconds. But it was recorded as a 2 second match. You might not want to wrestle with me.

Actually that is a funny story. I am friendly. I bet you hadn't noticed. I like to talk and I talk to people a lot. You might have guessed that too. I had an opponent who was built like me and we would spend our time together when we were at the same tournament. We liked each other more than our teammates. We almost always wrestled each other for the Championship each tournament for a couple years. One tournament we were talking about and he told me my next match was a man who had beaten him. So I was prepared and I came at this stranger as the whistle blew and tried to catch him off guard and be really physical and intimidate him. He went down and I got the 2 second pin. After the match my buddy came up and told me he had lied to me. The man wasn't really very good and he had beaten him last week easily.

Graze, caress, faint touch. tickle, I understand the feeling and action you are describing. Not petting but gently having your finger tips brush against them almost undetectably and each contact ephemeral. Subtle intimacy. I am sorry your sexy secretary is of no help.

Am I allowed to send a picture? Can I have my shirt off?

Struggling is good. I have found that is how you advance. My friend said she can get "LaLaLand" on her TV. Here we call Los Angeles La La Land.

I will share more about my life next time.

I am well. I will survive.

Sleep well.

Calvin

*

January 28, 2017

Good morning Calvin,

I could hold your back flat for much more than three seconds! Heheee. All the dirty minded guys cannot turn me on. I am just working totally absent minded, faking to be horny. But you can.

Ohhh, there are two voices in my head, one saying YES I do want a picture of you without a shirt! And the other one is quite scared of how that will make me feel. Bringing back the horniness without the romantic side effect is tricky for me. Just give me some more time. I want to keep that comfortable safety distance I feel so good at.

Thanks, I slept really really well. I went to bed super early, woke up in the middle of the night, drank some syrup for coughing (I am not coughing but it makes one sleep and I thought I need it to be able to go back to sleep) and I woke up at 9 a.m. I slept more than 12 hours. It was GREAT.
Somehow I feel sleepy again. I can barely keep my eyes open.

I tend to forget that Lily is small. Most of the time I spoke to her as an adult friend. But, damn I have to remember she is still a child. I left her alone with my pc and sure enough she broke it. She broke the charger, it is extremely hard to replace. Why isn't every charger the same? Damn it. It stressed me out. A small accident like this is more than enough for me to feel like a failureBut good news for you: I'll be online only in the mornings, sometimes very early too.

I love your story.

I feel like something is wrong in your life? Otherwise why would you write that you'll survive? I guess you are not speaking of surviving to read your annoying friend.

Elle

*

January 30, 2017

Elle,

Nothing is wrong in my life. If my mom died or was sick or

hospitalized that would be something. If I lost my job that would be something. I will survive having a house expense that costs me some money and taking a couple cold showers. I don't want to make more of this than it is.

Two parts and again this isn't even a bump in my path of life.

First part is that with the rains something might have shifted under my house. Whatever happened, my natural gas line is leaking. Rather than tearing everything up to run a new line, and the expense, I have shut off the natural gas to my house. I will simply change from a gas stove for cooking and a gas hot water heater to electric. The house was already set up for either gas or electric cooking. I just have to finish testing all the electric circuits tomorrow and the specs on the water heater I will be buying to make sure my electrical system can handle everything. If I decide to change back someday I might fix the natural gas. Basically nothing changes just a couple days without hot water, cooking with my microwave and doing a lot of work. Not what I would consider something wrong.

I will survive.

The second part is more personal. But it really doesn't apply. I sent you a picture once of a bench here on my property and the green around it. There is a natural water spring there and it is always green there. it was also one of my wife's favorite stops and her happiest part of her life was here with me on this property. In the picture there is a rock with words on it. My wife's ashes are buried there.

I can't lose my home. I worry about not being able to stay here. As I said, I am not going to have to tear the walls out and run gas pipes down the walls or under the house. But for a while I worried about how I was going to pay for the repairs and when they shut off my gas because of the danger I worried they might not let me live here until it was fixed. When fixed they might have to inspect everything and find more problems. I over think sometimes and go to a scenario that would be worse if not impossible. My wife used to say "Don't bounce until we get to the bumps in the road." But I sometimes spend my energy worrying about things that might never happen.

When we bought this house it was very simple. I have many memories tied up in fixing this house up with her. When I tear something out we built together and change it I feel I lose some of those reminders. The same with my life. It is good to repair and improve, but I still feel some loss. When a change is obviously needed you make the changes and don't live your life without hot water. I am trying but it isn't simple.

So really I am fine. Nothing is wrong in my life. I just have some work to do.

Now tell me about you.

Still Calvin

*

February 2, 2017

Calvin,

Handyman.

Thanks for cheering me up especially at times where you are not really feeling your best. Highly appreciated. I know the feeling of being poor and then going even more poor. You are right. Loved ones suffering is something, losing someone is something. The rest ... we can handle. You are very wise, but you learnt from the best.

Your Hawaiian shirt and the checkered one with blue jeans... you shouldn't wear those in public. Public danger. Fortunately I don't have time to dig up those pictures from our mailing. But they are burned into my retinas. And the one where you are sitting at the sunny window in white shirt, and the one where you make an utterly excited "Here comes Santa" or "Come here Santa" face.

Elle

*

February 3, 2017

Elle,

I already took the pictures of the handyman and they are waiting whenever you wish to see them. probably the shitless picture you should try first to see if you are ready yet.

I have the stove on and the hot water heater was frustrating. When I turned off the water valve it started leaking. I had to shut off all the water to the house and go back and put in extensions and tighten everything. So I have water again but not hot water yet. I placed the new hot water heater in place and have hooked it up but before I wire it and turn it on I want to make sure it doesn't leak and is full. I was very stressed today. I couldn't find tool's and tape and things I knew I had. I have three drills and none of them have chuck keys. I am sure they are with the drill bits. I broke a drill bit building a stand for the new lower heater. just many many frustrated moments when I felt I was making things worse rather than better.

I didn't say and swear words, eventually I stopped and ate because being hungry and without energy wasn't helping. School is great, it just takes up my time. I have a small coffee maker in my bathroom I have been using to make hot water to bathe.

Will your husband allow you to Skype with Lily while you are away in Hungary? I think you are feeling better about yourself and also better about what a good mom you can be and what you find important as far as loving her and putting her needs and not using her as a tool between you and the boss. I think as you feel more confident you are getting closer. That is a regret but it also allows you to focus on the move and getting your life set up as you wish, not just what's available.

Big hug

Calvin

*

February 3, 2017

Calvin,

All is good here.

Yes, I am allowed to skype with her and come back to visit whenever I want and can allow it financially. He will bring her to me in Hungary for school breaks and all summer. I am hoping for them to move to Hungary from September though. If not and I am accepted at the uniI might not go and just move back to France in a studio.

I am ill again. Nothing serious, just a cold. I used to only be ill once or twice a year but this year has been rough for me mentally and my body is not at its strongest.

Lily's dad is quite aggressive. If he discovers me writing to you he will try to kick me out. I could go to the police because he doesn't have the right to do so. But I would rather avoid that trip.

He seems to have many phone texts and hidden things on the internet. I hope he is not just playing with me but really having someone or something private in his life and is moving on.

This move is a good thing. I am sure he will calm down and realize it is easier to have me not too far and help raize Lily.

I have to go.

Wow, sorry I know you are stressed out from all that, but how incredibly sexy is all that description!

I don't fully understand!

Kisses

Elle

*

February 5, 2017

Calvin,

I'm sorry the last one was not really worth being read. Bad habits... I overdramatized probably. There is still some drama going on here, sometimes, but definitely less and less. I feel very hopeful about leaving it behind. I like the "boring" feeling of happiness and feeling safe. I am ok and safe and I can take whatever comes.

I had a great time with you at the last session. Mission accomplished. Thank you! It was like having your best friend come over and just not being able to stop laughing.

Why would it be easier for me to see you shirtless than in clothes? I am afraid. So... No, I am not ready. You know that I find you very attractive so it's not a lack of desire. I just treat myself well and avoid going back to the pain of being emotionally involved. It's just a matter of time, I have to get things a bit more clear in my head and feel more confident about my current approach to sex. I really feel like I made progress. My thinking about men in general changed. Now I think I don't need one. Being alone is a happier place than being involved with someone who is not right and ready for me. I absolutely love being friends. I want to get to know you and stay comfortable teasing each other and making fun of each other and telling eachother things that the other might dislike. I feel like I am more open, being open to many directions. Not having any preference. I don't care if you can or cannot imagine still being in intense contact in 2 years because we still don't know a lot about each other, not enough to know. This is where I was wrong. I gave you, several times, the wrong impression of needing to know what this is. I assume my behavior. It was nonsense. Yes I know we have chemistry, I'm not trying to pretend there isn't, I'm not playing with you, I need to figure out what is "just sex" and "making love" and "physical attraction" for me.

My charger arrived. I spent the day... well very glamorously blowing my nose and sneezing but also doing tons of research to find out what makes me feel passionate, now that it is just me. This feels great.

The rest of the time I'm trying to decide what bank to choose and on which website to freelance. Whether I want to sell my panties (I know it sounds like a very ambitious career choice...), teach French, translate, write books. Do I feel comfortable stripping on a webcam? I am massively confused about me and sex. I just have to put things in place. For a very long time I needed strangers to desire me in order to feel worthy of love. Now I don't feel like I need to turn on the cam to feel attractive. I like me.

I feel full… of potential and things to offer. This is such a weird new feeling, not needing the appreciation of a lover, my dad or a friend to feel worthy and confident of my choices.

Next Thursday I have a legal appointment. Just making sure that legally it will be clear that I did not want to leave Lily. Lily - flowers . Ohhh! I'm booking my flight ticket after that appointment. Huge changes. Exciting new life. Not perfect but more hope and peace and just being me. Your "for now" made my week! Yes, it is temporary. I will work hard to have her closer to me. I want to be strong and stable and ready to supply for her. I will spend summer with her! That's amazing. It will be all about the ice cream shop while she is in summer school and we'll be together at the beach in the afternoon. I don't think I'll do my masters if they don't accept me to move to Hungary. But it's ok. Being able to hug her in the mornings and tickle her when she is naughty is worth spending money on a french studio.

How is your gas-electricity situation? Still having showers with water from your coffee machine?
My grandparents have a tiny vacation house with no running water at a fishing lake. We walk to fill up water bottles at a pump and we wash ourselves in a small tub, heating up water on a small gas cooking something. And there is a dry toilet in the woods just behind the house. But it is charming and not stressful because it was always like this. It is not like your stressful event, where something breaks and everything has to be replaced.

Could you break down your answer in two for me? If the tiny number next to "sent" is bigger than the one next to "inbox" I feel like I am a burden. Don't make fun of me! I know it is silly.

You are an appreciated master of vegetable jokes.
(but what I love the most is when you are just spontaneously funny just by being you)

Elle

*

February 6, 2017

Elle,

I won't make fun of you. But you are silly. You are not a burden. Honestly if you felt like an obligation I just wouldn't write. If I have written less recently, and the 15th through the 22nd I might be away from the computer, it is because I have been busy and stressed with gas lines. Also I will admit to adjusting to both of us trying to not get too attached while still staying close and keeping all the good stuff. Well maybe not all the good stuff.

I use this page to contact people I see giving things away or selling them, also my spam is filled because I use it for restaurants and businesses that offer deals. Right now my scent is barely behind my inbox but they are about the same. I get more spam here than my inbox. Did you have a secret message in this I am missing? or were you actually asking about my inbox vs. sent? I'll answer the question, I just didn't get it. I enjoy your emails but I was told you can't open them right now because of the boss and stirring up things with him best left alone. Out of kindness to him you don't want him to catch you checking email from me.

No, I probably won't email you every day even when you are in Hungary. but I might. I don't plan on losing you though. ok? answered?

I have hot water!! I might rewire the connection. I am not thrilled with the wiring I did. Electricity is more expensive than gas so I will wrap the heater insulation, also I built a stand to raise it up higher so I might strap it to the wall so it won't tip over during an earthquake. But everything is done that needs done. I will fiddle with it over time. No stress or deadlines. My blood pressure was very high. I had a water leak in the main and then I couldn't get a tiny tiny small leak to stop but didn't want to crank down and over tighten. I am always too gentle. But everything went well. I learned some too. So it was a good thing, just frustrating.

Question? Why are his video games so loud? thud thud against the wall?!

I unselfishly like that you don't need sex or to have men like me want to see you naked and sexy. You are being healthy.

I started a business once building a computer component. Great idea but the industry changed. But I understand proprietary information. So without giving me the plot of your great ideas so I can publish them under my new nom de plume "El Electrico". What would these books be about? If you have time I think writing books and about your own life are both good. sharing with me and even more important your new psych friend is a great way to sort through things. So even if you don't choose it as a career or ever choose to publish I encourage you to write books. That's something you can enjoy when 90 years old.

I know you had ideals about translating and you seem overqualified so it might feel a loss to not use your studies. I fought, still fought a little with that. But I tell myself I owe me. I owe it to myself to be happy and the best me as I define myself. I have classmates who are more successful than me. I was a better student than them. They chose to do things differently than I did. Different priorities. My priority is to be happy and care for the people who love me. I honestly could be happy living at a place like your grandparent's vacation house. I am silly and regret not having things I don't want. I could drive a fancy car in a tuxedo to a fancy place and try to impress strangers or be loved by people for being just me. I like just me.

Ok I will SUC.

Always just Calvin

*

February 7, 2017

Calvin,

First of all, You do enigmas. I don't! I didn't phrase it well. It is simply that this email address is only for you, nothing else coming in or going out.So when I see Inbox 6 Sent 9, my little sick mind freaks out that I wrote more than you did. One of them was just a link so that doesn't count. And yes I know you told me it's not I wrote you so you have to write me back. But I just thought I will give you a little tour in my dark space and let you help me. I thought you could just cut your next email into 2-3 pieces and send them in separate emails. So that this crazy girl feels appreciated. But maybe I should just write to you from an email I have most of my spam. This way I wouldn't constantly see how much more I wrote. Am I a good or a bad deal amongst all your other mails?

Sorry, I need to work on my self esteem. I am a little bit annoying always questioning whether you are still interested, aren't I? I have confident days but then the hostile environment and constant bringing me down sometimes takes over my ressources. I try to charge back myself by spending time daydreaming or speaking to people who think I'm not a mess.

I accidentally left the stroller at preschool yesterday. Went with it, left the toddler in class and by the time I got out of the building I completely forgot about the stroller. And I never realized. I was already asleep and Lily too, her dad suddenly came into the room, switched the lights on and asked me "where is it?" I was half asleep. He was really angry at me. I had trouble remembering. He started to rage about how irresponsible I am and how I fuck up things every day and he spent years just correcting my mistakes. I had a bit of a hard time going back to sleep after this. I ended up calling my family. My mom is not much of a help. Whatever I say she rarely reacts. I don't know why she cannot just say "It is gonna be alright, don't worry, you are a great person, you didn't do anything unforgivable". She is always just listening sadly and making me feel even worse. I always think she is not reassuring me or stopping me when I tell her how much I worry that he is right about me because she thinks that he is right about me. Fortunately I got to speak to my sister too. She is in severe depression now :/ She told me things I know very well and understand but she cannot share them with people who've never been through it. I wish I could do more than listen and reassure her that it is not her fault, she is doing anything she can, depression is a liar, it's telling her that everything is awful and it's only getting worse. But of course that's impossible. When everything is so awful there is only better coming. I hope that helped her somehow. She did help me by saying "Agi, you just forgot the stroller at preschool, it is not a big deal. Even if you'd lost it, who cares? I have trouble focusing on everything. I would have forgotten Lily... and the stroller." Wow, she is funny even at her worst.

So yes I am forgetful, I have my head in the clouds, I overthink and overanalyze, I have difficulties trusting people who seem to be nice. And on some days I have so little confidence that I just phase out and stare at the wall until it comes back.

But I do think I would feel better in a more neutral or positive environment. And I hope, I really really hope that not everyone sees my default and mistakes as a reason to get angry and see loving me as a huge sacrifice where one has to sign and try not to swear at me or hit me. He got angry every day at the beginning of the relationship too but always had a "good" reason. He very strictly told me what a bad person I am and I remember him having to leave the room often, he told me that he has to go away a bit otherwise he would get physically violent. I always thought that is just the reaction I get out of people. He didn't hit me until now. And even now, he had a good reason and he didn't bruise me. It was more about humiliation. Could have been sexual, like bdsm, but completely out of context, without my consent and Lily being there encouraged by him to throw things at me and hit me too.

It was quite traumatizing. And I hate myself for writing about this to you. Because I am ashamed I let it happen, and ashamed that I cannot get over it.

I don't want to be this person who tells stories like this to you. But I kept it in and I felt fake. I guess I wanted to prove to you and myself that this is not what I am.

I like to hear you say I am healthy. I like to hear you say I am worthy of love. When you get very sweet like this, when you describe how you would touch me, when you send a photo and I put together the image with your words...I am scared. It is extremely hard for me to just take it and believe it. My mind starts to search for a reason why you'd be so kind and gentle to me. So I am either telling myself that it is the way you are with absolutely everyone even with a rotten person like me. Or I am telling myself that you would get just as angry at me as everyone else. You could hold it back better and for more time but eventually it will burst out. Maybe you won't bash me or hit me just sign me out of your class.

Deep inside I hope someone would find my lightheadedness funny and would just laugh with me about things I do wrong and just always gently cuddle me when I am sad or afraid. Not be offended and push me away, not say horrible things to me, not hit me... just understand or want to understand or just suppose that I am doing things at my best not at all out of desire to upset someone and punish me for it.

I was imagining your photos and already crying. I am so f* up. because that brought back your fantasy stories. I am craving you. But after a very poor emotional environment, it is very overwhelming and hard to take in. Once you asked why no sex in skype? hm... because I will most likely embarrass myself by bursting out in tears. Which would be very inappropriate. You would take it for something else and push me back. You would think I don't want sex with you or whatever you are able to overthink in your mind. And I know you are very good at that!

Will we skype when I am in Hungary?

CONGRATULATION on hot water! Clean man, mmmm. Just kidding, I know about your coffee maker.

"Question? Why are his video games so loud? thud thud against the wall?!" Sorry? Whaaaat? I am just staring at this and have absolutely no idea what this could mean. Should it make sense to me? Oh Calvin! What is this?

I don't need you to see me naked and sexy. I want you to see me naked and sexy.

My ideas about what to do for a living are just for the next few months, I will probably do all of them. I would be a terrible teacher, but I'd be good at giving private class to just one. This is what I am planning to do. Last summer there was someone interested in French at my lake so maybe I'll find interested people. I won't stop writing books. The first one is missing its end, I'm waiting for life to go on and bring me one that I feel would fit nicely.

I like your priorities.

I like you. I like just Calvin. I like the Calvin I know. I'd like to know more about Calvin.

More about my book ideas and also my green tiny home dream in my next email.

Elle

*

February 7, 2017

Elle,

Ok. I will allow your insecurity. I don't think who writes more or more often matters. But I will send you a few emails to assure you that I want you to write to me.

I will leave the topic of having someone humiliate you by physically dominating you for the next one. That is not a small thing. Shut up about the "Had a good reason". There is never an excuse to hit you. You know that. THERE IS NEVER AN EXCUSE TO HIT YOU. It is about keeping you down. You are not a child, this was not a punishment to instruct you because that's the only way of learning. You don't need to lie to yourself. You know it was wrong and not about you. Not about anything you did. Unless you came at him with a knife and he struck you to keep you from stabbing him, THERE IS NO EXCUSE FOR EVER HITTING YOU! EVER!

They tease me because I am an absent minded professor all the time. I am always asking my students to remind me to pass back tests before class gets out. I think some of it is about passion and priorities. Math is a discipline. It is a great way to expand your thinking and it expands your universe. The topic of my lecture and the problem on my board before them is important to them because it is their homework and on their next test. But I get side tracked about talking about what I think is truly important to their lives. I am trying to open a window to this great universe and they want me to describe the curtains to them. I forget the things I am doing that are less important when I touch on greatness or something that will expand their world.

Hello! Your daughter was more of a focus than the stroller. You are passionate about what you are focused on and lesser things get skipped over. I am a theoretical mathematician. Applied mathematicians and engineers hate that. They need each step done properly like robots. If you try to jump around to the big picture they get confused and say "Go back to step 3 after step 2. We don't care why it works, just show us what to mindlessly do in order". We dreamers annoy the robots. They don't get it.

Isaac Newton would forget to eat for days and wear unmatched socks. Most great thinkers in math were lost in thought. One of my favorites was Archimedes. He was the "give me lever and a place to stand and I will move the earth." He built all these ingenious weapons to protect Syracuse from the attacks of Rome. Giant arms that would pick up the enemy boats out of the water or lasers that would burn the sails. But while he was working a math problem in the dust he failed to notice that his city was being attacked and overrun by Roman soldiers. As a soldier was running through the city killing people he almost stepped in the dirt Archimedes was writing his math solution in and Archimedes pushed him. The soldier killed him.

So you are not bad or evil for being absent minded. I would pay attention to see if you are in the middle of a war though just to be safe.

Hug

Calvin

*

February 7, 2017

Elle,

Ok now your inbox is closer to your sent box.

When you are at work. I don't know why even in emails I tend to use this code about "the boss" and "Flower" and "at work". But when I see you sometimes I hear this loud bang from the other room. You say he is playing video games but it is loud. It's like he is kicking the wall.

Find your passion and be happy. Teach French or another language, write, sell your panties, (not interested), do what brings you joy then change careers. You don't have to be locked into a decision you made for the rest of your life.

Ok I will send you a third email before you write me back if it will make you feel better. Trust me I enjoy writing to you and reading to you. My life is good right now. I am busy and not in my head so much right now. I think maybe right now you have things trying to explode out of you and NEED to write to someone to get it all out. I am privileged that you think I am the person you want to share it to. I tend to write more when I am lonely and missing someone or when I am about to explode or sexually frustrated. I am none of those things right now. I am just writing because I enjoy you.

Did I cover the whole thing about lying to yourself about it being your fault someone hit you? Forget the hit even. What he did was lower you. steal your authority. but you down. take your power. It wasn't about you, or if it was, it wasn't about that moment. it was about him and power over you. As you describe it it wasn't a fight, it was intimidating you to gain the upper hand and dominance. Sometimes I would wrestle around and be playful and just because I wrestled in college I could control my wife and she kind of liked that, but she was always laughing and tickling me and if I won I kissed her and let her go. Also she always started it by tackling me or something. She got away with a lot because she was so small I would never hold her too tightly or squeeze her wrist or anything. Also this game always lasted much longer than I wanted. She never gave up, just waited for me to let go and then attacked me again. Sometimes losing has its own rewards for me too.

Life is good. Really.

Calvin

*

February 8, 2017

Calvin,

Thank you for the mountain of messages. I wasn't expecting meaningful content. You overdid the favor I was asking for! I really like the subjects and the "Calvin in your inbox" Yes I got it. These are one of my favorite kinds of jokes of yours!

Ok. Thanks for the part on physical violence, it is very sweet. But it is not what you think.

No it wasn't a fight. I was phased out, he told me too many mean things and I couldn't bear listening to him anymore so I layed down on the bed, curled up , fixed the wall... for very long hours. It is certainly not a normal reaction but I just switched off to somehow survive the day. He tried to get me out of it by asking nicely, by shouting at me, calling me by names and throwing things at me, took the blanket and the pillow, and put the light in my face. He hit me on my butt. So I wouldn't say that he attacked me. Oh, I just got a flashback from my lovely childhood. But let's not speak about it. Breath. Ok. He kept hitting me with a cloth or something. So he didn't punch me or kick me or anything. Anyways. Your words still helped.

I started to tell the psychologist but she wasn't really empathetic about it so I ended up just keeping it in. Thank you for listening. We won't speak about this anymore.

Thank you for the Archimedes story. And the hug.

That's not him kicking the wall! He is usually asleep when I "am at work". It's the neighbors from upstairs. I don't know what they are doing but it's like they are constantly moving furniture.

I have to take your word for "life is good really", it feels like hell here most of the time. When I'm sick, weak or sad he is like attracted to me, he can smell it and he appears right away and keeps pushing me down until I feel like there is nothing good in life. When he catches me smiling or being peaceful he just comes up with something that might hurt me, says it and goes away all happy. When he is enraged (most of the time) I try to go into another room with Lily but he follows us and just puts me down until I am shaking. If I am strong enough to not be affected by it, he just goes on until I'm not anymore. If one set of insults doesn't work anymore because I talked out that special insecurity with the psychologist he gets very frustrated and I'm left alone for sometime but he ends up finding something else that crushes me.

I do feel empathy for him and understand that he only recently realized it's over for us. That he wants me out of his view. But it is still not an excuse for his behavior.

I will forgive him. Every time he gets tired of being an asshole I feel so much relief and I just want to hug him and say "everything will be fine, I'm so sorry, but I have to leave you, you'll be fine, you'll be happy. You are doing great. Someone will love you so much. Us....it was a mistake. next time choose better." But it's only a few hours and the devil man is back.

Oh my god. I got so much experience from this. I am terrified now of everyone though. Because I just couldn't see all the red flags until recently. When I met him, I didn't really had any good sex to compare to, he knew more than my previous experiences (well, the best one was my very first love and boyfriend for whom I was the first and he only took time and effort to discoer his pleasure. I was lucky he was gentle but we were very young and the sex was ery basic) At 20, a man who was all about my pleasure in bed was more than enough. I immediately jumped to the conclusion that he is generous and kind and loving. He was unusual. He was French. Most of all he wanted me. The very first person who wanted me. Not my sister, not my body for a night, but my whole self just for him for something serious. It felt like I hit the jackpot. I made sure he wasn't a serial killer or drug addict and after running all the tests I could think of on him, I allowed myself to fall in love. Dumb me. I really liked the feeling and not really liked myself so when problems kept turning up I just brushed them away and continued to adore him like he was my god.

Why am I rambling about this? I thought I was over it, but I'm afraid it's a work in progress.

Wait what, you can say cruel and thoughtless things?

You have no idea how much of an issue is that you find me desirable. But I want the same thing as you. So, I have an idea.

Let's take it easy in a playful and enjoyable way. Prepare me. I want to get used to seeing you and you seeing me. We will just start small. I made you something. Something I feel comfortable to show (not much), I don't promise any sexy attitude.

Try to guess what you see! I'll send you a video showing what part of my body it is after you guessed.

"If we both decide the relationship should change we can make new rules. and then you can break them." Ohh, you know me so well! Thanks, it is very considerate of you. I love breaking rules.

Have fun guessing

Elle

*

February 9, 2017

Elle,

Warning! Sexy pictures, do not open!

Inside elbow.
Don't look at my shirtless picture.
Guess what body part is not real?
Too far? I put in a warning

Calvin

I will write later tonight.

Attached: picture of a handyman and Calvin with a wig

*

February 9, 2017

Elle,

I still believe it is your inside elbow, but because I am obsessed with this part of your body and dream of a video of your legs in tan pantyhose I will guess the inside of your knee.

Honestly I will write a true message after I go buy groceries.

Hug and a smile

Calvin

*

February 9, 2017

Elle,

Ok not much to say. No pictures. Sorry if I crossed the line. I honestly don't want to mess with your brain and I support you not making decisions or dealing with sex until you get straight in your head how you feel about it. I want you to be healthy and I want me to be healthy for you. I understand what I really do.

So now I am going to talk about sex...

But in general terms. You told me about your different sex partners and what made it better and how it effected your thinking. I am trying to do the same and share my thoughts. Trust. I think that is when sex became best for me. She loved me. Even with my faults or things I saw as less than perfect. We could enjoy a night of intimacy and understand that the other person was going to enjoy it also. I wasn't worried about if I was going to hit the button to stop the bomb from exploding. If one of us was tender or numb the other was glad we had all the fun it took to make the person too sensitive. It wasn't about if I was still hard or if she had an orgasm yet. It was a great night. We appreciated the other person trying to turn their partner on but we would have called Bull Shit if we faked a moan or pretended. maybe I am naïve but not every night did she orgasm and some nights many times, but they were all real. I wasn't concerned about pleasing her and she wasn't having sex to please me. We were being intimate. We were having fun. She would tickle me or I would say something dumb in the middle of things and kill the mood. but we loved that. It was us. it was who we were. I could be me and I knew she trusted me. I wasn't going to do something she didn't like. She could let me experiment and feel relaxed because I paid attention and before she could say "no" I already felt her and had stopped. The same with her. I enjoyed when she wore sexy clothes. But I didn't need that. I didn't like wrestling around and being too dominant but she did and we kept it playful. I trusted her. I could just enjoy it and not try. We could enjoy ourselves and just be us. We thought we had the rest of our lives so we could try again in an hour or next week or in 20 years.

Boys are sometimes not ready for affection or whatever level of affection the girl is. So if you care about a guy you will not pressure him or do anything to mess with his head if he is not ready. If a guy likes you he won't pressure you to leave your comfort zone either no matter what it is and no matter how far against your comfort zone you have gone. When you feel uncomfortable it stops. If you press him past where he is comfortable and mess him up for the future, you are a jerk. If he's a jerk who cares if you hurt his feelings. He's a jerk who tried to pressure you out of your comfort zone.

Ok that's all my sex talk for tonight.

-What is orange and sounds like a parrot?
-"A Carrot"

Vegetable joke king Calvin

*

February 11, 2017

Elle,

Why do bad things happen to good people? I came home to a wet floor. I couldn't find the leak and thought maybe the washing machine leaked.. really bad. Finally I found water coming out under the wall. I found the leak. it is small and I can cap off where it is going. I just don't like to disturb the main water line and cause more leaks. So I have no water again here. and my weekend will be fun working to get to the leak, try not to get electrocuted by the electrical outlet next to the leak that is now wet and shocked me twice. and a lot of work. I can do this just not the weekend I wanted. I have committed to helping friends from the 15th till the 25th who are going away for romantic vacation and need animals cared for. Then again for two weeks in March. Now I worry about coming home to a leak in the house and also wanted to rest up and be stress free before.

You said good things about how you see your relationship with Lily's father. Maybe your dad supports you more than you feel he does. I understand but I also appreciate that you were thoughtful enough to reassure me again that we are fine. We enjoy what we have and things happening in life don't always have to be about you and me. life happens. You said it in a very sweet way and I took every word as a compliment.

More on your books later.

Stressed and worn out. write when I have water.

Oh and I loved that it was cute and funny and sweet.. but your elbow in my favorite pantyhose was kind of hot! But I liked the way you did it. healthy. Plus I guess correctly! yay me!
Stressed out tired Calvin who appreciates you.

*

February 11, 2017

Elle,

I am not good at not thinking or worrying and just getting sleep. So it's 4 in the morning and I have been working on the water leak. I can't go to the store and fix anything but I can't seem to just sleep. I turned off all the water to the house but the valve still lets through a drip plus the lines have to drain. So I opened a valve next to the leak and let that drain into a big bucket. that will probably overflow but I will have saved the floor some water. I am a little nervous. The electrical box next to it bit me pretty hard when I touched it trying to turn off the valve. I am going to turn off the electricity to that area and hope I can check and know it is cold. That shock scared me a little. made me come inside and decide to wait until it is light before I work anymore. If I make things worse I don't want to have to work in the dark around water and electricity. I planted 4 trees for the donkeys. Actually for my view. When I first planted them I had to carry buckets of water everyday from the creek to water them. One had an animal dig under it and eat its roots. I tried to nurture it back to life when I found the hole but I couldn't. The creek is now so high it has flooded around the trees. Before when I used to water them I couldn't even see them from the creek because it was so much lower. No damage appears to be done, just a lot of water.

I agree with you not spending extra time making yourself think dark thoughts by writing a dark story. maybe make a note for later if a great idea comes. but don't spend too much time trying to get into that mood or get caught up writing that. At least not now. My advice is to follow it or not, it is up to you. I can't really think of a bucket list. There is art and architecture I have admired in photos I would like to see in person someday. But it's not a big deal. It is like historical artifacts. I would love to own a meteorite. Something from outer space, something not of this planet. But what would I do with it? it costs millions of dollars and I would want to show it so why not allow it to be in a museum and just visit it. they could dis[play it better and show people better. I have seen some interesting historical things that I found neat but again why would I want them except to know I have them? I saw a nice display with pictures of the first astronauts on the moon and below they had the actual read out from the monitors on earth of their heart beat. neat but not worth anything to me. my bucket list I guess is like that. things I would find neat. but not worth the money or of great value to me. I guess the trees and your bucket list go together. I like to see my job finished. I would enjoy a time machine and see the trees I planted when large, see the kids taught to be successful. See the little girls grown and happy and careers. Seeing the work I do was worth my time. When I die I would like to think my time was well spent. it resulted in something. I was dumb and dangerous when I was young and got that out of my system. Now I look at the things I did and wonder why I am still alive. Rock climbing, driving fast. jumping off cliffs into the water, just for the excitement.. I prefer living and not getting injured more than excitement now. I like me and don't feel I am missing a lot. I would love to see the Northern lights. (Aurora Borealis), I wish I could just sit down and play the piano amazingly like the artist I see, but not enough to learn. I wish I could fly a plane. but....

Ok I will write more. I need to try to sleep. Did that help you get to know more about me? I liked that question. Feel free to share your bucket list.

Calvin

*

February 11, 2017

Elle,

Don't bounce until you get to the bumps in the road. I stressed about the leak all night. I woke up this morning and figured out where it should be leaking and why. unscrewed a valve and screwed on a cap. took me about 5 minutes and it has been dry for three hours so far. Problem fixed. I hope so.

I was thinking today I have all these stresses and worries but I have few real problems. My blessings far outnumber my problems. I received texts today from two old friends. Both are rare people that are great people and who love me unquestionably. I am so lucky.

I enjoy reading but I don't seem to do it as much as I would like. I seem to have the weight of small things that don't matter on my shoulders. Having a clan house doesn't mean I am a good person or a bad person. but I feel irresponsible if I am lazy and don't keep it clean. My property needs to be kept up in case of fire or flood or weather. But I care too much about people seeing it. I try to worry less and realize things seem to work out ok. But that is not me. I stay awake all night worrying and thinking about a small leak and can't wait for it to be light enough so I don't explode from stressing about it. Even now when I know it is fixed I want to go check to make sure. Why don't I just sit back and relax and read more often? But I also mention this because I want to hear about what you write when you finish but I am not a good critic or a person who reads enough to offer an opinion. Oh I talk all the time and you will hear my thoughts. Shut up Calvin. But they are not thoughts from someone who understands and recognizes good writing.

I did my pen trick in class the other day. It didn't really fit with the lesson well but I made it relate. It got the class's attention and it was time for a magic trick. They are fun students. I stab a piece of paper with my ink pen. poke a hole through it with the pen sticking out from both sides. Then I said I wished I hadn't done that. So I slide the pen across the paper. So I slide the pen across the paper, they watch both sides as the paper doesn't rip and there is no hole but the pen is complete on the other side. They are sure it is a fake pen and so I offer to show them the pen. but before I hand it to them I say, "Will this prove it's real?" and I stab it through my tongue. They are all shocked. Then I pull the fake tongue out of my mouth and hand it to them. I say " See it's a real pen" Before I stab my tongue while they are staring at my tongue I switch pens from the trick pen to a regular one. Just another day in my math class.

Ok have a great day. Nothing clever to say or sexy. I am being good and not sending the next handyman picture. I will send one of me when I was young and skinny. I was still in my growth spurt.

Still Calvin

attached: picture of young Calvin

*

February 11, 2017

Elle,

I was tired, stressed , overwhelmed and distracted when I wrote to you last night. Here are the pictures of my trees I meant to send you. Sunny day today, no problems, just water in the creek.

See I can send sweet pictures that I am not naked in. I won't say if I am wearing any clothes right now as I send them... but there is no nudity in these pictures. unless you count the trees. They are naked.

Smile. You are cute when you smile.

Goofy Calvin

Attached: picture of trees

*

February 12, 2017

Calvin,

Try not to die electrocuted.

Don't get too excited about the videos. You sounded so desperate in the "why bad things happen to good people". I wanted to do something. These are pity videos. To cheer you up. You feel better now but the videos are here, I might as well just send them.

Ok, you got me worried. Stop working in the dark with water and electricity! I'm glad you are still alive. It is really hard to listen to you being stressed and not being able to help you to go to sleep when there is nothing else to do. Once again it is so freaking amazing to me that you manage to write about your feelings and know that you are worn out and frustrated and stay kind to me. I am so glad that your mood changed and you feel relieved and hopefully can enjoy the rest of the weekend. Well done!

Bad things happen to bad and good people too, all the time. Life is about dealing with shit. You are great at it. Life is also about "being wise enough to see beauty around us". Very well phrased from one of your first messages. You stay yourself when suffering instead of turning into a raging monster and hurting people around you. You get put down but you get up every time and make good use of the "no shit" time.

I tried to do a session. Ughhhh. It sucked. I can't shut up. And I am afraid of all of them. Having the screen between me and them and distance is not enough to feel safe right now. I'm not ready to go back.

Right now I would love to speak with you. Just enjoy your company and feel cuddled. I feel horny but only because my body didn't have sex in a while. I feel tempted to say that I want sex. But it is not true. I just want to feel loved for a moment. This week was so much. I just want to rest and breathe and feel safe.

When that aggressive scene happened, I just couldn't even realize what's happening. Now it hits me. Flashes are coming back. I feel constantly in danger. My brain knows I shouldn't. It's over. I remember my surprise at that moment when he jumped up from the chair. Enraged is a good word to describe because he was completely different from his normal self. I like to watch him sleep or enjoy a video game. His face is like a little boy's. So peaceful and sweet. And it turned all dark suddenly. He often has this threatening look that creates a shadow on his face and disforms his features. I didn't have the time to be conscious about my feelings. It happened very quickly. After the push and my wrist I instinctively moved away from him and cried out in a high voice that didn't sound like mine. It was over in a blink of an eye. I was still in shock and my whole body got extremely tense, fight or flight mood. My mind sharpened. I could feel his mood and focused on him to try to foresee his next move. Not even realizing how little of a chance I'd actually have to do anything if he continues. I wasn't conscious of feeling helpless and the giant fear in my stomach. And right after I just focused on Lily who got scared by my voice screaming. He didn't continue, I took her immediately in my arms. He tried to take her, but she didn't want to go with him. He came after us and continued threatening me but I could feel that he wouldn't do anything. He was getting out words not burning inside silently and preparing to hit. In the following hours all I felt was the desire of him being normal again. And when he came back I was shaking and crying. But oh my god that relief, when he could speak calm again. And seemed to have realized that it went too far and that what he did was actually a bit exaggerated as a reaction.

You know, my relationship wasn't good. And I've wanted to get out since october. We didn't have sex these last weeks. We don't do anything anymore together. We hardly even look at each other. And we only speak when it is inevitable. But it was something. Something that helped me to maintain the lie that I am not lonely. Now. I'm just lonely. Period. The psychologist kept saying she thinks I love him. I denied it every single time. And now I think about the aftermath of the break up. I start to realize that I do love him. Not him. But the person that he was rarely, the person I forced him to be or imagined dhim to be when he was silent, asleep, pleased me.

I want to be touched so much. I would hug anyone who comes close enough to me. Great. I guess my journey of "finding happiness on my own " starts now. I am a little bit afraid that letting him go only starts now and will be an emotionally complicated task.

I feel like I have understood so much about myself since I met you. I was just struggling and being stuck in a vicious circle and you stepped into my life and started to gently say to me "no" and direct me into better directions. Things keep getting more clear and at the same time I realize how little I know. How much I still got to understand and discover. How generous that you didn't let me self-destruct to flatter your ego. I can't believe I actually got better psychologically and how much my thinking changed. It is overwhelming.
Ok.

Enjoy the pantyhouse. I'd love to have sex with you but only if I can be sure that I enjoy it as just sex. My mind has to understand that sweet and kind people are sweet and kind in bed. And my heart has to understand that enjoying being treated gently is not necessarily being in love.

Pfff. I have absolutely no filter. Stuff is coming out of my mouth, it doesn't necessarily mean that you need to know all these. But it helps to share, otherwise I will explode.

Thank you so much. I know you won't see me differently or say something inconsiderate when I'm being vulnerable. I am trying to speak about it with my family but the reactions crush me. They just don't know how to react. It is not their fault but sharing is not worth it if I feel worse after it.

Take care!

Don't get electrocuted!

Elle

*

February 12, 2017

Elle,

I am glad you don't have any filters with you. I wish you weren't right though. I LOVED the video, but sex is not your solution. I am not your escape. You are strong and can handle this. You are doing everything you credit me with. It happened when you decided to change your life. maybe you just decided you wanted to be someone different, maybe Lily had her effect, maybe he got worse or you became more aware. Maybe it was diet. who knows. But It was and you are changing things.

Ok I'll stop being so selfless and be a little selfish. The leaks are all fixed. I have not fixed the electricity but I am watching my friend's animals for 7 days and don't want to start a project tearing things apart electrical and not be home. That's my excuse for being lazy. Plus even though the leak is stopped I like to have everything dry up first.

But my selfish point was.... Life is good and I am not stressed, you didn't need to send a video but you know I loved it! Even if you wanted to make them playful but not orgasmic. I mean even less than the last. maybe just heels and a long dress to your feet, or a blanket covering your legs. that would be innocent. maybe show your ankles, or lower leg. Or maybe even lift it slowly to show knees while you smile that seductive smile. That would be innocent and nonsexual, not clearly nothing I would masturbate while watching. lol. I am selfish and will mention Video 3 came through but videos 4 and video 5 just had the names and number but no video. I mean if you already made them it wouldn't be any of you relying on me telling you that you have worth because of them if you sent them now.

You have worth because you were kind, the generosity and thoughtfulness and the fact you did it to be kind are what has value. The sexy part just happens to be what I like. I am the reason it was sex. You have value beyond sex and you did the kind act. I am the reason the kind act involved pantyhose. Thank you.

Of course if that's what we do now. If one of us is stressed, the other sends something nice to distract them. handyman picture 3,4 and 5.

When I get stressed and frustrated I tend to become short. This can be hurtful because I shut people out. I don't try to but I get caught in my thoughts. Having someone tell me to relax and eat bugs me because I feel like I have a fire to put out and lunch isn't the solution. I think you feel that way when people offer easy solutions to your problems. They don't respect the immenseness of the problem. Go take a day off and have your nails done doesn't change the fact someone at home scares you. It isn't that I don't appreciate help. I love video help. But seriously, I tend to focus and be frustrated and be quiet rather than act out. I turn my disappointment onto myself, but I also believe in myself. I know I can do it. I can figure it out. I am just angry at myself because I haven't or I am overwhelmed because it is so big. I think you are overwhelmed right now. You are not looking for me to fix it. you give me credit but you want to rely or believe it is not you. I don't know what I am talking about. I just know I believe in you and as much as I would love to be selfish you are too correct. Sex is not your solution. I want to make you a video, I want to write you a sexy story. I want to comment on my video. But I won't.

Elle you have value and strength and power. You can do this and you know it. I am some guy in California, you are dealing with this. I can say things to make you feel held and cared for and caressed. But the reality is you are great. You are going to survive and just want to credit something besides yourself. You are hurting. I am sorry. I want to help. Ask and we might agree. but I think you know sex is great for me but a replacement for you. I admire and care for you because of how wonderful you are. charming, sweet , considerate and caring. You give and think of me when you are suffering. This is why you are lovable not just because I am hard thinking about my video.

Ok Sunday. I am going to church then lunch with friends. No worries or electrical shocks or leaking water here. the world is not falling down over my head and Elle made me three pantyhose videos.

What do I always say? "Life is good"

What else do I always say? " The greatest gift and show of respect and flattery a woman can do for a man is to remember his words, value them and quote him."

You are too good to me.

Thank you!

Calvin.

I am not sure if I am supposed to comment on your wrist. You know and I think you need to get it out and write to me. My telling you he was wrong isn't needed. It isn't because of my words. it is because you already know and have said it to me. I do understand and can picture what you describe. I have not felt that but I can imagine and you describe it well. The shock to your system. the fog of the suddenness of it. Trying to piece it all with your memories and view of him. trying to make sense of something and not wanting to think about it but can't stop. I get it. But I hear you and you are right. You don't need me to say it back to make it true. Your voice is more powerful than mine. And if it isn't to you. Fix that so it is!

*

February 13, 2017

Calvin,

"Maybe it was diet?" Oh, wait, I actually changed my diet not even a year ago.

Ok, I got it. I am changing things. We both like to underestimate ourselves, don't we?

I laughed at your pen trick with the fake tongue. Just imagining it... it sounds so ridiculous, I can totally picture you doing it. Watching you this is what would go on in my head "What? This guy is unbelievable. I can't believe this is a math class. This is just so random. What?" It is so unexpected. It reminds me of your math papers with the encouragement and wise thoughts in between the exercises. Oh my god, I can't stop laughing!

Those pictures. Hahaaa. I love the misleading wood!

Sorry, I did something wrong when uploading them. By the way, I filmed them yesterday. I won't backhold videos from you. The snowy one is an exception, we weren't speaking at that time and I remembered it recently. I unfortunately already deleted those two. But don't worry it was just some random blabla. I will make some more.

I felt like I had to "pay you back" for taking me on as a charity project. I feel so bad for suddenly becoming uncomfortable to put on a sexy face. Because you got to know me always horny and always interested and I feel like you invested time and effort into that person. I wish I could feel that I am enough without the sexy part. You keep repeating it, thank you! It bothers me that I can't please you wholeheartedly. Thank you for the video suggestion. I like the little innocent script. Heheee. Feel free to introduce me to your other pantyhouse themed fantasies, I am a little bit lost not quite sure what exactly you'd enjoy.

This is what we do, we distract each other from stress? Aww I like this! Yes!

Sorry, I get why "go to sleep because there is nothing else to do" was not helpful. I get how frustrating it is when people seem to not respect the immensity of the problem. Thank you for explaining! Good example with getting your nails done. I sense that you are not hurt by my easy solution. In my head it was a distraction, a funny scene that I didn't develop enough. The "help you go to sleep" was a winky eye kind of thing. I tried to express that I am concerned about your sleeping hours too. It seems to be all over the place. You write to me at very strange hours. But I would never send you to bed when you can't sleep. Hmmm. I am realizing now that I could be vexed in a situation like this. I tend to be at my best in emergency situations but if it is something like an electricity problem I have no idea how to solve or even not make it worse... I guess I would be trying to make sexual jokes or forced sarcastic optimist jokes. What is a woman supposed to do in this case, in addition to not making the problem worse? I am just asking because I am curious. Also I wonder how to behave around a not aggressive man. An aggressive one would prefer you to disappear and not say anything, just make yourself invisible until the problem is solved and also for the next few hours/days, the time he forgets about the problem. So, how about a kind one, who is still focused on the problem, stressed, disappointed with himself but optimistic? Is "getting out of the way" the best help? Encouragements? Or just tap on the shoulder afterwards? Patiently waiting for him to solve it, knowing that he can? Preparing a sexual treat as a "thank you, well done"?

Lily's dad used to tell me I look like a cocker spaniel when I am sad. I didn't take it well. I don't want to look like a cocker spaniel. Last time Winnie the pooh was on, he glanced at me "Actually you like Eeyore. hehe. Yep. That's it." I found that very accurate.

If I'd want to make fun of myself I would compare myself to him too. :) He has this reaction when his house gets demolished by the wind "Well, houses are like this, they get demolished by the wind" His gloomy pessimistic optimistic approach to everything... It's so me. He always made me laugh. Watching Eeyore is like watching someone make fun of me in a cute way. I love Winnie The Pooh, all the characters have some psychological illness going on but they are so lovable.

Please write me a sexy story, if you feel inspired *.* (sparkling eyes) A sexy story would be a great great distraction!

Yes, sex is a replacement for me. But I just need time to get used to it again. I want it to become something great, something light and fun I can enjoy. Not an escape. No I don't want sex. I just want to feel safe again. Your words are perfect, I did feel held and cared for and caressed (wow This word turned on my body. You are smart!) and my confidence is back. I just miss feeling safe. Right now I can't imagine being able to feel safe. I am afraid I will spend my life highly aware of people's mood around me, checking all the little details all the time, getting worried about an eyebrow raising or a voice changing. Realistically it should get better with time. But I can't really rest and let myself go feeling so unsafe all the time. I am so exhausted. two more weeks, he can easily find another reason to get mad however hard I try to avoid everything I can think of. "Don't bounce until the bums come on the road" Quoting your wife again. This one is incredibly helpful.

I got my hug! Lily woke up too early to my taste this Sunday morning, I succeeded at putting her back to sleep. I could hold her in my arms sitting for quite a while. Then we laid down, she was wrapped up in my arms and legs. oh my god... isn't this the best feeling ever?? We slept on the couch like this. Octopus mom... Sweet sunday morning.

Bucketlist another time!

I went back to sleep this morning. I will film something the next

time I look presentable.
Thank you for the many many messages. Your short ones are different from the long ones. They are more raw and less censored. I like both. The short ones give me a better insight to how you function and react in situations and I can picture you better. The long ones are like the best version of you I think, where you put time into phrase it well and take a step back from the happenings, think before writing. I like both. Getting closer to know "the worst " version of you is always very reassuring because it is so not scary. Just human. And still adorable.

I fell asleep this morning fantasizing about life being different. How different things would be if the man I'm cooking for would be sweet and kind and gentle, someone like you. What would my life be like if I had met someone like you 5 years ago? But it is not the case. And what I take away from this huge life lesson is appreciating experiences, good people, little things, the desire to learn. But mostly appreciation. I will never take kindness for granted.

Quick kiss on the cheek

Elle

*

February 13, 2017

Elle,

Honestly the "top and eat something" was not a reaction to you. You did exactly what I was commenting on. I know the people are trying to help. I don't feel like I am mean or angry, I just am not appreciative and I am cold. you are so in tuned to me you heard the coldness I hate. I hate when people are trying to help and I am so focused I am cold. I wasn't commenting so much on the fact it doesn't help, but on the fact I know they are trying to help and I return their kindness with coldness. I tend to get mad at myself because at that moment I am so self absorbed. I don't strike out but as you did I don't let my frustration be contained and instead of stopping and eating I brush off kindness and act cold.

Wow this is sounding cold now. But I will give you the answer to your question. It is just a difficult situation when a man is not at his best and you can't help but feel you should. it is difficult for both. What my wife did and you can do this. I am talking generally not about me or you. But when a man is frustrated, don't act. Try to be as positive as possible and still honest. Pie in the sky doesn't help. But when I felt overwhelmed I started to doubt myself. telling the man he can do it, only works if he can, and you believe wholeheartedly he can. Things like, " You are incredible and you can fix this and if not we will just...." that's the tricky part. Offer a solution that isn't impossible. "You are wonderful, I believe in you, yay Calvin. And if you fail we have x amount of money saved up to fix this." Don't say I can live like a cavewoman and you are a lousy husband I am willing to live IN horrible conditions with. But stop the man from spiraling down to the worse case scenario and help him believe in himself again. Sometimes playing dumb is ok. I had a coach who would always build me up by asking dumb questions. " Didn't you beat the guy who beat this guy?" Didn't you win last week at an even harder tournament?' "Wasn't that you I saw beat the guy bigger than this guy?". So asking, " So is this job like the job you fixed before? Is this harder than the time you amazed me?" "I know this is totally different but will it cost as much as the last disaster we lived through and are fine now?" I can't speak to all men but there is a little boy inside. We think, "I am just pretending to be a grown up man, if I was a real adult I could do this." Men feel they must provide and protect. Sometimes the big picture is that you bought us this house and gave us a place to live that is going to be wonderful someday. This is not the end. We can live without a roof for a couple days. You are not a failure, you just are in the middle of doing something great. The sacrifice is worth it. I don't mind and I believe the dream is going to get done somehow. You can provide by paying someone who is more of an adult and more of a man to do what you are not man enough to do for yourself.

I am trying to expose the frailty of the man more than giving you words to say. But it doesn't work when the man calls Bull. You know I can do this?!!!! How?!!!! I have never done this before and have no training. Why do you expect me to be Superman all the time? I never said that, but I have thought about it. Also it hurts when you hear doubts like they are saying they believe in you but they are booking a hotel for when you fail.

Out of the way? I love strong women. I am not threatened. So being there to hand me a tool and being ready to jump in and lend a hand and get dirty and not worry about your clothes or fingernails makes me feel closer, We slew the dragon together! I think with anyone there has to be a relationship. I grew up working with a lot of older men. They don't want to treat you like an idiot who doesn't know anything and you don't want to treat them like they are weak and useless. So working alongside them and neither of you dismissing the other's value. Maybe that's a life lesson. Wow I am deep. But the man has to value her suggestions and let her look because she might have the solution. But she still has to be thoughtful of his ego and not tell him to get out of the way and let her do it right. Again it is not even a man woman thing. Just being able to accept that you both bring something to each table. Something I might be better at, and some things you might be better at, but we value the input even if it is uneducated and off target. That is why I hate when I am cold. I don't try to shut anyone down, but I don't hide that their kindness isn't helping and I am too self absorbed at the moment to appreciate the spirit the gift was given in. Like the little kid who hands you the wrong wrench. Appreciate that he wants to help.

I can't help with your situation but this little boy keeps handing you tools that he has no idea what they are used for. Appreciate my useless off target advice, just don't follow it because it is harmful.

I will consider a story, but I tend to make them personal. It is the way I write. I don't think that I am healthy right now. And you don't owe me sexy. Isn't this what you and the psychologist are working on. I love that a sexy video is a tool you handed me and I used my hand and it worked. But it is not "All you have to offer." It is not something you owe me because I "invested" in you. I know who you think you owe for 5 years and all he has done. I have enjoyed and gotten plenty from knowing you. Love doesn't keep account of who's ahead and who owes who. If I have a sore shoulder, you can massage it. when your neck hurts I will massage you. Maybe one of us will get a massage two nights in a row or many more massages. That's not what it's about. You have repaid everything I have ever done and then some. Just do what your heart feels is right. You never do wrong doing what's right. You might be guilty but at least you know your heart and that your intention was to do right. That's easier to live with, even with failure and setbacks.

Ok late for work!

Hug.

Calvin

*

February 14, 2017

Elle,

I read your message and peeked at my videos. I checked and you just went off line at work. If you are on a break I am monitoring the site if you choose to come back.

Calvin

*

February 14, 2017

Elle,

I will start on your soft sensual loving story that may have some sexual content. But right now I am in a more content mood and just don't feel like going there. Let me write this and watch your black outfit video. wow. Thank you. You did that perfectly.

I sent a couple songs. Yes, They are religious, but that's not why I chose them. They are not meant to preach or change your thinking. They are just nice songs. The message is there, even if the religious message is there too.

You ask hard questions. I didn't want to get married, Maybe that's a guy thing about being tied down and scared to make a choice you must stick with. Fear of regret, hoping for some better life playing the field or with a better woman. Part of being an adult is you have to make decisions and deal with the consequences. Not making a decision is a decision.

I chose this small house surrounded by nature to be surrounded by beauty and I like the lifestyle. But I planned to have a family and entertain and have friends come up and spend the weekend. It was very much a show place to let people from the flatland and the city come up and spend time in the woods. I love hiking but I love grooming my trails and making them easier for guests to go on. I like to open up little look outs so they can see over the hill side then go back under the trees for shade or if it rains lightly. I don't know if I am putting my fears onto you, but I fear I am living too much like a hermit away from everyone. Luckily I work on a college campus filled with people. I don't just live alone away from everyone. Also I very much depend on my neighbors. I stop on the road and chat when we pass each other and they all feel very comfortable coming to my house. if I am not here they go through my tools and take what they need. I am not a hermit. But I was hurt and being alone was a bad decision that felt good. My friends forced me to go out with them and be active and social again. I don't want you to build a small off the grid low emission house and be alone. You don't have to marry again. but make your family relationship stronger. heal, don't run away because you have been hurt. I wanted to do that. I am glad I didn't and I am more isolated than I like, but this was not planned.

When I am down I am just optimistic. Maybe I love you so much because I adore Eeyore so much. Ok, let me take another step. Hopefully I will come back to what I do when I am feeling down. I love Eeyore. I really didn't think a lot when I said I love you, and I didn't mean that all deep. I am not going to take it back because I didn't mean anything by it and what I did mean I don't mind saying. I am not in love with you. But that brought up your other question. I tend to be trusting. If a woman says "no" when I ask her out, (I can't remember that happening so I guess it didn't bother me too much) I tend to believe her excuse. I think if the girl explains it and has a good reason it doesn't have to hurt. I like to have a woman love me and it is good for my ego. I mean in love with me. I think what hurts is if she gives me the idea I am not good enough. I could never have someone like her. If it is because there is something wrong and unworthy about me. Probably any woman who made me feel that way because I offered to take her somewhere and buy her some food and be nice to her and allow her to have a good time sharing something I find fun. If she is someone that makes me feel bad and dislikes myself because of that, I am glad I am not going to be spending time with her. I am glad she said "no." I think my ego can handle someone not loving me. I think it is a gift. If she chooses not to give me this precious diamond and just cash gold. I might be disappointed because the diamond was something more precious but if she doesn't hate me or dislike me. Even if it becomes awkward and we drift away from each other, your question was, does it hurt my ego to be told someone doesn't love me? No. Maybe not my favorite thing. Hallmark doesn't sell a lot of "I don't love you" greeting cards, but it is not that negative. I guess the way it is said and the real feelings I believe behind it. The sky is blue, water is wet, I still admire who you are and know you to be the same person, I am just stating a fact, "I am not in love with you." I wish the sky was another color and the rain didn't make me wet and every woman in the world was madly in love with me and found me absolutely irresistible. but the fact is that they don't.

Ok I love Eeeyore, I am an optimist. If I worked hard in wrestling I became better and I won. I recognized when I was in better conditioning than my opponent and won because of the time and work I had done. I got my diploma from college and smarter classmates didn't. Even when times were dark I knew eventually I would win. I am destined for happiness and life is good. Maybe I am an idiot to believe this. I have no evidence to prove it. I just have faith.

I am Calvin.

Life is good.

Everything turns out ok in the end. if it is not ok, it is not the end yet.

Hug

Thank you for the videos. This is what we do now, if it is good and it is healthy and doesn't cause confusion or pain. If it is a problem I can keep the dog in my pants.

"Can I see the dog"?!!??? what?!!!?!?

Calvin

More Beautiful You by Jonny Diaz
Breathe by Jonny Diaz

*

February 14, 2017

Elle,

You like wood?

Thank you again for the videos.

Please, I will not be upset if my distractions are a bad idea. Don't do this for me. Don't feel guilty if you need to avoid sex for a while. I am offering to stop. It is my idea. You don't have to send mercy videos.

I am going to babysit animals. mostly cats this week but they are going to feed them before they go and said they will be fine until after work Thursday. So I will be home an extra day but they asked me to stay extra because they were able to get tickets for Thursday. So I will be gone Thursday night till Thursday night. I will be coming back a couple times. Saturday for sure, probably early next week at least. They just live closer to work and it seems odd to drive the extra home. I will have wifi but I am not sure if I will have internet, free data.

Video ideas for you and story ideas for me… mmm.

I love pantyhose and the way you went slowly was awesome in that last one. I loved the orgasm but it doesn't have to be that much. Just soft touching and knowing smiles. I like the teasing too. Don't just do something. pretend you are going to do it then don't... then maybe do. I love your voice but it is dangerous for you to say my name while talking dirty. plus there is a reality of your words being sweet in stead of "Fuck me Calvin I hope you are stroking it hard and cumming Calvin." My story will be too real I fear. But nice if it's a story from me. I don't know. You can't go too far, but my stories always tend to be sweet instead of total hard core.

Ok see I didn't write anything sexual or send any sexy pictures.

Good Calvin.

*

February 14, 2017

Calvin,

What?

The dog means dog, because when you told me about watching friend's animals you mentioned a dog! But thanks for the porn anyway, bad Calvin.

Elle

*

February 14, 2017

Elle,

Me with dog.

Calvin

Attached: pictures of Calvin with a dog

*

February 14, 2017

Dear Calvin,

Happy V-day!

I am not in love with you. BUT I do find you absolutely irresistible. I appreciate you for being sweet, loving, caring, considerate, incredibly funny...being you. I'm grateful to know you. You are lots of fun to be around.

Here is a vegetable for vegetable day!

Soft hug

Elle

*

February 14, 2017

Elle,

You are fun and funny also.

-What do you get when you mix potatoes and onions?
-Watery eyes.

Calvin

*

February 15, 2017

Calvin,

I am really confused about the last photos. I'm so sorry.

As far as I understand myself I think I prefer the fantasy story because it is tendre and leads to sex and that is how I imagine it and it just fits t my fantasy. So that's nice.

A picture without context is a bit shocking. They keep coming back in my head and I really like what is going on in my head. But I feel like I am adding a context that you wouldn't and so it makes me feel like we do not have the same fantasy. And my insecurities kick in and I feel not enough and just a freaking body that makes you hard. Yay.

I definitely cannot handle your dick picks out of nowhere.

I do absolutely love your funny pictures with sexual content. But cumming that's too abrupt.
I mean flattering that I do that to you. But taken out of context it makes me doubt myself.
I hope I managed to explain it somewhat understandable so that you don't feel rejected. Because I obviously really really like the content just not like this because it results in not 100% positive feelings.

My body is craving you but my ego or heart or brain is confused and it is not nice to have them disconnected.

Elle

*

February 16, 2017

Elle,

I think you are referring to Ben? You asked to see pictures of the dog. It is the dog I will be watching in march.

I understand. No more dick pictures.

Life is good.

Calvin

*

February 16, 2017

Calvin,

Yes, I was referring to Ben. Watching the pictures I thought Ben was your dog though. You looked young. Thank you, really nice photos.

I loved the songs. I didn't hear a religious message in it. For me it speaks about beautiful ideas, but really if you don't mention god it fits in my religion too.

When I read your line about how Hallmark doesn't sell a lot of "I don't love you" greeting cards... I realized how inconsiderate it was (how much of a dick I was) to send something like this just before the 14th. Wow I suck at timing. It didn't even cross my mind what date it is. I am so sorry. I hope I am just overthinking right now. You didn't seem hurt and I liked how you understood it.

I love you so much too. Nothing deep and dangerous or heavy or painful. I am a little bit confused with "love" expressions. What would be the intensity scale from I like you to I'm madly in love with you? I feel like "I love you" is so versatile and confusing it can be used in too many different cases.

I LOVE your philosophy of everything turns out good in the end and if it's not good it is not the end. And that you are destined for happiness. I could listen to this all the time. So that I feel less of an idiot, I am being told all the time that I live in my dreams and chase the non-existent perfect idea I have in my head. But I like to be that idiot. It feels good. They are real to me.

Thank you for sharing your thoughts about being isolated. I will think about it.

Have fun with the cats! Write when you'll be back,

I won't disappear.

Elle

*

February 16, 2017.

Elle,

When I am with Ben I will try to send you a more current picture. He is older and lazy and fat now. But when I go for a walk he is always excited. His owners used to be my neighbors but they moved away. After I lost Woody I used to take Ben on hikes to be safe. He had a greyhound in him and used to run up hills and loved being out running full speed. He would chase animals. When he caught them he would bark but never hurt them. He just loved chasing things. They spoil him but also they are busy and they don't live in a place they can just let him run free in the woods now. When they go away Ben understands they are packing and gets very insecure and upset. When he sees me he always thinks I am going to stay. If I just come over to visit he whines when I leave. They tried to have another friend watch him and he tore the house up, So they put him outside and he broke a window trying to get in. An anxious dog. But I am very strict with him and I reward him with long walks so he is better behaved for me than his owners even.

I think you are confusing yourself with the dick pictures. I don't feel bad about my intentions. But I respect that your confusion is real so I'll stop until you figure things out and send me another video. I think I made it clear, you don't have to send me sexy videos. my secret message was. when you try to turn me on and send sexy videos they turn me on.

Another positive this trip is I will be closer to my mom's and I might be able to drop by her place. I still have repairs on my place but I can live with it. She feels helpless because she can't fix things herself. So I will work on the repairs a little.

As you said Valentine's Day was never a special day for me, us. My hardest days are her birthday because I also miss my mother in law and celebrating with her, our anniversary and Christmas. Also the bad day shows up on the calendar but they are just dates, no reason to get down. I am doing great and they barely pass notice. Whatever happens that day fills my thoughts. I tend to be busy. But valentine's day was never special. Yes I got sex, but I remember getting sex a lot more often than now and not just with myself.

We are mathematicians, that makes us dreamers. the circle doesn't exist, it is a perfect idea. a concept that cannot exist in reality. Before cantor' work on set theory people could not accept the number 0. They couldn't imagine nothingness, a vacuum. But Cantor explained having no apples doesn't mean nothingness, just 0 apples in the set. The idea of a negative amount of something was unacceptable. Even Steven Hawking stated that matter goes into black holes and they get bigger so black holes will always get bigger. He resisted the idea of negative matter making them get smaller because the concept of a negative amount is so difficult for non dreamers. Analysis is dealing with infinity, Irrational; numbers like pi and square roots were known and used by the Pythagoreans but not considered real because you couldn't write them as a fraction and couldn't hold them and they can't be perfect. Then my guy came; Bernhard Riemann, and said, fuck all of you I am going to use numbers that don't exist and call them imaginary just to mess with you. Yeah they aren't real, deal with it bitches!

So it is good to be a dreamer and not everything has to be real to be valuable and a focus, and things can turn out great or awful. They have a 50-50 chance to think they will be great so much harder for others to accept. Prepare for the worst and expect the best. But why stop imagining the best I ahead? I think making your life better is hard to avoid. Your life has been getting better. You see it. you have been getting better. Even if I don't get to see you in tan pantyhose, I still think you are getting better.

Ok I will try to write from their house and if not I will be home Saturday night. and maybe Tuesday or Wednesday. maybe more.

big hug. Life is good. I am happy and life is under control. Doing for others and being upset that my stuff is not getting taken care of is silly. I am happy. I like what I am doing and I like myself.

Happy Boy Calvin

*

February 17, 2017

Calvin,

These little breaks are a good reminder that I am not dependent on you. I feel functional, I don't need to lean on you to handle things. I'm strong. I'm getting more stuff done when we talk less. It seems less appealing to work on something when I could have fun with you instead. When you are busy it's easier to concentrate on my tasks.

This safety distance (9350 km) is actually very convenient for me. It's like I chose to become close to someone who is so far away that cannot be threatening or too real for me. Interesting.

The countdown started. I'm leaving in a week. My family is excited to see me and I contacted friends to see them. One invited me to sleep at her place on the 25th right after I landed in Budapest.

Lily's dad is joking around. We are constantly admiring and hugging and kissing Lily. We are both very happy to have her. We wanted to have a child so bad, that's something we don't have to worry about anymore. We'll always have her. Really, now I am not worried about my future at all. I already had everything I wished for. Now I can just let things happen, no pressure. I feel complete even if nothing major will happen while I am growing old. I will always be a mom. He thinks he is too old to have any other children, by the time he finds another woman. I think he might have more. He really loves being a dad. I don't know if I'll have more. It really depends.

We joke about me having to pack away everything because the moment I step out a woman will take my place. He is so impatient to see me gone, it's like he already found a replacement for me on craigslist. He wants everything to be gone that is mine. Even my soy products from the kitchen cupboard! It's funny. His jokes don't hurt me. We are both relieved and happy to put this behind us and start focusing on the future. Life is good.

Right now Lily's dad is laughing and singing a french song while playing video games with virtual friends! I am so happy to hear him sing again. This is the guy I got to know and was afraid I broke.

He will be ok.

I feel like I am a flower about to blossom. Go out in the light and open up for whatever comes. Right now I feel like I want to meet new people and do new things. I remember how anxious I was last summer going to work with my sister in the ice cream shop thinking it is not really my thing. I thought I am an introvert and that I don't like to interact with so many people in one day. And I discovered that I changed and I felt at the right place and I felt like I was myself. I thought I was dark and I was there joking around and smiling, asking people questions. It lifted me up.
I want to get that feeling back. On lj I am so lost now in my own dark place I cannot even concentrate on the members. It doesn't feel good. It doesn't help that I cannot see them. I often feel very alone. If I could see their eyes I could notice how they are feeling and would start to think about them and not myself.

On Saturday I am going to my god mother's to have a chat about me leaving. I am a little bit anxious but it's better to speak and try to explain things nicely instead of just disappearing and letting them guess what happened. The challenge is to state facts instead of bashing myself, of giving away dirty relationship secrets, of revealing their son's defaults. We'll see how good I'll do.

I am so happy I had an occasion to put on that dress. I love to wear it. It makes me feel like a lady.
How casual. I should go grocery shopping like this.

Elle

*

February 18, 2017

Elle,

Wow to the red dress. I love it. and the cute way you tease without teasing. love love loved it.

Not sure if it is my side but I can only seem to get one video at a time. Casual didn't come through just the numbers again.

Do you give good back massages? I slept on a couch because they have cats upstairs. Then I found work to do there and tonight my back needs a beautiful woman to run her hands all over my back gently.

I was thinking about your question about what to do when a man gets frustrated. It takes time to know the man, but my wife had a way about her. I appreciated that she knew sometimes I didn't want to talk. I would tell her after I was over it when I appreciated her. But she was careful not to move things I had in a certain place for a reason and she would let me see what she was doing but not really ask my permission. But she would find a way to help. I would always tell her that even if she didn't shovel as much dirt as I did, every shovel full of dirt she dug was one I didn't have to do. So she would stack the wood I was moving to make it easier for me or something out of my way but still showing she was doing something to help even if it was small. just to show she cared and wanted my problems to be easier.

Yes you are strong and getting stronger and more confident but still as great.

Calvin

Home for the night.

Thank you for the red dress. Great.

*

February 18, 2017

Good morning Calvin!

Yes, I'd love to run my hands on your back! Am I a beautiful woman? Awww.

Ok. I cried all Friday night. I'm grieving. It's good. I want to move on. I start to remember the good moments and miss the feeling of loving someone who loves you back. I started to see him as human, as someone who has value, as someone I loved. loved so much. I am still so sure about my reasons to get out of this and wanting a new start, a better life, new chances, hope. I still know that we are unhealthy for each other. But it still hurts. I still miss what I had. I find myself gazing at him, my heart squeezed and remembering what I used to feel when I watched him. He was my everything. He was the only good thing in my life for very long. We know each other like no one else. We slept, ate, and laughed together. He became a part of me. We did absolutely everything together. I barely went out on my own ever. He wanted me to still be in the same room even if I was busy on my pc or reading a book and he was busy watching sport or playing video games. It was a presence. A constant in our life. I was clinging on to him whenever we went out, holding his hand, sitting on his lap. I felt like I couldn't do anything without him, I felt scared of everything.

Wow, this sounds really unhealthy.

He was nice. He came to check on me at around midnight and saw I was crying, asked whether I wanted to talk about it and stood silent with red shiny eyes at the door. I smiled and said no thank you.

He touched my knee and walked away. It would be cruel to cry on his shoulders. I am not quite sure at what phase of letting go he is. It was a very tender scene.

There are boxes next to me on the bed, I'm filling them up with my stuff. Actually I'm just sitting on the bed crying, staring at the open cupboard. I know I am pathetic. But this feels huge. So many memories.

Deep breath. I can do this. I have to clean up, leave space for new things to come.

Oh my god. I think I am happy.

Elle

*

February 18, 2017

Elle

Yes, You can do this. Yes he was great to you when you needed someone. You are not to blame that you got healthy. it is ok that you are not that same person. You gave and tried. He was what you needed. You recognize that and appreciate him. But you have the right to get better. You have the right to get healthy.

You were strong enough to climb out of the flames into the boiling water. It felt good to have him pull you into the boiling water from the fire you were in. But the boiling water still burns.

Stay in the boiling water if you are falling back into the flames. He did a great job of being there when you were falling apart. But it is still boiling water scalding you. He is welcome to love and be with you in your healthy safe life. He just can't pour scalding boiling water on you. you have the right not to be burned. You are strong enough not to be burned by flames. You are strong enough not to allow yourself to be burned by water. You aren't being cruel because you want the water to be warm. If he can be warm and not painful and healthy, when you are strong and not burning you decide. But you do not deserve to be hurting. Yes you are better than when you broke down and he was there to pick up the pieces. Yay you for healing. Yes, you are better now that you are dealing with things.

Yay you.

Give yourself some credit, not the boiling water. It might have had the best intentions and pulled you from the flames out of love. But you deserve not to fear, or hurt, or be trapped in a cage. You are so much more.

late for work again

Calvin

The videos didn't come through.

*

February 19, 2017

Elle,

I read your message again and something fell out. I don't mean this in a sick way, obviously. But you want to be loved, to be held, to feel gentle caress and compassion and love. You say you need to find the difference between love and sex. You would hug anyone who would let you close.

I understand it is so hard. But Lily would allow you to hug her. I never knew a kid, especially a little girl who felt they loved us too much and didn't want to be hugged. I even bet she will return your love. Hug you the way you need. Someone who loves you and admires you and you are her world.

Next step is harder: You're a mom and know how hard it is to hold your daughter and not worry what she thinks or want to hug her longer or just to have her hug you for no reason. When you get to Hungary can you hug her even when it is awkward? If you need love,it is pure even if she disapproves, I think a mother always gives love.

Last one is the hardest but I will say it. One of you has to start. You know your family but does a lot of this start with the way your dad treated you. You are searching for his love? You are looking for affection and admiration in sex from California and you know I would love to.

After that video OMG I have trouble saying "no" to you. But I think I hear you saying you want love and support not some guy shaking his cock in front of a camera. I know I am more and you are not body parts to me either. but I am trying to make a point. The impossible to do might be what you want most.

Elle I don't have a filter either so please don't listen to me too much. Just say "Calvin cares and he is trying to help and offer ideas, but he is a clueless idiot and doesn't know what he is talking about." I am not a psychologist. I am just trying to help with my lack of knowledge.

I will send a sweet hug and nothing sexual about it. just a soft hug from a friend.

Calvin

Video four and five are already made? Pantyhose in them? I am a man not the saint you imagine me as.

*

February 19, 2017

Calvin,

Yes, Lily is the perfect little thing to hug and kiss. My therapy helped me to realize that she is just like me. She won't beg for hugs and kisses, she won't come and start it but she wants it. It was an amazing experience to see her get more and more comfortable with this. When she was a baby and cried so much I thought she was rejecting me, she pushed me away a lot and hit me often and I thought she didn't want me. I am ashamed now to admit that I gave up on her thinking she prefers her dad. She still pushes me away and hits me every day! but now I know it's not rejection, it's playing and testing my love. If she doesn't let me hug her I can tickle. She is not my husband, she won't get angry at me for being playful. He just wants blowjobs. I thought it was my task to save him. But it hurts too much. Takes too much time of my life. He seems like he doesn't want to be saved. It would be different if he'd want the same changes for himself but he proved that he is not looking for answers and he likes to be like that. And you are a living proof that not all the men are like him. It is silly to take one and hope for him to change when I could just wait some more and find one that is already the way I'd love him to be, no changes needed.

You are right. I NEED to get closer to my dad. I put this off for so long, being too scared and it is eating me up and still affecting my life. Living with someone like him, the boss, being in an intimate relationship helped me to understand my dad better, thus forgiving him. He did his best and didn't want to hurt me on purpose. Yes, I will try to hug him in a week. I don't really feel comfortable saying I love you yet. But I want to say it, I mean it. I am just very nervous. I will fix things with my family this time.

Strangely what I really want is to hug my husband/ex husband now. We hurt each other so much and I want to tell him it wasn't my intention to do so. I told him crying at our last fight but I want to hug him so badly to end things on a positive note and not with our last touch being a violent act. The last time I touched him was weeks ago and I was punching him on the chest. I didn't put my strength in it and he catched my hands very fast and kept me immobile. But still, that was a violent act from me. And his last one was pushing me and squeezing. He did stop and it could have been worse but the intention was to hurt me. As silly as it sounds I want my happy end. Make peace and keep finding compromises with good intentions.

It is my fault I see you as a saint. Obviously if I am acting sexy it will result in a sexy reaction. It is normal. Me being confused has nothing to see with you. And you were wise enough to understand that. Of course there is nothing wrong with your reaction. I am sorry if I made you feel like there is. In my head everything is a little bit messed up. I start to understand that my dad is my dad and no one has to/could take his place. The boss should only have been my partner. Not my dad and not my kid and not a charity project to work on. A partner is a partner, not a replacement for other relationships.

Thank you for saying no. I wouldn't have thought I'd be happy to hear "no" one day. I needed your "no". It might be hard to say but you earn to be respected.

Silly right? But someone always saying yes to me just to please me short term, would mean a yes by cowardice. And that is really not working out long term.

Shut up Elle. Ok, end.

Elle

*

February 19, 2017

Elle,

Nothing much I can say in response but I like you. I respect you. I think you are getting better and better and your life is getting better. You always saw life positively but now you can live it the way you see and follow your heart. You are not reacting but leading now.

As far as "no" goes. You are welcome to send as little or as much as you wish. If you feel I am enjoying your body and your sexiness more than who you are, stop. Yes I enjoy your looks and those tan pantyhose I will never get tired of and they ALWAYS do the trick for me.

Always.

But we can go as long as you wish without that part of our relationship. That is not necessary. I love it. But you have great value to me without it or besides it. If you start to doubt that, prove it to me. I will miss my videos. But we won't change. That is not who you are.

That being said. I love what you do.

I am sorry if I gave the impression I thought you could fix everything in an hour. Your father and ex husband and mother will take years maybe. But you are healthy wanting to fix it. I hear your heart. you are giving. you are loving them. You are helping yourself get healthier but you also want to do things just because you want to. You want to hug the boss for him. You want your dad to know he is loved and forgiven and you don't think badly of him, for his sake. Yes it will help you but you are driving me more. I like you. I like who you are. I respect you. I see the good.

Calvin

*

February 20, 2017

Calvin,

Do you remember how I wrote that I get so much done when we are not writing to each other? Well, I got absolutely nothing done these last few days. Besides filling up my suitcase and boxes. And gathering all the videos and pictures I got from you to one place. Oh, yes. Now I'm just enjoying the freedom of having it all within hand reach. So that I can choose whether I want to see the cowboy, the handyman, young Calvin, your ass or your asses...

I am obsessed with your dick picks. My lower belly has tiny cramps right now even just thinking about them. Thank you. My insecurest time is gone. Wow that was probably the least sexy I ever felt. I won't be disappointed if it never happens again. Don't try to understand me. I try all the time and just get a headache.

Your dick picks were like a time bomb! They are working now. I very much enjoyed them. Wow. I'm trying to breathe here and get some blood in my brain.

I love the long sleeved casual black shirt, it feels so intimate. Looks like a comfortable clothing piece one throws on after a tiring work day when finally at home and has nothing to do anymore. Or maybe on a rest day when one has no plans and stays home to rest. It feels like relaxed, improvized sex. Nothing of it was planned, no one had to get ready. It feels like real life sex with someone you know very well and for long. Someone you feel comfortable enough with to approach with a teasing look on your face. Someone who knows what's under your comfy clothes and that it is worth unwrapping.

The handy man has different underwear from the ones you normally wear! I noticed. And yes, the handy man look is for me. Ahh, you realized a dream of mine.

I just watched back the cowboy videos. I didn't remember how well made they were. It's crazy. Your attitude is so sexy. Your personality really comes through. This is powerful stuff. With each little bit of video I'm dying to see more.

You mentioned somewhere that I can prove I am worthy without or besides the sexy side. I see why you wrote that. But I will ignore the word prove. There is just something wrong with it. I feel like proving has a temptation of trying to figure out what the other one wants you to turn out to be. And it makes things unnatural and forced. If I try to prove to you I have worth other than being a pervert, that's not gonna be me anymore. That's gonna be me trying to be someone you find worthy. Maybe time will prove it. Or not. And that's ok. I don't need you or someone else to see worth in me. Without sounding pretentious, I am often in the extremes..., I do see worth in me.

I watched a TED talk about highly sensitive people. That was one huge insecurity I had. I denied being sensitive because it seemed like a default to me. But I listened to that speech. I am not crazy or defective. From my point of view, actually the steel elbowed, aggressive ones are the unhealthy ones. I have a strong intuition, I can empathize easily, I have an urge to help people in need. That is rather good for society. I can speak up, I have thoughts, I have ideas and I do things. It's just that the world is overwhelming for me, because I can feel people's feelings, like everyone's in the room. I remember talking about this when I was younger and being taken for crazy. I am so glad I came across this video. It explains exactly how I feel every day. And how I cannot change that I am like this. Hearing someone say it's genetics and no matter how many times people say "you shouldn't be so sensitive", it's like having blue eyes.

Lily started to play "I am sick, heal me". So cute. She makes a poor little face and I have to ask her where she is hurting. She tells me and gives me a healing tool (random object). Then I have to put it against her painful body part and hold it there. I think she is into alternative medicine! I'd love to play doctors with you. I'd love to check your body parts and hold my stethoscope against you…

Here is a video of pajama talk.

In case you cannot tell, I am back in the game!

I had an awesome session Wednesday night. Awesome because I felt like myself. Livejasmine became a fun and safe place to play again. I enjoyed getting ready, I really liked my look and felt excited about putting on another outfit next time. I felt so good in my skin, I took photos for my feed. And for you!

Aren't you home yet? It's Thursday night.

I'm flying tomorrow

Elle

*

February 20, 2017

Hello Elle!

I got home yesterday and was tired and just wanted to sleep in my own bed and not be bothered by cats. I liked the bla bla bla and the pictures. Also I think it is great that your mother in law loves you and hopefully you can see that you are lovable and that not everyone blames you. She of all people could have something against you and she understands and thinks you are good and normal and there is nothing wrong with you and it isn't your fault.

The fact she still wants to be your mom and be close tells you that you have done well.

I will send pictures of the cats tomorrow. By work I meant I was late to go cat sit. I usually fed the cats in the morning before work and in the evening. I came home and so they didn't get fed the night before. I know they are cats and they will survive, but I told my friends I would watch them and feed them and I had planned to drive down earlier to feed them. I just enjoyed being home and writing to you.

I have things to do around here having been away but I wanted to write to you quickly. I will write more tomorrow.

I want to hear about flying Friday and what happened. How you are feeling and what you are hiding and not telling everyone else.

That's my job. Halfway around the planet you can be open and honest with me.

Calvin

I will still trade you a shoulder massage for a body massage.

Yes, I saw the hugs in the picture and I will write you a sexy story. Just not today

*

February 25, 2017

Calvin,

You are a great cheerleader. The best.

How is your pet sitting going? Were you working on Sunday? (late for work) Everything is ok at home with the electricity situation? Of course you found something to repair even though no one asked you to do it! Does your back still hurt?

I don't have anything to say, not with words. I know things are a little bit awkward between us, adjusting to not... So here is something to make it even more awkward!

I dreamt about us making love. Khm. Is it because I fell asleep in the middle of stress relief? Maybe. Like during, just after the first orgasm. Woke up naked in the same position. I don't sleep naked in the winter.

Did you get the videos? I'll insert the links just in case. It's just blabla but if I already made them, I'll want you to see. Mostly to show you my face because I felt like my make up turned out ok and my hair looked fine. So obviously you have to see.

Well, I think I started to type this like an hour ago. And I got like five lines written. Khm. This is what I am speaking about when I say awkward. I censor all the time. I still like what we have but oh my god it's a lot of staring at the screen, typing-deleting.

I am feeling another kind of 'why sex might be an issue'. I am dying here. I am so horny. And the only person I want to sleep with is you and no one else.

That might be an issue! Get used to it

Elle

Shut up Elle.

Oh my god, how much I will regret sending this.

Elle

*

February 26, 2017

Elle,

I am considering having my stories travel across the state. If we start at the northwestern part of the state it is cliffs and trees and waterfalls. I think I have told you about Fort Bragg and Glass Beach. The movie "Overboard" with Goldie Hann and Kurt Russell was filmed here. I hope you like whales.. That's going to be the theme. We can take a small boat out and ride the waves up and down and in and out until we get close to the whales and then enjoy them. Then come back to a nice restaurant overlooking the ocean and the bay from the cliffs. Then watch the sunset and go back to our hotel room.

The room overlooks the ocean and by the moonlight you can watch the white spray as the water crashes against the rocks and the whales mating and jumping out of the water. Up and down in and out of the water, our bodies still feel the water rolling off the ocean even though the bed isn't moving under us.

It is actually a nice place, not just a fantasy but I will tell that story tomorrow.

Here are the cats and I was feeling a little horny while I was gone.

Big hug. missed talking to you.

Calvin

What does KHM mean?

Attached: cats and Calvin with horns

*

February 26, 2017

Calvin,

Hello! You are back!

Calvin, I missed our conversations. Thank you, you know you don't owe me anything. I appreciate you coming here to listen, giving me a chance to speak about what I want to hide. Even though I have now people in my life who listen and care about me and love me. I still miss our connection. I still love having you.

I feel now how lonely I was in France. It feels nice to talk to people who see me as a human whose feelings matter. I think my feelings matter.

It was flying Saturday, not Friday. When I wrote to you I will fly tomorrow it is Thursday night, it was Thursday night at your place but Friday morning at my place.

I am ashamed of how stressed out I was on Saturday. For days I was explaining to Lily that I will leave. She took it well, a bit upset but she said "all right" every time. The morning of travel day I was so pissed off at her dad, feeling like he pushed me to leave my daughter. I felt like he got everything and I'm leaving behind the only thing that matters.

With the usual stress of traveling I got every time I was quite unpleasant to be around. I was crying and walking up and down in the flat until noon, finishing packing.

They took the bus with me and came with me to the train station. We fighted for the whole time. Very ugly. I apologized in the last 10 min. I got some one-on-one time with Lily to say goodbye...

She wasn't crying when I waved to her from the train. I was. I felt like I'm pregnant and my child is being ripped off of my belly, the skin tearing. I still feel like that, a constant pain like strings are binding me to her and they are forced to be longer and longer, but it's a body part. It hurts.

The flight was alright. I actually enjoyed being on my own. It was so easy. Guys checked me out without shame. They were hungarians. I take staring as a compliment, I actually miss men checking me out when I am in France. Different country, different culture. I felt lonely and sad leaving the airport all alone.

My mom offered to come and pick me up by car. But I wanted to take the train. I love traveling alone. I headed to my friend's place. The airport bus was a culture shock. Looking out through the window, I only saw rusty old buildings and couldn't believe my eyes when I noticed cars parked around them and lights being switched on in them. The subway was so different from the French one. Not all clean, new and shiny like everything in France. No elevator. I struggled a bit carrying my whole life in two suitcases. My friend waited for me at the subway station. I felt welcome and loved. She left me in her flat alone and went to a concert.

I started to feel shitty. I Stared at myself in the mirror thinking "at least I look good". I thought that's funny. Because it's so superficial. But at least it made me smile. I skyped with my sister, then with a friend. Cooked pasta and sauce. Watched John Oliver trolling Donald Trump. Found myself laughing. Watched some tv series about a strip club owner. Documentation for work, right? The girls were moving wow really good.

She came back at around 11 p.m. and we chatted until three a.m. On Sunday I had a very late breakfast, some more chatting and left to take the train to the big lake.

The train man helped me with my luggage. I couldn't stop smiling and was so happy. Ok, I know I am a young good looking girl but still. The French wouldn't care, I lived there and watched them not caring and just walking by or watching down on their lap. Hungarians are so much more likely to offer their seat to a pregnant lady or old person. They are also more likely to offer help to a stranger. Not all of them. But most of them.

The moment I sat down in the train a man started to talk to me. He talked nonstop for 1 and a half hours. It was touching. He is an ugly carpenter whose life had a rough start and a not fairytail like following. I liked listening to him. He really opened up himself. He thanked me and told me he was boiling inside and felt relieved now before he left. I think he would have spoken to anyone really. But I was happy I was there.

My mom waited for me at the train station. I live at the southern side of the lake, where it's flat. But when you are at the lake you have a beautiful view on the northern side, little mountains. I skyped with Lily tonight. She was shy first but opened up slowly. I managed to "play" and laugh with her. So damn cute. She was staring at the screen and showing it things, speaking to it. I tried to hug and kiss her. It felt good. For me. I don't know how she feels. I try not to think about it. I cannot change it anyway. So I try to focus on what is happening here. Even though these strings from my stomach are pulling me towards her.

I think I'll make her short blabla videos and upload them so that she can watch. Maybe every day or almost.

You know what? I think part of me is happy in a mean way, imagining Lily's dad struggling to do everything I used to do in addition to his tasks. I don't like this feeling. I find myself thinking it is only fair that he has to take over jumping out from the bed four times each night, the mornings, the cooking, the dishwashing. He never respected what I was doing. I don't think he ever will. But if he gets exhausted and overwhelmed well, I'm ok with that. That means the little monster in me is tapping its hands. He hurt me so much. And didn't even care that I was hurt. He might think differently but he deserves to be left by me. I am not an object or a slave or an employee. Even an employee deserves better treatment than what I had from him. He did behave like a very bad boss.
I don't have to toughen up and be strong enough to take his

bullying, his mean "jokes", his "help" to better me.

I have the right to leave someone who hurts me even if he doesn't do it on purpose. He might be doing it from love. A strange way to love. I don't have to keep offering my life to someone who doesn't want to listen, who thinks my feelings don't matter. Who thinks only him can be right. Who treats me like I am his thing, and I have to obey at all times. The number of times he shouted "Come here! Right now!" "Don't ask why? I need you! When I say come you have to come!" "Just do what I ask you to do! That's all you have to do."

I am worthy. My feelings matter. I don't deserve to be told every day that I am not good enough by being myself. That I am not trying hard enough to please.

I'm whispering now. This is what I want to hide. I don't know if I can function without him. I don't know if I can function without someone telling me what to do. Without rebeling against him by putting on the pants he finds ugly or realizing a project he finds stupid. Being happy and confident was an act of rebellion against him. It gave me motivation. See, even in my good moments it was all about him.

I'm ok. I have very contradictory feelings but I am surrounded by people who love me and care about me. I am free and busy. I basically don't have to worry about anything for the next six months.

even though the bed isn't moving under us... nice wording

Who is giving a massage to whom? :) Ok, I'm excited to read your story.

I'll sleep with my sister tonight. Yesterday I slept with my girlfriend. I don't feel ready to find myself alone in the dark, in an empty room with only my thoughts. How will I do this? I feel panicky even just imagining finding myself alone. Ok, Elle calms down. You are not alone. You just moved into your family home where 4 other people live. You are not alone. I'd love to love to be alone one day. That's the goal. But right now it would be too sudden of a change. I am so used to always having either a supervisor or a little being to take care of with me. I'll be ok. I'll keep myself busy.

Tomorrow, for example, I will go to my mom's yoga class. She is teaching yoga in the evenings. I have to change money and do grocery shopping and declutter my old room and arrange it for the webcam. Do some work on the internet. I'm so grateful to have things to do and people to speak to.

hope to speak to you soon

Thank you for the quick messages and the cats!

Elle

*

February 27, 2017

Elle,

You sound stronger now. Even when you told me you were afraid of being alone you state your weaknesses differently now. You are strong in saying, "This bothers me." or " I am glad I don't have to face this yet." But not scared or overwhelmed like before. You don't sound overwhelmed. You wish you had Lily with you. But it is a painful regret not hopelessness. You are confident even if it is not the very best possible or what you would choose, everything is fine between you and for now this will work.

You always want the best for her and for you and her, but again, this is not horrible or hopeless. This is skyping and playing and her smiling and looking forward to time with you and you sending her videos. You want more but you have joy still and no worries. You are strong and not scared.

I think you want to be loved. It is nice that he will appreciate all you did. But you want to be wanted. not because you woke up in the night to take are of your child, not as a cook or house cleaner or for sex or to raise his daughter. You want him to see all you did. You want him to see how much harder his life is without you. But you want to be wanted for you. Not for all you did.

I think I try to have my heart open. You sent out a feeling. I think that you are warm and caring and appreciate people. On trains I always see people looking at their phones/ A whole train and no one speaks and no one looking up. I am in the hills where people stop in the middle of the street and talk. I wanted to get past so I got out of my car and walked up to the drivers blocking the road talking, recognized them and stood between their cars talking. Duh, Calvin talks a lot. But I think if you look at people they can see if you care and are willing to listen. You appreciate the people of Hungary. I hear this. You cared and enjoyed listening to the man on the train. I think you did a good thing. People don't understand that joy is not from buying a new video game or getting drunk. Joy is from being appreciated. from having pride you helped someone. In seeing "an ugly carpenter' and getting to know a person. Your world becomes more beautiful. You have pride in yourself. I saw an old man with a walker struggling to carry his lunch and guitar case. I came over and offered to help. It was small, just a short distance. But the look of gratitude was priceless. not because he was handsome or rich or seemed like someone I would profit from knowing. just because I liked being kind and him appreciating me. I think you understand happiness and are way ahead of the people on the train who missed this beautiful person inside the ugly carpenter. You allowed him to exist.

You are beautiful Elle.

Thank you for sharing what you were hiding. I really hear your fear differently now. You are strong. But I enjoy that you are open and tell me. You see how much healthier things are. You just recognize doing things for pleasure instead of to spite him is different and a change. Change is always hard even if it is better. Some people go back to the bad because the good is just to foreign and difficult to get used to. Some people feel anxious when nothing bad happens. they are always waiting for this bad thing because their whole life something bad happened every week. The anxiety and fear is so overwhelming they prefer to make something bad happen rather than suffering waiting for it. I knew a guy who stopped doing drugs but still always waited for the police to come arrest him for it. he couldn't understand that if he had no drugs he didn't have to worry about being caught with them. He ended up stealing plants from a store just to be arrested. He knew he had no reason to fear getting arrested but he felt uncomfortable waiting for it and it never came so he basically went out and found a reason to be arrested because they wouldn't come to him. My point was even when you go to a country filled with love and people that are good and no worries. it is still a shock to your system and a change. A good change is still different and hard for you. it is natural and ok to feel this way.

I am better now but in college I had a roommate and then my wife and I weren't alone taking care of ourselves for a long time. I could take a dog and go for a long hike and not worry about being alone in the woods far away from anyone to hear me. I was brave about bears and mountain lions and poisonous snakes. But when I had to live alone for a long time it was hard. I would hear a noise late at night. I would sit there in the dark and listen to hear if it is someone there to do me harm. I would keep listening and realize it was just a tree branch or a small animal. but still I would stay awake and listen even though I knew what it was. Just a little fear remained. When I was sick I had someone by my side. Someone to get me medicine or a cool wet cloth for my forehead. Now I have a stomach ache from eating spicy food and I stay awake worried. I am sure it is heartburn or gas but I worry since I am alone, what if I am having my appendix bursting, what if I am bleeding inside. what if I pass out and don't have the energy to get to the phone. These are stupid thoughts and not real. I know they are nothing to worry about but still it is hard to ignore them and sleep when you are alone. My brain can console myself but my emotions don't listen to my brain.

Ok sexy story coming soon. I loved your message. Thank you!

Strange that when you lived with two people you were more alone. Now that you have a friend who goes out to a concert you are less alone. You know when the people you love can, they will love you and want to hear you and value you.

I value you in my life.

Calvin

*

February 27, 2017

Elle,

I will try to make this whale watching story interesting

There is a nice restaurant with windows looking out over the water where we can eat a nice vegan meal and watch the sun slowly set into the ocean and the full moon come out. We always enjoy talking and it is fun and joking and comfortable without thoughts or nervousness about what might come later. We are enjoying our meal and in this moment enjoying the present instead of missing this thinking of the future. We enjoy the food and laughter and smiles. We touch hands over the table as we talk but almost unintentionally.

It is a short walk across the parking lot to our room but the air is cool and wet. You slide in against my side as we huddle close against the change in temperature from the restaurant out into the ocean air. Our room is at the far end of the motel and at the end of the cliff. It had a large window that faces the ocean and we quickly walked to it, opened the door and rushed in.

I am going to have many many fantasies about those beige pantyhose, but tonight you can be comfortably dressed with a warm jacket. As I light a fire in the fireplace you undress and crawl into the bed almost unnoticed. I watch you out of the corner of my eye but you are quickly getting under the fresh soft sheets and the warm fluffy comforter. You leave on the warm long shirt you were wearing because it is already warm and you start to get comfortable as the bed warms up. The fire is lit and the glow fills the room. I go to turn off the light and you jokingly, but not jokingly say, "Don't turn off the light yet" You give me a cute smile and I understand. So as the room warms up from the fire I take off my coat and my shirt and then undo my pants. You give me an approving smile. I undo my belt and pants but then quickly and not too sexily pull off both my pants and underwear. You smile as I go to the light switch to turn off the light and knowing you are admiring my naked body makes me feel my penis getting harder and growing. When I turn around after turning off the light I am not fully erect facing straight up but it is sticking straight out and filled so it is thick and its head is swollen already. I crawl into bed with you and we snuggle close. My body is cold but I am like a heater and I give off a lot of heat when I am cold.

Our eyes quickly adjust to the light from the fire flickering darkly in the room and the moonlight outside is brighter than inside the room. Just outside the room we can see the water crashing against the rocks and you slide against my side as I wrap my arm around you. We lay there quietly enjoying each other's heat and the calm quiet of the room and the scene outside our window. We both smile each time we see a whale surface or water spray up from one's spout. The water splashing white and the spraying out a hole in the whale is a little erotic and reminds us we are naked.

I run my fingers through your hair and you relax and get

comfortable against me. As I run my hand down your cheek you hesitate trying to decide if you want to be excited or to enjoy this comfort and fall asleep and have me later after you sleep. My touch is very soft and loving but as my fingers glide under your chin I trace your smile with my thumb barely touching your lips. Spontaneously you go to kiss my thumb but instead to take it in your teeth. Your lips cover it and you tease the end of my thumb inside your mouth with your tongue. You slide your lips over my thumb and slide up and down my thumb like you are imagining it is my dick. I enjoy the view watching your face as you smile at me and look into my eyes and I get an up close view of your talent with your mouth.

You slide your hand down inside the sheets and over my stomach until you find my now fully hard and throbbing dick. You grip it lightly then caress the head mirroring the exact same actions as you do them to my thumb with your mouth. As your tongue circles the end of my thumb your finger circles the top of my head, as you bite my thumb your fingers pinch around my cock. As you slide your mouth over my thumb and suck on it sliding up and down, your hand slides up and down my cock stroking me. I am both watching your mouth and feeling what you are doing on my penis.

You kiss down my chest and slide the covers off me running one hand over my body as your lips slide down and replace the other hand on my cock. You rest my hard cock against your cheek as you gently lick the base of my shaft and just above my cock. You then slowly slide your mouth up to the top of my cock and it jumps when your lips hit my head. You cover my head and give me a suck them slide your lips back down my shaft to my balls. You hand cups my balls as your mouth slides up and down my shaft. You take my shaft in one hand and gently stroke it into your mouth as your lips suck me and slide down the shaft following your hand. I am about to cum when your hand on my balls slides down. You caress very softly the area just below my balls sliding up into the balls feeling my lower cock. You taste my precum as my eyes are rolling back in my head as I try not to climax and just enjoy what I am feeling. I imagine your face doing what I just watched you doing to my thumb and think this can't get any wilder. But you always surprise me.

Very softly you slide your hand down from my balls still taking my cock deep in your mouth almost covering my whole cock but it is a little too big to fit completely inside. As you caress under my balls I realize you are now circling with one finger around my ass hole. I am not sure about this but I trust you and everything is driving me crazy. You suck and stroke faster your lips against my head as your finger presses against my ass. You look up at me and smile as your finger slips inside me. It doesn't go in far because my cock is full and your lips quickly cover me as I cum.

To be continued…

I need to rest my cock and let it feel back in it but my mouth and fingers are still available and you are very wet now.

*

February 28, 2017

Calvin,

OH MY GOD! Calvin. You know me too well.

Elle

*

February 28, 2017

Elle,

Nice day today mostly. I have a sweet lady who I help. She is very small and almost 80 years old. Her kids saw her standing on her roof with a chainsaw trying to cut the limbs of a tree. Since then I have come over with my weed eater and chainsaw and cleaned up her property for her and cleaned out her rain gutters and those things she shouldn't be doing anymore.

She has two grandsons. The oldest lived with her for many years. He had some emotional problems and his parents were alcoholics. He had a substance abuse problem and the drugs and alcohol caused his emotional issues and mental illness to worsen. She let him live with her in his early 20's and would bail him out of jail and let his girlfriend live with them and tried all she could to help him. She invested her heart and energy in loving him. Finally when her husband got sick she couldn't take care of them both and made him move out on his own. This was about 8 years ago I think and her husband died soon after.

Last night her grandson who had been off drugs and alcohol for 3 months got upset and found an old friend who sold him drugs. He overdosed last night and this morning they turned off life support. She called me early this morning to ask me to come over this week as it will be sunny and the grass should be dry enough for me to help her clean up her land. She has told me she thinks of me as a son and she is not the type to sit and cry. I think she wants to work and deal with her emotions that way but also I will not give her advice or pity her but she feels comfortable talking to me. I am not sure what will happen but I am glad to spend time with her and help her.
But otherwise it was a good day.

I think I will continue my story about the whales in my next email tonight. This suddenly doesn't sound like a great lead into my trying to make your nipples hard performing oral sex on you.

But I will continue my story tonight.

I hope you are well and see the happiness you have inside.

Life is good. We are blessed and even when we suffer we have strength and tools and people to help us deal with it. We are truly blessed when we think of what others deal with. I am sorry your life is not as wonderful as it will be in 6 months or even better in a year or that you will be in the next year. but I like you now and believe in you.

Calvin

What can I do to help?

*

February 28, 2017

Calvin,

I woke up to the wind. There is a storm.

My first thought was, I want to write to Calvin!

I'll eat my breakfast, get ready and come online!

I had a busy day yesterday, it was good. I'll tell you more about it later. But I also understood that it would still be a good idea to go to a psychologist. Your story with the guy who continued to be scared of the police coming helped.

I am happy and feel good here. But it will take some time to relearn to feel safe I guess. I feel good, I just have a lot to talk about. Ok, see you in a while maybe.

Kiss.

Elle

*

March 1, 2017

Hello Calvin,

I just finished streaming. I am exhausted. Cannot really think anymore. I set up a website today.

Khm is the sound of a little embarrassed noise from the throat. In Hungarian we often write it in conversations to express embarrassment, things we don't say..

The movie overboard seems like fun to watch. I will keep it for a dark day.

The pictures with the horns!

"I will try to make this story interesting" You made me laugh , then smile, then daydream and get nervous. I enjoyed it. By the way, I absolutely love the little details. So many sentences that will stick in my head, they are so memorable.

The room is ready.

This is khm. I'm doing it at the end. Khm...means.... "you know what I don't say"

I didn't get it. You go over to her place to help but come back at night? Or You won't be available to chat but you can write emails?

Anyways
do your stuff I can wait
you are amazing

Elle

*

March 1, 2017

Elle,

You are funny that you trapped yourself in your room, almost. You definitely can't live alone yet.

Thank you. I like knowing what your room looks like. When I see you now I will understand better. It will make that time more enjoyable to me. Nice wood floors. I also liked the fact you acted like you were working and " Oh yeah by the way I am naked." lol Thank you. I am considering a hug. I am selfish. I like being able to choose when you see me. We will discuss Skype again someday. I very seldom check it now.

I will try to work on the lady's property after work before it gets too dark. maybe Thursday and Friday both. When I am in Pioneer watching the dog I should have full internet.

Ok interesting night tonight. I was going to write to you or check if you were online about 10 PM and I got a phone call. I almost didn't answer and felt I was stuck. My friend for so many years called. While I was away with the cats she had reached out to me but I didn't know. It was the woman with the big breast I dated. I haven't spoken to her in a very very long time and she had shut me out of her life. I was glad with this but I knew her feelings would be hurt if I did the same to her.

We talked about her daughter and her life and my mom. I kept it a nice conversation. She had invited me to a party for a mutual friend that was leaving. I didn't go or respond to her. So tonight as we were talking she sent me some pictures from the night. I figured it out she was sending me pictures so I could see she still looked good. I really don't want anything to do with her. But I am glad I answered her call. When I answered she said, " Hello my friend," but I still think she was not in a friendly mood.

She was depressed and I got her laughing and feeling good about herself again. I tried to end the call a number of times and she wouldn't let me. But I made my attitude clear and by the end she saw me as an old friend and seemed to have the message that was all I would be. maybe she was just testing to see. It was awkward for me but I am glad I answered.

I saw the Khm at the end. I get it now. I will try for some more details on part 2 but that might take time from the sex part. I am sorry I write so long and nothing happens. I always have to make it part two and part three and it is a lot of bla bla bla. But that is me.

So here it goes:

You slide up and rest your hand on my chest as you look at me from above me. My breathing is under control but you can feel my heart still pounding quickly within my chest. You smile down at me proud of the reaction you just got from me. You lay your smiling face on my chest as I pull the cover back over our naked bodies. I put my arms around you still trying to regain my composure. You have just made me cum hard so I know there are no expectations for me to do anything with it for a while. For now I am content having you laying on my chest and holding you in this warm bed and the moonlight.

As my senses return and I am feeling less exposed after seeing my reaction. The light from the fire is now red from the coal of the burnt wood. I can hear your breathing and you sound calm and content like a cat purring. But the soft sheets on my legs are interrupted by your leg sliding on top of my leg. I feel your foot sliding up and down my lower leg. Then I become more aware of your entire leg against mine. Your inner thigh on my leg and I can tell you are starting to straddle my leg. As your thigh brushes against my testicles I can feel how wet you are.

I slowly slide my hand down your back. I trace the beltline of your bare back under your shirt. Over your hip bones and lightly run my hand over the top of your ass. Then using both hands I reach down and with a little assistance I slide your shirt up off of you.

You scoot from beside me over me almost presenting your hard nipples to my face. I gently place my mouth over one and then the other. Not sucking much but mostly just to make them wet.

The cool air of the room and the fact your shirt that was keeping them warm was just removed makes your wet cooling nipple pucker and get hard. I place one hand on your back and roll you onto your back gently and slide down to suck your breast.

Your nipples are sticking straight out but I still cup my hand under your breast and massage your entire boob. I run my tongue in a circle around each nipple then flick them with my tongue. I start sucking one and my tongue runs across the end of it inside my mouth. my fingers are pinching and pulling very gently on the other nipple. It seems more sensitive so I give the nipple I am currently sucking a soft bite and run the front of my teeth across it. Then I grip both breasts and squeeze them together slowly licking from one to the other. As I suck the tip of the new nipple my hand runs softly between your breasts.

Without warning I lift your breast slightly and suck as much as much of it into my mouth as I can fit. Your nipple presses against the roof of my mouth and my sucking motion slides my mouth stroke by stroke down toward your nipple. I bite my lips down periodically until I can feel your hard nipple deep within your breast. I suck and pinch my lips on as many nipples as I can.

As I do this my free hand slides down your front and over your closed pussy.

Part three

*

March 1, 2017

Calvin,

I like your bla bla!

I didn't work this morning. I turned the alarm off and slept. I was even too late for skype. A big mistake. He always manages to place a few hurtful comments. I don't react but I am hurt.

So obviously now that I was late he felt in power. He doesn't show the videos to Calliopée, the ones I made for her. He tells me that I can stop speaking to her if I don't want to. That I couldn't take care of her for a whole day. That I am free to disappear from their life completely and forever. These kinds of things really hurt and scare me.

Ok, deep down I know myself and I know I can take care of her. I know I can make money to pay what I have to. And I know that the fact I need a psychologist now doesn't mean I am a mess incapable of being happy and taking care of myself. Ok. I will go and hug the people who love me otherwise I will start crying and let him crush me and win again. I have to stay strong and continue to build up things for later.

My sister's ex turned up after six months of silence dating someone else the moment my sister stopped going to the psychologist, stopped taking the medicine and started to have feelings for someone else. But I believe in everything happening for a reason, for a good reason.

If someone reached out to speak to you, it was needed. I'm glad you answered. Maybe all she wanted was nice words and she knew you would have those. Or she met someone she could feel for but wanted to check first if it is really not possible with you, just to be sure.

By the way my sister won't go back to him. Thank god. I wouldn't blame her if she were because I needed five years and things turning dramatic to finally be able to leave. But I am happy she won't need many more years. But she still needed him to contact her and speak with him again, to be reminded why it didn't work out. She got what she needed to move on.

I like Calvin! You have all the rights to choose when I see you. I wouldn't let you see me on a bad hair day! Stop worrying about skype. I let it go. I am really happy with our written conversations and I like things to be slow. I am more cautious now. I know that what we do now feels good so I don't really feel like risking it. Also... even just seeing your name makes me nervous.

I will try to relax today. I became aware of how hard I tried to keep myself busy to not feel or think.

I feel like I am trying to escape. I had two fairly good sessions. There is a couple who is interested in taking french lessons from me. And I am setting up a photo/video/panties business. It sounds so funny. But I am. I have more success on LiveJasmin I guess because I feel better and it shows. I never got up to 100 in only two days. I am not even working more hours than in France. I will try to squeeze two effective sessions in a day.

Maybe both at night with a small pause to refresh and eat. I don't know. I still want to have energy to work out, visit my mom's yoga classes, spend some time with family and go see friends from time to time. I just had so much time so suddenly. It always stresses me out. I feel like I shouldn't waste a moment from it.

No filter, whispering time. I cannot relax. I don't know how to do that. Lily's dad had such calm vibes around him. This is why I got so addicted to having him around. I tend to just get excited and frantically work on things non stop. His presence calmed me down and he made me sit down and relax, taught me how to switch off and allow myself to just watch a tv series, how to do nothing without feeling ashamed, angry at myself. It is time to find a way to do that myself. My stomach is constantly shaking.

I feel so bad. My mind is like a truck wheel sometimes that gets trapped in mud. The harder you try to get out the deeper you get trapped in mud.

I am not asking for you to calm me down. I want to be able to take care of myself. He is wrong. I can take care of myself. Oh, no. It's about him again. Great. I will book a psychologist appointment...I will relax today, try to not think about anything work related until tonight. I think I'll eat and work out and in the afternoon I'm going to see my grandma before yoga. Mom has some errands to do. So normally that will keep me away from work until 9 p.m. Good plan.

I'm sorry if I am a bit absent, I feel so caught up in "building up my life". I worry about not being able to go back to France in september. In Budapest I can find a job so easily. Few people speak good French here. I see about two new offers every day. Office jobs that I would love to do.

In France it's so much harder for me. I feel pressure to have a well working system to earn money working from home. So that I know that I can work when Lily is with her dad or in school and still earn enough to pay for rent and food and internet and phone and pharmacy. I know for sure that he won't help me. Not arranging time with Lily if an office job requires it. Nor financially, for sure not. He said he doesn't care about me getting financial aid from the state or not. Which I won't until we are officially divorced. Procedure we cannot start yet because I have to be there to go see the lawyer. Shoot me.

When I was in the victim's house or what they told me to go seek social assistance but it will take many, many appointments (time that I could spend working) and it will take very long to actually have the money. I won't get anything while we are married. Great.

So it really feels like I cannot count on anything but myself. I prefer to think so and get prepared.

You know if I send you pictures and videos I send them because I feel like doing so? It is not to get something from you in return. It's because making them and knowing what you will see brings me joy!

I know I can be overwhelming but that's me. You can be you and take your time.

Elle

*

March 2, 2017

Calvin,

I will be gone tmr morning (wednesday night for you). I got a psychologist appointment early in the morning and right after I went to my friend, the same one I spent my first night with. She is at her parent's too. I'll go there and we'll cook a nice vegan dish for lunch. We went to school here. She is from the same town as me.

I just realized you wrote me a whole boobies fantasy just after mentioning your big breasted friend. Ok, maybe I am a little bit insecure about my breasts. Thank you. That's funny how considerate you are!

Having casual sex with someone is dating? Did you go on dates with her? Or you just used the word dating because it sounds better?

I had a pretty bad day. Yoga was like a massage to my muscles. Very nice. It felt good after a dumbell workout. My sister was there and at the beginning during relaxation we had an urgent need to laugh and couldn't stop. She had to leave to calm down. It was weird. The kind of laugh that has no reason really and can turn into crying very quickly. At the end of relaxation I just started to cry, I went out in the bathroom. Maybe because the yoga session took place in a kindergarten and seeing all those sport tools for small children made me heartbroken. I remember thinking: It is not fair! He was abusive and I have to leave Lily behind, this is not fair! And just crying.

We went to my grandma afterward. Some more crying. But also hugs. She told me things like "He said bullshit, you are smart and strong and beautiful..."

This is a small town, I know quite a few people and everyone knows me. My parents are very active in the community and they speak a lot about me. So even people who I never met saw my pictures and knew about me. And now they ask " Ah, you are here! And the small one? Where is your daughter?"

I tried to find something funny to answer. I could only come up with "she jumped out of the airplane", "I put her in my luggage but it got lost". My sister suggested to say " Fuck you!" and run away. We are dangerous together, next time I'll put my mattress in the other end of the room, far away from her. We make eachother laugh.

It's so bad. I just forced a huge smile on my face and stood there speechless. What could I say? I ended up saying she'll come later.

Someone reacted: yeah, I understand I fight sometimes with my husband and feel like leaving my family behind for a few days.

No she doesn't.

I am glad I got an appointment so quickly. I am in so much pain right now. I have absolutely no idea what to do with it.

Before you write part 3. You might need some additional information :P I cum rubbing my clitoris with the fingers of one hand and putting the fingers of the other on my (what is that called?) vagina, kind of circling around or just putting some pressure on it without penetrating.

Here you go. Now you know ;)

I wanted to make a video demonstration but I am not in the mood.

I could cum in my privates tonight but I felt like it took longer than usual (the guy said wow you cum fast. WTF? that wasn't fast) and wasn't nearly as much pleasure as it normally is. I figured it is not the perfect time to show you how to.

Sorry.

I will write more when feeling better

Elle

*

March 2, 2017

Elle,

Wait! Are you saying you are a human being and you sleep? You missed one Skype appointment. Forgive yourself. Lily has. If you really want to over think it and examine it to death go ahead, but in the end you'll find you love your daughter and look forward to seeing her and care about her and make videos because you want to be in her mind.

So your grandma is right. That stinkin' thinkin' is bull. You know only because it affects you is why he went to those crazy words and crazy ideas. I am an idiot and even I know you made her videos and miss her because you don't want to be away from her. You are the only one who doubts that, and you know better.

He doesn't doubt how much you love lily, he just knows it is so untrue, it is something important to you so it hurts because someone said it isn't important to you and doesn't hurt. Kind of disproved his own theory. Proof by contradiction. Quod erat demonstrandum.

Thank you for your generous videos.

As I have said, the simple little teasing of lifting the dress and gently touching and undressing works for me. if you want to do more for your pleasure I don't mind.

I noticed in your video earlier you tend to slide your fingers up and down your entire clit rather than wiggling it side to side, twirling your finger in circles or trying to get under it. Long quick stroked and not so much about penetration. Some attention to the entire vagina but not so much about slamming four fingers deep inside or trying both holes. You like up and down a very precise area. bring a little moisture up and keep everything wet, but up and down the clit. Also the entire clit from as high as my fingers can feel it to sliding down under and rolling back the sensitive clit. I will touch the sensitive area and flick it upwardly with my tongue and suck on that part of your clit but when you are turned on I am going to slide up to the very tip top of your vagina and caress as much as I can.

By part four I will be hard again enough to...

Calvin

*

March 2, 2017

Elle,

Don't bounce until you get to the bumps. I had plans to try to get rid of my car and get a newer one this year. I have to get the license renewed and to do that it has to be checked. So of course my car is running great but the light says to have it checked. I wouldn't bother or spend any money on my car except I can't get rid of it unless it is registered and I need to fix it to get it registered. I am just stressing a little because this was nothing. I just take it in and send money.

Now I have to decide within 180 days what to do. I probably am going to find it is a very cheap fix and I will get it checked off as planned and drive it until I find a new car and save enough money. But I can't wait until the last second to start paperwork. I must decide what I wish to do. But I won't worry or think about it until I know what to worry about. I will first find out why the service engine light is on. No need to worry about the unknown when I can know soon enough. it might be nothing so why worry about it until I know if it is worth worrying about.

So part three in length even though I seem to have been on the right track in my overview.

Thank you for giving me feedback. I am not the greatest at sex but I had a good teacher and learned to read women and always cared enough to want to know what they were feeling. I had the freedom to be myself. When I felt like being selfish and just doing what made me feel good, I was loved. When I was enjoying her being turned on by me, I was loved. Whether I was trying to please her or trying to please myself or both it didn't matter. That was not why I was loved and I was loved as just me. I didn't have to be the world's greatest lover and I didn't need to be more than myself. But feedback always helps. Remember that so you can do it again. Good Calvin

I am leaving my time on your breast not because I like the breast of the girl I used to date better than yours. Hers were nice but bigger than I like and not as perky. I am leaving because I love your ass and legs! You already knew that. Stop overthinking and coming up with more than what is there. I start at the top and work down. always. Not because I got a phone call. and yes we went out. But I used to take her and her daughter to the fairs while my wife was alive and before I did anything with her. I tended to do work on her house or some manly thing that she couldn't and that turned her on. Then I would clean up and cook outside and we would eat at home. Then go upstairs to her room. But we did go out also.

So we are laying in soft sheets in a darkened room lit by a bright moon. Our eyes have adjusted and we look into each other's faces as my hands travel down your back enjoying the idea that you are naked now. Your head is higher than mine as you look at me but still close enough that your nipple still brushes against my chest. I like your breasts. Get it? Good!

Your leg is warm and against my testicles just enough to drive me crazy by hinting they are being touched but maybe not. I can feel your wetness straddling my hip and thigh. My hand has traveled down to your pussy but has only brushed against it. My fingers follow the inside of your thigh higher and higher. I brush by sensing where I am on your body but careful not to touch you as I slide from one thigh to the other. I circle between your thighs and the region swells as I rub close to your pussy but not over it. Just close enough to get a response from the region between your legs.

As my whole palm makes contact with the inside of your thigh it slides up over your hip bone then back down your hip and leg. it slides back up a bit more to the inside but this time my thumb extends and softly slides up the crack of your pussy. At your clit it enters you. It slides down your clit but then along the soft wet pink edge inside it pinches softly the puffy skin between your legs and pulls your pussy lips to the outside. This pulling action on one side allows you to feel the air against your wet inside but my thumb does not touch inside you. It just pulls your shriveling swelling lips outside. My thumb pops out at the bottom and explores the area between your pussy and ass. Then my wrist twists and my thumb slides inside barely at the bottom of your pussy and opens and pinches the other side and stimulates the lips on that side. When I reach the clit again it is a river flowing inside you. I run my first two fingers down either side of your pussy barely touching the wet pink and staying on the outer edge. I scoot my body down so you can feel my breath on your pussy. As I slide my two fingers back up the edge of your pussy I open it with my fingers and slide my tongue inside and lick up to your clit. Your clit is easy to find and I come at it from below catching the most sensitive part with the end of my tongue. This causes you to tense up but I want this to last so I slide my tongue down each side. Then using your entire pussy as my surface I write each letter with my tongue inside you: A,... The top of the B circles your clit. C licks mostly the left side of your inner wall. D both sides. E and F get a reaction from you as your clit is wiggled side to side. G circles and continues on the clit but when it reaches the bottom and the line sideways I insert it deep inside you. HIJKLMNO.. You like the O... P and q get your clit so ready I can't help but find it as I write, You are excited by q so slide my tongue inside and as I start to lick up I stop my tongue just below your clit and cover my lips tight and suck. Your entire clit is being sucked and my mouth is even slightly above your pussy. My tongue is busy. I remember you like my tongue sliding up and down and only moves your clit when it goes up one side of it. I gently suck one side as my two fingers take over caressing up and down your clit. At the top above the pink I have to press and roll my fingers across your clit to find it but it is swollen and definitely there. All of it. I slide my tongue inside you at the bottom and up to your clit again. My fingers are sliding up and down your clit faster now and I end up licking my fingers a little as they slide down to the tip of your clit where my tongue is under. I have a finger on each side of your clit and it is getting messy between your legs. You lift your knees for a second and I slip my tongue deeper into the bottom of your pussy still rubbing your clit with my fingers. When I get to the clit again I begin sucking again and your legs straighten as you take a deep breath. My other hand not on your clit slides two fingers massaging around your lower pussy as my long strokes and sucking continue above. You put your hand on my head and grip my hair. Suddenly your thighs try to pinch together as you orgasm. I stop moving but still keep pressure against your clit and my other hand inside you. As you shutter you move and your sensitive clit reacts to your movement. After a couple shutters I take a hard suck and flick the bottom of your clit. Your legs bend as if you are trying to put your feet on my shoulders and push me away from your sensitive pussy while still holding my face close with your hand. You are sensitive and where I am touching you is causing a reaction but still you are enjoying the orgasm. I slide my knees up between your legs and gently caress the edges of your wet and messy pussy with the swollen head of my now erect penis. I don't put it in just run the head along the sides and against your now slightly numb clit....

Calvin

*

March 2, 2017

Calvin,

What?? How? Seriously, just watching that stuff from beside you, you could figure out this much??? What? How? Why do you know this? I cannot wrap my mind about how easy communication is with you. And about the fact that you figured out all of this with as much as you got. I don't understand. If you wanted to distract me, well done! I am just sitting here, I cannot even function, I am speaking to myself but it's nonsense because I just keep repeating "Ok. How? What? How? I can't. What?" I am ridiculous. I have to go and get ready for the day. Wow, did I say you know me too well?! Oh my god, shut up elle. I just can't... Ok. Bye

Elle

*

March 3, 2017

Calvin,

How are things with your car? How is the lady doing? You must be exhausted with everything going on.

You don't have to be the world's greatest lover! But after what you wrote and how you described your approach to women you seem to be pretty great. You meet my description of the world's best lover!

I think I understand why I feel like making you leave. Every time you announce that you'll be busy I feel it. You know, just in case you are not busy, just tired of me. I get ready to be dumped and try to end it before. I am struggling with this but at least I am aware of it. I try not to hurt you sorry.
By the way I love your "I am busy with this and that, will write more when I'm done"

You have nothing to prove. You don't have to write long messages when your life is crazy and you barely have enough time for yourself. I know you want me in your life. Right?

I don't know... I know you had other reasons to say no to your friend. But still it reminded me that you spend all your free time writing to me. Instead of giving yourself a chance to meet a body you shouldn't write fantasies to but could actually have it be real.

Beautiful sunny morning. Sun always makes me think about the Christmas tree and the sunshine on your sweet face in front of the window. Very nice picture.

I think skype bothers you. Especially if I am the one to bring it up because you feel pushed into it. And knowing your first sex experience, that might have something to see with yor preference of keeping things under control and making sure to take the decision yourself about when and what happens. It's ok.

I might be horribly wrong and overanalyzing and seeing things into it like I usually do!

The devil is teasing you!

kiss

Elle

*

March 3, 2017

Calvin,

This is just a youtube video about the difference between the action of loving and the feeling of love. 0.36 Made me think about you. The difference between nice and kind. Being kind is harder than being nice. Unpleasant. Awkward. I like that although you are a nice person who tries to avoid confrontation you manage to do the kind thing.

From 2.03 it helped me so much to work on how I feel about leaving the person I loved and who loved me. He did have the feeling of love. But he didn't do the action of love. Oh my god, the sentence "it's ok to leave someone who hurts you after explaining and asking to stop if it doesn't stop".

I don't think I can hear this enough. I still remember his mom looking at me "But he loves you. You made him so happy. He became so much more open and joyful as a person". As if that would be enough of a reason to not leave. As if me being hurt by his "love" wouldn't matter.

I am also thinking a lot about how he always told me "it's a joke" when he said something cruel and I felt torn down. I guess I know

now that it was funny. It wasn't kind though. He chose to be funny over being kind. He could have chosen to uplift and encourage. Also there are so many ways to be funny. He could have made a cute joke that leaves me feeling loved. I guess what bothers me is that his choice was self serving, not selfless. That he chose power over kindness.

This is not my approach to people. I do mess up and hurt people unintentionally by thinking I am funny or just not thinking before saying something. I know, I know. I hurt you by saying "I hate you, I don't want to speak to you". It was selfish to exaggerate a feeling for a quick relief not thinking about how it makes you feel. I don't want to hurt you. Not a promess (quoting you) But still I care about whether you are hurt or not.

Someone just wrote me in free chat:

-I am a vaginatarian.

-...And I am hungry

I had a session from 10pm to 3 a.m. It was very cool. I had a very surprisingly good one that felt like actually having sex. I learn every day. I was so scared to consider having sex with you online, thinking we couldn't get comfortable, that it would be weird. Maybe I was wrong.

He said he had a domina woman 50 years old and she taught him how to do things. I think I enjoyed it because he stayed kind, he gave me instructions but also many compliments and at the end of the instruction there was always a soft word. Plus he praised me for everything I've done even though I was just doing what he told me. I didn't feel humiliated at all. I felt adored and respected and flattered and even spoiled because it was all about turning me on. It was a game. What I also really enjoyed. We started with c2c and I wasn't allowed to touch myself and he did things and told me I lose if I do touch myself.

I thought: easy! Let's play! It was so playful and so much fun. Sometimes he told me "ok, now you have 60 seconds to touch yourself, you stop when i say stop " It was so funny and sexy at the same time.

Guess who would be fun to do this with?

The psychologist was really sympathetic. She is very distant and professional, young, pretty. I felt better when I left the appointment. At some point she asked me how I feel when I hurt myself. What makes me do it? And toward the end when I was still telling my story and getting a bit into those feelings she, on purpose, said something very positive that stopped me from going into that dark direction. It felt so good! It is not fun to tell my story. I am so glad someone knows what to say to help me feel better about it. The thing she said was "You know, nothing's carved in stone.

Everything can be changed. She told me this because I confessed I often feel trapped, like there is no way out, no solution. She is cool.

I'd love to have another session and chat with you, when you get home from the lady but I might be too exhausted. I don't know yet. I had a nap so I should be ok.

On Friday we are going to visit my grandparents for the whole week-end. I will be gone from lj but I will have the internet. I'm coming back on Monday in the evening.

Sorry I got weird after you told me about the interesting phone call. I know everything is not about us. None of my business that you two went out. I'm sorry. I know you don't want to be with her. Even if you would, it is still whatever. Can you feel how I am digging a hole under myself? It's only getting worse. Oh, me... That's muddy ground. I don't have to drag myself there.

Also: no man ever used "too big" and "boobs" in the same sentence. Also: You like my breasts. Got it. Ah, you make me laugh! The A B C made me laugh too. Why do I feel like it wouldn't be the ABC though but rather some stupid vegetable joke spelled with your tongue.

I noticed that I have a little issue with this fantasy mentally. Now strangely what makes me feel the most uncomfortable is being the one who is served. I don't want to find myself in a position where I could feel superior. It's so weird. I don't feel comfortable with this. Because in my stupid mind there is no connection like when I am on top and we are having sex together. This is different.

It's so weird. I still have plenty of privates where I obey and I don't even mind being treated badly, it cannot possibly be that bad as at home. Because it cannot get personal.

But I am absolutely unable to do Domina things. No way. I don't want anyone to become my object.
I know it is all silly. But this is where I am at right now. I need time to process.

Wow this email is weird!

I feel so weird. Honestly, I have this urge of making you leave. And I just don't understand where this comes from?? I don't want you to leave. You can, but I don't want to.

Elle

*

March 4, 2017

Elle,

The last two nights I have worked out on my friends property until dark then talked to her about losing her grandson for a couple hours each night after. I am glad I did it, but It wore me out physically and mentally and emotionally.

I will try to write to you later tonight or definitely tomorrow. I worked at her place because it has been dry all week and today it was supposed to start a set of storms. I need to get out and take care of my work before it rains. I had planned on waking up to rain, but since it is dry I need to go take care of business. I think I fixed mine already.

Life is good. What is more beautiful than people being beautiful? This is the video I mentioned to you.

Oh and the fact I told you about my phone call from "the woman with the big breast" should assure you that I am not going to just disappear one day. I might get too busy to be able to write as often, you might meet a guy who can spend all day/night depending on where he lives chatting with you while you work and decide you don't want to spend as much time with me, but I am not worried about you leaving without warning.

Trust me, Even if I disappear for a few weeks, I am not planning to do that. But if I break off our friendship and stop our writing you will see it coming.

Don't try to read into things. If a woman I used to date calls me I will tell you. If something happens between us or in my life, you will know.

So stop trying to guess. I like you. I feel I am getting tons out of our relationship. I write to you a lot. Everything is fine.

This idea of escaping before you get sent away isn't a worry. We tend to share a lot and if I am upset you know. I am not upset.

I love your videos. I love hearing about your life. I love sharing my life. I love having someone to share my emotions and frustrations with.

Did I mention I love your videos?

Ok so relax. Life is good.

Calvin

Attached: Video of Compilation of acts of kindness recorded by Russian car dash cams all over the country

*

March 5, 2017

Calvin,

I started to write again. In the car and on a bank in a shopping center while my family was shopping. It's the "whose funeral is this" story. I sat silently staring at the blank paper for an hour until the pieces finally came together in my head. Then another half an hour to find the first sentence. But once it was done the story wrote itself.

It felt like I am just a tool, like the final thing already exists and my brain and hand try to grab ephemeral (ahhh this word) bits and pieces to recompose it. I thought it would be a funny sketch, stand up comedy like but the story wanted to be a slightly funny but mostly sad short story. I don't know, it's strange. It became something completely different from what I envisioned but I love it.

I totally forgot to take panties with me. How?? I thought of you when I put on the dress and the pantyhouse. It was very exciting to go out like that. I loved walking around in public thinking "You have no idea, but I have no panties on." I filmed a short and cute video for you but cannot upload it from here.

I was crushed after skype, laying on the bed, curled up. My sister came and spooned me and she stayed and talked to me until I started to feel strong enough to sit up and speak and make eye contact. We spoke about our exes who didn't come to hug us when we felt down, not even after asking them to do so. She is not depressed anymore and she is a wonderful support. She gained back her confidence and optimism but she also has a new way of empathy from her experience and a sensitivity she didn't have before.

Alright I want to tell you something. Remember how you mentioned that you got lucky because you came before the others. I do not have much or any experience with kind guys. I met some at my internship but I just avoided them on purpose because I didn't want to find myself in a situation where I could be tempted to compare him to the not kind dad of my child who waited for me at home.

You bothered me so avoiding you would have been my normal response, block delete and forget. But I didn't do that. I feel like you are much more than kind. And that we understand each other so easily. It makes me feel good when we are communicating in some way.

I didn't tell you right away but I made up my mind about dating people. I feel like I want to try. I feel curious. Does this sound horrible if I say "I want to know whether I like you so much because you were the first kind man to me or because I like YOU" Yesterday I signed up to a website. It's really special.

I honestly do not understand how and why I get myself into these kinds of things. But I'll try to explain.

It is a sugar daddy kind of website. I like that I can be very selective and try to only pick the ones who seem to be kind and intelligent. I also like the fact that meeting them won't mean I won't earn money that day because they will compensate me for not being able to work the day we meet.

I don't want to go on regular dates while I am stressed out about saving money to raise my child. I want to meet several people I like chatting with and choose one I can have a relationship with, rare dates but regular, always the same person. I am absolutely aware of how unhealthy this should feel. But it doesn't. I cannot stop myself. I want it so bad.

I don't want to sleep with anyone who finds himself in my way when I am horny and too weak to stay away. I want someone I like as a person but someone who doesn't want me to be her girlfriend, who doesn't want a future with me or own me in any way. Someone who respects me and appreciates me but isn't in love with me and won't go crazy possessive about me.

I have no idea about what's wrong with me. I have no idea why it doesn't feel like being a slut for me. Maybe I want the illusion of feeling safe. Maybe I just want regular safe sex. I am very maniac about sex being safe. It is so much easier to keep safe if the overall number of people you slept with is low. I don't know why I am even counting. It matters to me somehow to have it as low as I can keep it.

I know very well that i should be able to do the next months without having a sex partner in my life. That would be cool. That would be healthy. But I am not. I don't want someone to love me. I want someone to treat me kinder than my husband and just enjoy that it exists. Get used to it, learn how to let someone do that.

I haven't met anyone yet. And I'd like to write about it when I do. If that's ok.

Is it shocking? Please be honest. I'm sorry if I disappointed you.

Elle

*

March 5, 2017

Calvin,

My sister knows about my research and obviously disapproves.

It got me thinking about why I feel so addicted to this kind of world.

I witnessed a whore house and cannot imagine my body being sold for money.

I tried the "champagne bar" while we weren't speaking in January and escaped after the first day when someone wanted to sit next to me and convince me to kiss.That was a definite no. Not being able to choose who is touching my arm even if there is no sex involved and it was all about making them consume more and more expensive alcohol. I couldn't do it. I felt an urge to slap him and run away.

I felt so relieved.

"Huh, I am not a slut. I just like flirting and making private shows protected by a screen and distance"

And here I am considering meeting someone and selling my personality and body.

I try to think with my French psychologist's head. She would say it's a pity I discovered swinger clubs and gained self esteem and felt seductive for the first time, all at the same time. She told me once this. Suggesting that things are really messed up in my head.

It is interesting how the swinger clubs, although they weren't about money, required my personality and body too. It didn't feel like people were interested in my body because things always started with conversation and it was a huge part of attraction.

Maybe she would say that I discovered unconditional love and gentleness in a porn environment, from a member, who paid me for a private but hugged me. So maybe unconsciously I tend to look for that in a similar environment.

You asked once whether I want more or different. When everything was different. I feel like you really want me to tell you things without a filter, even if it's too much.

Of course I want more. Who wouldn't? You are so perfect. Of course I want to listen to you confessing your worries and frustrations before you go to sleep, feeling more relaxed because you could speak it out. Of course I want to have a casual, smart and funny conversation with you, build up the sexual tension between us, our heart racing and heavy breathing. Of course I want to touch your cheeks with mine. Of course I want to feel you in me. It's so easy and evident to love you.

But it's all just a fantasy. And I am telling myself that I have to let it go. And then I get so frustrated because nobody is like you. You are like you. How to move on when nobody looks like you, I won't have this connection with someone else, he won't have your story, neither your personality. I want this. I want the whole package. Closing my eyes and seeing you inside might not do the trick.

I understand if you feel upset and don't want to speak to me. But please don't go. Please stay in my life. I enjoy fantasy. I love your contradictions. I just love admiring from afar how incredibly kind you are, how strong but also vulnerable and so smart, you stimulate my intelligence and everything is so much fun with you.

I hurt for you when you are hurt and I am so happy for you when you feel good. Even if it's someone or something else that makes you feel good.

This is not really clear or coherent but I am confused so this is all going on in me.

Elle

*

March 5, 2017

Calvin,

I'm meeting someone tomorrow.

I am getting that feeling I am so used to having, the excitement of getting my body prepared to fight or flee. Crap.

I am addicted to feeling in danger. I think I don't feel alive when I am safe.I feel like I can't breathe and I have this urge to just do something, anything new and different.

I don't feel good. But I can't stop.

It feels like... if I don't choose the danger myself I am not in control and it could come at any point unexpected and I won't be ready to protect myself. But if I create the danger on purpose I know about it and can get into that ready function.

It is strangely so familiar and makes me feel safe.

I feel overwhelmed.

I don't know how to change what I thought I wanted to but it doesn't feel like I do.

Elle

*

March 6, 2017

Elle,

Ok. That was a lot. Let me try to reply to a few things. First your words about me were very kind and generous and I know exactly what you meant. You don't have to be clear. I understand. I am not a first time reader, I have read all your novels and know the characters intimately. I am being poetic. I understand how you feel and don't worry about difficulties explaining inconsistencies and contradictions in me or in our relationship. I understand.

I am not disappointed. Please never feel you have to fear being honest and open with me. I like you. the real you. I like hearing what you feel and what you think. Sometimes I hear more than you do. normal doesn't feel normal. You want me because we connect and are loose already. You want something else but not to replace me or to lose me. My advice is simple. I want for you what you would want for me. be as kind and generous with yourself as you would be with me. Follow the advice you would give me. because I know it is from your heart and caring and from love. You want to feel compassion and love. I get that. You want to feel sexy and attractive. You want to know you are desirable.

Here's part of us also. I am not seeking physical contact as much as I would be without you and your videos, partly because I would be dating and looking for someone to admire me and make me feel I am a good guy and lovable and everything I am trying to be. I don't know if it is healthy but you give me so much of what I need. Even without physical contact. You don't want to lose me because what I fill in your needs you fear no one else will. I know this because I am the same as you.

But here's the thing. I am here. I am not leaving. If you meet a guy, hell yes I want to know. I want to know all about your life.

That is who I am. That is who we are. Follow your own advice. You wouldn't want to hear I am in love, but you would want to hear I was in love. I wouldn't want to not be able to tell you what I am feeling. Both good and bad. If I asked a woman out and got shot down and felt bad about myself. You would want me to write to you. I want you to write to me. If I have a great day and am happier, you want to hear. Don't worry about being open and real and honest. Plus I know you and might call Bullshit if you lied.

As far as the slut comment. Where did we meet again?

Of course I hate the sugar daddy idea.

Of course I see everything you see about wanting to be bought instead of loved because of your value.

Relationships are scary. But you meeting a real man and you flirting and being the sexual person you are and maybe being horny and wanting physical sex, I understand. My only concern is that your heart is fragile right now. But I don't think that the fact you really want sex, and to be held and loved and feel kindness, makes you a slut.

Maybe in a way a sugar daddy or swinger's club you feel is safer than falling in love or being expected to be treated a certain way or have expectations you don't have enough self esteem to accept you and give to someone.

I think you are obviously wrong. You love Lily, you treat me extremely generously and beyond what I could expect. You just beat yourself up for not being as perfect as the perfection you want from a man. But you are human and perfect doesn't have to be superhuman.

Maybe I am still a perfect fantasy, but I think you love that I am flawed. It is my pain and my struggles and my mistakes you love. Let someone love your imperfections. I get it. You paid for the private you don't have the right to expect more from me. You can touch my arm but don't expect a relationship.

That's too hard.

I get it. You are not lost. You are lonely. Duh. Like you shouldn't be lonely? Look at your situation. I think it is healthy getting love from people in your life who don't want sex... and from me.

I want sex. I want to not feel old. I want to be admired. I want to feel like I can still be sexy and found attractive. I want to be more than a math teacher. Why would I judge you? I hear your heart. your real needs. I don't judge you by your actions.

I have never judged you by your words or actions. I judge you and our relationship[p by the way you treat me. I am very content. Based on us, I adore you and enjoy having you in my life as long as you allow me to be.

Calvin

*

March 6, 2017

Calvin,

I read back what I wrote while waiting for your answer. I know you will react to "you are so perfect" by reminding me of your flaws.

I know you, I know who you are when you fold up your blue shiny outfit and put on a black long sleeved T-shirt.

Thank you. That was really sweet. You treat me so well.

Elle

*

March 6, 2017

Elle,

I did find someone with sexy underwear. But you are so much more than what the eye can see. You have a beautiful heart.

Calvin

Attached: photos underwear target

*

March 6, 2017

Calvin,

You are so silly!

Elle

*

March 6, 2017

Elle,

I am reminding you that it is normal for you to feel that; calm and sweet and kind and loved and not dangerous and no drama is not normal. I totally accept that you feel anxious waiting for the drama that never comes. You want to drive me away before I drive you away. I understand and accept it.

But be safe.

You are loved and don't deserve to be treated badly. Part of you wants to be treated as though you are owned or controlled or not worth intimacy. Part of you feels safe if it is just sex. Part of you feels comfortable in a bad relationship. but you deserve more.

I respect that you are a grown woman. I am not always proud I went online and found you there. I can't judge you for having a sexual outlet. I had one. Just be safe. Emotionally also.
Remember you have value and this is not what you want. If you can enjoy something besides what you want. I am happy for you. But you deserve to be loved and can handle a real relationship and deserve more. But it can be more also. It doesn't have to be any more instead.

I did get a little turned on thinking of you in pantyhose and not panties.

After having said that and admitting that is part of us. I might sound like a hypocrite but honest.
You need to feel successful and talented and that you have worth as a writer and a great mother and a great sister and a great friend and translator. I think right now, and I fully admit I am part of the problem. But right now your main compliments and affirmation is for being sexy and flirting. Don't believe us perverts. You are great at so much more also. I have never actually had sex with you. But
I think you are great at other things too. Don't let our affirmation dictate who you are. You know you are more.

Your Identity doesn't stop because I can't fuck you. Your identity won't stop if I can't see you. I like who you are. Who you are is more than sexy clothes on a mannequin. Who you are doesn't need excitement, drama and bad things. Who you are can be positive and happy and what you want, Not what you feel you need.

Sorry this felt very judgmental and hypocritical of me. That is not how I think. I trust you to do whatever you want. I just want you to be healthy and safe. I felt I needed to speak up once.

Maybe I am feeling I love the sexy and am trying to absolve myself of any guilt if my obsession with your body and sex with you causes you pain. I don't know. I said it. Now I will go back to being me.

Really I understand you are an adult and I am not talking down to you. I spoke up. You won't hear anymore. Enjoy. You are sexy. You are a great flirt. I love all those parts of your personality. But when you reread your emails they were unsure and asking my thoughts.

Life is good. We got some snow and it is fresh and beautiful here.

Calvin

*

March 6, 2017

Calvin,

I am flattered you want me. I would be really upset if you wouldn't! I would cover my whole body in nylon and put on my "unattainable woman" face. .. and quote smart things you said. Would that do the trick?

I don't think you are part of the problem. We had one private and I think very soon we both felt uncomfortable with money being involved and it didn't feel right. I think this sounds healthy. I don't want to get rid of sex and my sexy flirtatious side. I probably couldn't. When I felt so insecure and not sexy I didn't feel like me. That didn't feel healthy. I felt like it was the other extreme.

I think sex is a healthy part of a relationship. It can be. And now I feel so too. Sex is not everything. "If sex is good it's only 20% of a relationship. If it's bad it's 80%."

You gave me so much to think about! Your words are healing me, they feel so good to hear. I try to get used to them. It's really... strange. It's a lot.

You are so silly. But my eternal question is "Who is taking these photos?!" You must have a very good friend who can bear with silly Calvin. I can't believe you did this. You really have no boundaries! I love the look on your face.

The date got canceled so I came home with my family. I'm going to see him on Tuesday after my psychologist appointment. We flirted a bit these last two days, I liked it because he brings out my funny side. When I speak with you, I care too much and it scares me and I freeze and I miss perfect opportunities to place a joke. I don't care though because you are funny enough for both of us, I don't need to entertain you. I can just relax and laugh.

It feels nice to be cool with a stranger. But he is not funnier than me. So, I guess I will have to entertain us tomorrow. I don't know much about him except that he seems to be turned on by me and communicates in a not scary way. The good thing about being a webcam girl is that someone wanting me is not enough to impress me anymore. I don't know what to expect. It could go any way.

We'll eat something out, public...safe. If I am not feeling it I will leave. I don't feel desperate to have sex. Also there is this young and sensitive guy I am supposed to meet at the end of this week. But everyone seems to be boring to me. They are like "ask anything that you'd like to know " and there is nothing I want to know. Why don't they tell me interesting things? They just ask questions and praise my pictures. They get ecstatic about everything I say. No one starts to explain the golden ratio! You raised my expectations too high.

I'm glad you get what I say and don't say and that you understand me when I am unclear. I think I can feel you, more or less based on your words but rather as a whole and it's more of an intuition than understanding every single sentence. Why do you write in riddles? Some sentences have several meanings and you do not give a clue how to interpret them.

Examples:

"I might call bullshit if you lie." Whaaat? You don't know me that well, do you? Mmmm...aren't you trying to make me get used to us being close and make it feel less scary? It is not working! :D You never did and I am pretty sure I wasn't saying the truth all the time. Probably to me neither. Does that still count as a lie?

"You wouldn't want to hear I am in love, but you would want to hear I was in love."

No comment. This is not even a sentence. It could mean everything or anything. This sentence comes from nowhere. It would never get passed revision and be published in a book. You are so annoying sometimes.

I found "Duh." so funny, it always makes me laugh when you use it. I wonder how you say it. Is it as funny as written?

I feel like I'd have so much to say in reaction to what you write but it's weird breaking it down in small pieces. I feel like reacting to every sentence. But then I can see how annoying it would be. You could never finish a thought if I constantly interrupted you asking with my "What do you mean exactly?"

Thank you for all of this, it felt like a tight hug. I didn't feel judgment from your words but I felt that you want to say it so that I can start to insert it and let it sit and grow and enjoy it when I feel ready. I felt like you let me heal my way even if it's not an exponential function kind of healing, rather two steps ahead and one step back.

I loved the video of the kind acts. The music is really good. I love the song "To build a home from the cinematic orchestra" . I walked down the aisle to this song. People tried to make me choose something more joyful but I'm stubborn.

How are you?

I was a little worried that the conversation with the lady would bring back pain for you.

hug

Elle

*

March, 7, 2017

Elle,

Here's a duh: “I'm a Mouse, Duh”

You don't have to cover your whole body with nylon. I really like when you uncover your body. But saying smart things... when you said "You let me heal my way even if it's not an exponential function way" I did get a little hard.

I must remember to go back to my math stories. Kurt Gödel I don't think we ever got to. The infinite hotel with infinite rooms and an infinite number of guests, does it have a vacancy? The shepherd who couldn't count. Mobius strips.

The lady who lost her grandson knows all about me. I felt she understood when I said things. I was not just quoting greeting cards. I felt I was sharing my heart, my life and she appreciated that. The one thing that surprised me and hurt a little was that we both agreed that we had done all we could. I made my wife's life better and she was happiest in her life with me. She had a great life but our time was the best to her. I truly believe that. The lady could identify with that. She had done so much for her grandson and had no guilt. But then she said something I wasn't expecting and it upset me a little.

I am ok but when she said it I was hit in the heart. She is a lawyer and her husband worked very hard and many hours and had to work away from home some nights. He gave up so much so he could have a life when he retired, after their children had grown they would have money and could relax and travel and have a good life. But their grandson was a drunk and got robbed and beat up when drunk and had depression and drug problems. So they let him move in just before her husband retired. She agrees that she feels at peace because she knows she did all she could for her grandson and his life was better because of it. I also reminded her that her husband wanted to make his grandson's life better and he chose to take his grandson in.

But then she said something that affected me. She said she had troubles because she resents her grandson for taking her last years with her husband. He wasn't able to spend time with her because they were always upset about the grandson. They argued and when he retired he had medical issues because of stress and died. They could never leave the grandson alone and never traveled.She blames her grandson. She knows it is not right but instead of being happy he is not suffering she feels guilt because she is still mad at him.

This bothered me because I am a little mad because she died. I am mad about my loss. She said that her grandson had problems that were not his fault. Her daughter had messed him up. She had raised a daughter with drug problems that affected him. She was never angry at him and he tried and did so well. She is upset he took his own life and mad about what her life is.

I have forgiven the drivers who killed my wife but I still feel bad. I get disgusted at myself when I am upset at her because she was killed. I know this is stupid. I am so healthy and past all these emotions. I was not expecting her to say she loved him and felt she had to let go of her anger at him.

Please don't worry Elle, I would not have brought this up if it still bothered me. read my emotions. you know me. This is a very small moment, not anything on my mind.

The phone call from the big boobed woman upset me, but I am past it. I was more upset about treating her right. We have a history. We were friends before we had sex. Part of me wants her out of my life. Part of me knows that is not right.

I broke away from her, but she also hurt me. Maybe it was easier to let go because our friendship was damaged and she didn't treat me well as a friend. But stop worrying. As I suspected she was horny and tested the waters to see if she still had a shot with me. She understands that it is never going to happen. She did look good though.

I think we do understand without words. but I will try to not be so poetic.

I want to hear if you fall in love. Please tell me about the men. But yes, part of me doesn't want to hear:

"He is even better than you Calvin, I am so much happier with him."

But also I want this to be true. For you to be happy.

Actually I took my mom shopping. She took the proud pictures of her son feeling up the mannequin In her bra and panties. Yes, the store was full of shoppers.

Life is good.

Happy Calvin

*

March 7, 2017

Calvin,

It was very nice to see your name in free chat! It didn't even get me nervous.

Kurt Gödel... Wow! How can you always make things interesting? Now I am curious. I started to research it but ugh it's better when you explain it, more fairytaily and exciting.

I understand being upset. Upset at her body functions and soul to give up and leave. You are not disgusting. Thank you. Ok. But for me it's new details every time so it is a strong, overwhelming emotion. It helps to know that you are not bothered by it now and could bring it up but still I cannot stop myself having a feel of what you could have felt. Thank you for sharing. I would never ask you to tell a story too hard to tell.

She did what? She hurt you? What did she do to you? Do I have to go and beat up the big boobed woman? I am quoting you, threatening is not my thing. But...what did she do? Maybe I could give her my death stare. I do that really well.

I loved your pictures!!! The "Duh, I'm a mouse." And Oh my God, the mannequin! I love your silliness, who does this??

The psychologist appointment was ... a lot. But helpful.

Next time she wants to get into the Borderline symptoms with me. I am afraid. I don't want to. It is on purpose I avoided going and getting a diagnosis. Until it's not said by a professional and there is no written proof of it it is not true. And I can live my life with the hope that it is not. I hate being borderline so much.

She mentioned attachment styles and suggested I look into it. I am currently doing my research on it. Looks a lot like I have the anxious type. And he was avoiding type. Anxious tends to look for avoiding because it feels familiar to childhood. Makes sense.

Actually I do understand now that I am playing with you. I am not doing it on purpose. I wasn't even aware of this until now. Because I did this my whole life, it was the norm for me. It is so shocking to me to face the ugly things I do. Somehow my childish brain is convinced that people who are not physically with me don't love me.

http://the-love-compass.com/2014/02/22/understanding-the-needs-of-the-anxiouspreoccupied-attachment-style/

Wow, this describes pretty well how I treat you. It's horrible!

“If you have an anxious attachment style, you will feel more stable in a committed relationship with someone who has a secure attachment style. This helps you become more secure. "

I am not unable to have relationships. Maybe.

“Heal your shame and raise your self-esteem. This enables you not to take things personally.
Learn to be assertive
Learn to identify, honor, and assertively express your emotional needs.
Risk being authentic and direct. Don’t play games or try to manipulate your partner’s interest.
Practice acceptance of yourself and others to become less fault finding — a tall order for codependents and distancers.

Stop reacting, and learn to resolve conflict and compromise from a "we" perspective."

I found this list of things to do to change my anxious attachment into secure. I don't really know what these mean but I'll look into it. The first one I know, I am working on it. I have no clue about the rest.

If you see me doing the manipulating game things could you tell me? And stop me from doing that. I'm glad I have to face this because I hate to be like this.

I spoke to the psychologist about the sugar daddy thing. She told me things like you did.

The date got canceled. Too late. I went for nothing. A little frustrating.

Hum....I am not angry at him because I wouldn't say it is mean to cancel it...again. But also I don't want to put myself through the risk again.

So, he is out of the game. The psychologist just asked me to focus on my emotional reactions. Well, I didn't like how I felt, unimportant. So I guess I want to avoid that.

The Lily situation is catastrophic.

He is less and less willing to let me skype with her. Disappeared for a day. And today he just said he is opposed to me seeing her during spring break. Also, he is still extremely abusive verbally. I didn't know it was possible but it's getting worse.

I am ok. I have enough on my account to buy the tickets for spring break. I am considering not taking her to Hungary but staying in France in a hotel. This is what he would prefer. Or maybe he just said it to upset me I don't know. Before I left he said I can come back anytime to visit and sleep in the flat. He is so opposed to that now, he scares me. This is so ugly.

Time will solve everything. I feel like I am doing the best possible. It is still not enough and very bad.

But what can I do?

It helps a lot to be so sure about my decision. I didn't run into or out of things. It was a long process of thinking through and considering all the other options. I am confident about my choice. He said I am certainly sleeping with the whole country and that the court will never give a crazy whore right to see a child. But I am not crazy. We spent weeks on this with the other psychologist.

I am not perfect, but no mom is. He slept with someone. I didn't even sleep with anyone. Yet. And if I do I have my right to do so because we are not together anymore and someone doesn't become a bad parent for going out on dates. It was actually so transparent that he tried to hurt me because he was feeling hurt.

After the mean words he said: Huh! I touched a sensitive point, didn't I?

It feels like I broke him and should fix him. But how? He wants to be fixed by me going back to him, but that is a life not worth living. Ok, patience. Our marriage lasted about two months or six at the maximum. So he deserves to throw a tantrum about how unfair life is.

Thanks for the hug in free chat

and the images you put in my head for the whole trip!

Elle

*

March 8, 2017

Elle,

You could read those symptoms another way: You could look at how you really don't like those qualities and you know you would avoid them. Look at all the ways you already do exactly what the solutions are. Be assertive, direct and honest.

I am not sure they are talking about our relationship but more about your partner or husband but you are very open, honest and outspoken.

Also Elle you know when you do something manipulating you almost always announce it to me. You say something then tell me to ask for another bite of your sandwich. You admit when you are teasing me and sending me something sexy to keep my attention.

Also recognize that most of the time you admit it, you really aren't trying to play games. You try to please me not to manipulate me, but because you enjoy pleasing me. If that's a problem it is my problem also.

I like pleasing you and I like when you please me. I get that pleasing me sexually is me reinforcing that your worth is in your sexiness and your body. But you also get that I don't think that's your only worth. Maybe I need to be less of a horny pervert. But I honestly think you want to please me and don't think of me as just a sexual person.

If I thought I was doing wrong by you by allowing you to feel I admire you because of your body and the way you tease me and how you turn me on. say so. I won't be as happy but I am not going away if the sexy stops. I think down deep you fear this, but suspect it is true. I like you and not just because of the physical part. hello I am on the other side of the planet and never had a private where you orgasm or anything.

Ok. I am not an expert about Lily. I think life is harder than he thought without you. He recognizes all you did and what he had. He is filled with regret and loss and is striking out. He wants to hurt you, probably just emotionally, but be safe.

Can he be protecting himself? Doesn't want you back in the home and see how things were. The contrast on how things are better with you there and bad when you aren't. He also sees that Lily loves you. Maybe with you gone he is more jealous of her attention and her choosing you over him scares him. He doesn't want to risk losing more.

Ok David Hilbert in the 1920's and then Turing.

I will explain in a more magical way. but this is an overview. The magic of writing computer programs before computers were invented. Looking at Artificial Intelligence ruling and making our decisions for us. then examine if there is a solution you can come to if you had enough time to look at all the options and decide the best. Then Gödel argued for the need in Faith. The need to see something bigger than yourself. The answers don't all exist in yourself. There are more true statements than provable true statements.

I will tell the story.

Also I recommend "Flatland". It goes to my philosophy of life after death. but is a good example of how you can see more completely from outside and understand better than from inside.

I enjoy you. and not just physically but also Physically.

Calvin. You like my body, but you have seen better bodies. You like me for more than my body.

You want me in your life, not just in your body.

Calvin

Attached : Flatland - A romance of many dimensions

*

March 8, 2017

Elle,

I hope everything is great.

This is because I know you love my math talks. Maybe a little too sexy so don't watch if you are not strong. You like me for more than my body. I just like distracting you and making you smile.

Life is good.

hug

Calvin

*

March 8, 2017

Calvin,

THIS IS NOT MATH TALKS!

Calvin, The first thing I will teach you when speaking face to face is how to pronounce "szia". This is still not it. Although I really like your way of saying it, maybe I will go and convince every Hungarian to start saying it like that. It's so cute. But it's so annoying. I keep correcting the screen as if you could hear me: "No! That's' not it! Say "see ya"! The "z" is silent." It's my fault though, I didn't explain it well enough. Teaching Hungarian is tough.

No, I have not seen better bodies, I've seen different bodies. I really like this one! I love that jacket...The bow tie is surprising but I know I should have except a funny touch, it's you!

YOU HAVE NO UNDERWEAR! And just when I am at my horniest you do the little dancing to make me laugh again. How you raise one eyebrow... and your voice.

Wow, it made me feel so much in such a short amount of time!

Elle

*

March 8, 2017

Calvin,

I am feeling down today. Fortunately I have a funny video to watch and rewatch and Flatland to read. I cannot focus now, but I love the bit that could get to my brain cells.

My dad just came into my room with my mom, handed me a chocolate bar saying "Happy woman day!" putting a leaflet about our town's accommodations in my hand. I was so happy about the words that I didn't even notice that I was on the cover!!!!!!

Nobody will recognize me but IT'S ME!!! My dad took the photos last summer. I am a cover girl!

I'm taking a train Thursday at 9 a.m. My friend wants to hang out so I planned a few dates but if they get canceled or turn out to be disasters I have someone to spend time with!

I will make a session before I leave, probably from about 6 to 8:15 a.m.

I don't feel down, I actually feel good today. This is a very bipolar day. I ended up working out, getting two dates for tomorrow. And.. tadam tadam tadam...

Lily sourit "Je t'aime maman"!

She was so freaking cute. Her dad got off his chest with all the anger in messages. It was good. I remained calm and confident and kind. It felt easy. I am so grateful for my psychologist sessions.
If I analyze a bit, obviously I love myself right now because three men are interested enough to meet me.

And that I love you mommy! It was so touching. Especially because no one is telling her to repeat it, for sure. I am saying it all the time. I felt like she is not hearing it or doesn't want to show she is. When I was at home she used to answer my "I love you"s . I cannot wait to squeeze her in my arms. Maybe her dad showed him the videos I made.

I will try to squeeze the dates in the three following days and that's it. Dating is not fun.

I love how big you are. It shows more in this video than in the others. So much Calvin for me! I could let my lips wonder and brush your skin with my breath. Start it innocent, leaning toward your naked body as if I would just move in my sleep to make myself comfortable. Eyes closed. Cheeky smile. You know me but you let me think you don't know what I am doing. That you cannot see my smile in the dark. But you can feel it.

You try to not move, not react but I feel the tiny change in your body. You get a tiny bit tense and your breathing is forced to the same speed but a little bit deeper breaths. My warm breath is making your hair stand up on your arms, as I slide up in the bed, my lips move on your shoulders, really slow, up on your neck. I playfully, very gently bite your earlobe and make you burst out in a laugh. You only open your eyes now and look into mine. Our eyes shine in the dark room. Your fingers find my cheek, slide down to my chin and you pull up my face toward yours. ... Shut up Elle!

I wish I had a sleeping buddy. As if anyone would want to just sleep with me! You look so comfortable to sleep with.

No matter how many times you say you are old. This is not what I see. Good luck trying to change the way I see you. Even watching you eating a steak wouldn't do it.

Elle

The cover girl..I am so cool!

*

March 9, 2017

Elle,

Whoever makes that magazine for your town is pretty smart. You are the best reason I can think of to visit that town.

I forgot to tell you before; I think you looked adorable in the picture with curly hair. Jumping was nice too.

I have a friend who moved away. I spoke to his parents today. They are traveling to go see him and his two kids. They retired from a job where they were overwhelmed and felt they were too old to keep doing it. But it was a job where they helped people. They were always surrounded by people who needed them and who they served. They say now they are adjusting. They don't have to get out of bed because they don't have anything planned to do that day.

They feel their life is empty now because you can't fill a hole inside with money or awards or drugs. But they were in touch with their spirituality and helping others and liked that they felt they were doing good. They are visiting their grandchildren partly because helping their son and being there for their grandkids gives them a purpose.

I think you have to like yourself, and when struggles and suffering and challenges you don't think you can handle come, you are introduced to who you really are. This is hard for them but they are learning about themselves. I think we have both gone through things that we thought we would handle better and things we handled well that we didn't think we could survive. But we discovered who we really are and what others think matters less because we have pride and have discovered ourselves.

No one can convince me I am less than the person I have proved to myself I am.

You seem to have taken over the next part of my whale watching story. I like it and I am enjoying reading it.

See ya,

Calvin

*

March 10, 2017

Elle,

I love Fuck Me Now Calvin. FMNC.

My buddy's place is funny. He has four deer that come by every night. I had a young buck I called Bucky. He had small antlers and ran with two dots. He wasn't the least bit afraid of me. I have deer that will come to my window while I am inside but Bucky would wonder down where I was working and if I slammed a car door or was banging on things he'd barely lift his head to look. He'd come within a body length of me and not be concerned.

The deer at my buddy's have been coming every night for over a year. His dog freaks out every time and runs to the gate and barks. They look at him like they know they won't let him out and they are teasing him. Woody, my dog, was mellow. Dogs would submit to him and he was bigger than most animals so he ignored them. He never got sprayed by skunks. But I knew if I had to be concerned. He could smell a bear or mountain lion and would get upset. If the bear was down by my trash barrels I always knew long before it got close to my property. He also knew snakes were bad but ignored squirrels. Smart dog.

Not much to tell here. I neve feel I need to write.

I hear a strength and even when you are unsure you are in charge now I didn't hear before. I like it.

I don't like you saying you wish people saw their interactions with you as an exchange. Yes you fill needs in me and support and comfort me, but not in exchange for anything I do for you. We both write and hurt for the other because we care. You want to fool yourself into believing you are fooling yourself.

You want to feel loved but not be loved. You want tenderness and kindness but because they are jerks who are being selfish and trying to get something. Not because you believe they are tender or caring but because they know they have to do certain things to get certain things. I have done it too and it is probably normal. But I didn't like hearing you write it.

Funny I said :"hear" but when I read you write "Calvin" I hear your accent and your voice saying it. Now that niether of us re using our mouth in the whale story sexually, maybe we will talk more in art 4.

I liked FMNC!

Calvin

*

March 10, 2017

Calvin,

I ended up having one date, in a restaurant next to the parliament building. The guy was cool. Very strong sexual tension. He had to run back to work and left for skiing this evening. But I think we'll meet again.

The date for the evening got canceled. The guy just disappeared. He never came and didn't react to my message. If I'd had a date with myself I'd go!

But I didn't mind at all.

I walked, admired the city lights and sang out loud. I felt like something ended. I let go of Lily's dad a little bit more by having a date. It wasn't only a sad feeling, it felt a little bit sad but also exciting.
I was extremely embarrassed. I didn't speak much. But it was a positive experience.

I liked to feel desired and feel excited and scared about what will happen. I wasn't flirty or funny. I was extremely shy and intimidated. For the whole time I was freaking out about what if he is like Lily's dad and I am attracted to this type still and again. Then I relaxed. If he is, this might be an experience I need to heal.

I'll see what happens.

I reread your fantasies this afternoon. They stick. Still as powerful as the first time I opened them.

I think the guy wants a relationship. He is single, has quite a bit of free time and is a bit too interested in me... I'd prefer to have an exchange kind of thing.

The other day I had a private show with a Japanese person. He was very romantic and I wanted to shout at him "stop" "YOU don't have the right to say things like this!" It was a little bit like your sex stories but unpersonal. There is this other guy who never takes me private but comes all the time to bother me with his stupid compliments and started to write hug. It got me really angry for no reason. Why does he think he can come and say whatever, without meaning it?? He gets aggressive all the time. I don't know how to send him away, he looks like the kind of guy who quickly turns his "love" into hate.

Something changed on LiveJasmin a few days ago. I guess your stories start to have their effect on me. I cannot cum anymore for the members unless I close my eyes and press my lips together to avoid saying outloud fuck me now Calvin. Great. Your stories are smart. Also I do look for you walking around in Budapest. Bad Calvin.

still sexually frustrated

it's like I have a monster in my lower stomach

Elle

*

March 10, 2017

Elle,

Part 4

We are still looking into each other's eyes, naked in bed with the ocean outside our motel room. Your attempt to seduce me by biting my ear made me laugh but also made me hard. It was partly a nervous laugh but now we are both smiling at each other. I place your cheek in the palm of my hand and smile back at you as I guild your chin and face toward mine. First I kiss your lips softly but just a taste. Our lips touch but don't press together. I feel your lower lip brush against mine.

I slide back to smile at you again. Your eyes are still closed waiting for the next kiss but you have a content and relaxed look on your face. My hand that is not against your face holds the back of your head with my fingers entangled in your hair. I kiss you deeply and long. When I come up for air I let out a "Whew!" You giggle somewhat proudly. "You're fun" I say remembering everything we have already done tonight. "Really Calvin?" you say pretending to be innocent and not knowing what I mean. "What fun thing do you wish to do next?" you say with a smile jokingly. I reply jokingly,"Fuck me now Elle!" We both giggle but I slide close to you so you can feel my stiff dick against your hip.

You turn toward me and I straighten my cock toward you and between your legs. " Mmmm you feel good." I whisper. "I know this Calvin" you brightly reply, "I feel myself all the time." I smile and slide myself close so I can feel your soft skin on my entire body. " I like when you touch yourself" I say smiling is my best attempt at a seductive smile. My complete failure at the seductive smile makes us both laugh and I turn it into a joke by raising both eyebrows repeatedly forcing my sexy attempt over the top. Out of mercy for my attempt to be sexy and because you are a little turned on that this feels natural and not heavy or self conscious for either of us you slide your hand down.

You take my swollen dick in your hand and slide the head of my cock past your clit and against your pussy lips. Then you play with your clit by rubbing yourself with my cock. My head is swollen and as you rub it against your still wet and sensitive clit it catches under you clit as you slide it up then point it inside you as you slide it back down over it.

I roll on top of you after one of your downstrokes because I can't handle not being inside you as you play with yourself using my dick. I feel how wet you still are, or are again. " Mmm go ahead and say it Elle" I say with a smile as I start sliding deeper inside you. "Fuck me now, Calvin" you quote with almost a growl. Slowly I slide inside you and almost out. My shoulders tense as they hold my weight off you. You are thrashing about a little and not sure where and when to look or open your eyes. You are concentrating on how you feel. I am looking into your eyes.

Our foreplay was not my doing something so I could obligate you into reciprocating. We both were enjoying each thing we did and enjoying the pleasure we were giving the other person. At this moment while I am fucking you over and over we are both enjoying the feeling in our sex oagans and our entire body. Suddenly and unexpectedly you are just feeling happy and loved and enjoying it when you're surprised with a rush. Your entire body, you would swear your hair and toenails had felling, suddenly an orgasm flows over your body like a wave from the ocean covering you. Drowning you. Your entire body tense up and you can sense my throbbing inside you. You make an odd squeaking sound you never heard before and explode.

Not literally. No cartoons in this story. No exploding or safes falling on anyone.
I slide myself outward but as I slide back in I recognise how sensitive you are and I pull out and lay beside you breathing hard and hugging you. I smile at you again and say, "wow!" I have no blood flow to my brain so forming even that word was something of an accomplishment. You cuddle against me and kiss my shoulder. Then you rise up and with a sudden sense of re-examination from your orgasm you feel my hard dick and say, " You're not done yet Calvin". I am not sure if you mean I haven't satisfied you enough or you just really want to see me cum again and don't want me to go to sleep hard.

Suddenly full of energy you sit up in the bed and cup my balls and give my shaft a firm pull. It gets fully hard again imediately.You straddle me facing away from me. I realize as much as you pulled me inside you with your thighs and fucked me, you were laying on your back and I was dictating the speed and how deep. Now as you stand my dick up and insert it in you I realize you are in control. Slowly as you move on top of me I feel you place your feet on my thighs and lean back. I reach up and support your back and massage it as you seem to speed up and slide back and forth. My balls have been filled since watching you orgasm and my dick needs only a climax to explode. You sit up slightly and speed up again. As I resist and my dick thickens and fills you, reach down and tickle my balls with your fingers lightly. This does it I cum hard and repeatedly.

Still breathing hard we both lay beside each other. I reach over and awkwardly grab your head and kiss your forehead. Forget trying to be sexy I am going to seduce you with my awkwardness. We both laugh again and you cuddle close against my side. I hold you and listen to you breathing as we both drift off asleep knowing we will wake in each other's arms in bed with no plans fo the next day.We might shower together, we might continue having sex, we might go get breakfast, but for now we are smiling and content.

Calvin

*

March 10, 2017

Calvin,

I am feeling happy and loved!

Instead of "You are not done yet, Calvin!" I would say "Calvin, I am not done with you yet!"!

Awkward is the new sexy!

WOW. This is the wildest sex I've ever had. You have a special place in my mind. I keep reading it to be able to go there. This is the best daydreaming I've ever had.

Thank you.

Elle

*

March 11, 2017

Elle,

This is not about me. You don't need me reassuring you or telling you how desirable and special you are. You know already. You need YOU to say these things. You can't lean on other people. You need to feel good because you are proud.

The facts are there. But you want others to tell you so they have value. Value yourself. Recognise the truth you know inside. I am honest and you know my words are true. But words from someone else are just words. The jerks on LiveJasmin can say words.

Ok but here's the thing. You are interesting and deep and fascinating. You are so much more. You are a full time mom! You have ambition and the ability to fulfill your ambitions. These are not silly dreams, these are books written, talent proven and value undeniable. Ambitions? You mean what am I doing? What am I achieving while dealing with moving recently and changing my entire life? I am kicking butt and growing and doing.

I get that you don't need to get into everything with a guy you just met. (I am not crazy about him going private with you.) You are more than a private. But you know this.

Why wouldn't a man fall in love with you?

Why would you not be a better choice than any woman at that party?

answer:

Because you are not looking to get married again right away.

I don't disapprove of your choice, just of you getting down on yourself because you met a guy at LiveJasmin, had an orgasm in front of him and then when you felt he was interested in you it was because of your sexiness. Duh. I know you like that word. So I get it.

Date, get healthy, understand yourself.

Get a little sex. (Safely)

I mean safe physically as far as disease and being alone with a creep or in a bad place safe.

But also emotionally safe. If you know you can't handle it, don't put yourself in an unsafe place emotionally. Why?

Spiritually safe too. He has to be on the same road as you. I am not completely sure what road you are on. I like that you are open but also that makes you vulnerable. If you tell the man how to trick you and what to say, He might say it. If he's good will that be enough? What do you want? What do you want for your future? Don't change to fit his needs and wants.

Be safe. You are smart and in touch with yourself.

I like when you touch yourself.

Sorry that was getting serious and sounding negative. I want to tell you how great you are right now. How lovable. How deep. How interesting. How desirable. How unlike the other women in that room. You know how much I admire you. Not your pantyhose but you. But as much as you want to hear those words. They are words from a man. Even me is words from a man. You need them from you. You are awesome. Able to, more able than most women because you have survived this once, but able to have a relationship.

You would be an interesting date that I would enjoy and stay until the restaurant threw us out talking to you. I would ask for another date the next day. You are interesting even if sex was not an option. Lol! How much have we written and physical sex really isn't an option. Facts, not just words from a man.

Obviously the sexual tension is there if you want it and men find you desirable. Duh 2
But also you are a long term woman.

Story time: No, not that type of story.

"Calvin's life" type of story.

My father was double majoring in Accounting and Theology and the Dean of the college came to his house to talk him into finishing off his degrees. My point was that he knew what he believed and was well thought of by the faculty. He had an older teacher who had retired as a Theology teacher but was still working at the college. My dad knew him pretty well and when dad graduated and moved away the old teacher asked where he would be going to church. My dad said a church in the area we were moving to and there was one church he had in mind. The professor said that the church was closing because the preacher left and he was taking over as the new preacher and moving when we did. So this old ex theology professor became the preacher at the church I grew up at. Eventually he retired after finding another younger man to take over.

That was the background. I spent a lot of time with this man and his wife. They would babysit me and sometimes my parents would go away for a week and I would live with them. His wife seemed very old but I was little and she might have been 80. But she adored me. Literally. I could do no wrong in her eyes and everything I did she loved. They had an old piano in their basement under the house. she would come down and listen to pound on it. I would try to learn chords and make beautiful sounds and create music. She wanted to encourage me to someday become a great pianist and she would rave about how beautiful my playing was. But honestly it was from my heart and her heart would brighten and her eyes would soften as she listened to this boy she loves so much. He had a garden and he enjoyed me working with him. They were fun weeks when I lived with them. I was loved.

They were a great example of love for me. My parents had a great love but these two were what I imagined as marriage and love. My parents were busy raising me and working and dealing with everything. They got mad or ignored me or each other. But the preacher and his wife were retired and they got their money from their retirement. They didn't work and he basically preached once or twice each week and that was all they did.

Every morning they would wake up early. She would make a simple meal like coffee or a bowl of oats. Sometimes he made himself breakfast or cereal. Then they went to separate rooms and studied and prepared for the day. Then they went outside and sat on a bench. This was difficult for me because I had way too much energy, but still I loved sitting between them and feeling their love. They have a flower garden with a bird bath. They would sit and hold hands and watch the birds and squirrels and small animals for hours. Many of the birds they had seen hatch and they seemed to recognize each animal as it came. They really enjoyed being together and sharing this time. Then she would clean the house and he would work in his garden and mow the lawn. I usually helped him but probably caused more damage than help.

She would watch and when he came out to pull weeds or clean up her flowers she would come out. They were both old and would help each other up when one knelt down to clean or plant flowers. It was her flowers but theirs.

He would come in and get cleaned up and go into his office to study and prepare his message for Sunday.. When I was there she would watch me. We would eat lunch and then I would go play all afternoon outside. They would watch TV in the evening and every night they played dominos on the kitchen table after dinner. It always amazed me as a child because my parents were so busy and did so many different things. Every night was something different. But they spent all day together doing the same thing every day; flowers, 3 meals, TV and dominos. Yet they never tired of each other. They loved each other so much and spent time together. They would kiss 4 or 5 times a day in front of me. They enjoyed playing that silly game at the table every night and would laugh and compete with each other and tease whoever lost. No matter how many nights they played, they laughed and enjoyed being together and playing was more fun than anything else. They didn't want to go out with other people. They didn't want excitement. They wanted to be in each other's presence. They wanted to hold hands and watch their animals. They wanted to stand side by side holding each other and watch this silly little boy run around outside. They always seemed to support each other. Maybe his wife was a little less strict and if he said no she might sneak me some candy. But they supported each other otherwise.

I think few people have the potential to live like that and have a relationship like that. Most people find that story boring. Most people don't understand or think they are crazy. But I think you are one of the few who are worthy of that and you know it. You don't want a fun time and a few laughs and then move on to the next husband. She didn't care if he was rich, or old, or exciting or successful. He was her husband.

Tell me again why you aren't leveled over every woman in that room? Tell me why you are only an object to fuck? Tell me why you are not deep? Tell me you don't understand love and want the truth?

I don't believe you. I know how awesome you are and how caring and so much more than many women can even understand. You read every word of my boring story about two old people. If he doesn't want a woman who listens to every word of that story and cares, then he doesn't deserve anything but whatever night of fun you want to give him. But he doesn't deserve you and you have my permission to safely, after you are sure what you want, to use him for what you want. Know your worth and not because I said it.

FMNE

Calvin who thinks you are awesome.

*

March 12, 2017

Calvin,

I didn't meet anyone else but him. I feel like it's already too much to handle emotionally and quite a big step.

I canceled the dates and stayed with my friend. The party started well, I got really good at smiling on command. It melts away just as quickly the moment nobody is watching me. the moment I turn off the webcam. The moment I escape from the room full of people and crawl into bed to hide under the blanket.

I met an exciting girl, had a very good conversation, she is weird and funny and it felt nice to talk with her. It really felt different than the other times I tried making friends. I usually have a crush on a girl and we both get really excited and it dies very quickly. This time I was more relaxed and cautious I guess. I was me and it was a comfortable talk.

I was drinking a tiny bit and felt dizzy very quickly. Then I started to feel less confident and just a mess. My friend came after me in the room and I had a meltdown. It wasn't bad. It still felt like I am strong and healing but have to get through these emotions and steps. I was crying about how my place is not here, because I am a mom, I am not someone who goes to parties and on dates. I spent years in a serious relationship , completely devoted to it and was always busy with real life stuff. Household and cooking and changing diapers and singing lullabies.

I don't feel at my place in a party full of girls who dream about having a wedding one day and their biological clock is ticking. I don't like the too much sound around me and the meaningless conversation. The dizziness and losing control. Not feeling safe. I had what they wanted. And now I don't. From now on I will only be a part time mom. And the rest of the time who am I? What's left if it hurts too much to identify myself as a mom with my child being away, as a webcam performer that's too shocking to share?

I analyze the date a lot in my head. I was so not myself. When he asked about my ambitions and achievements I was rambling and always making it seem less important and unsure. This is so not me. I have achieved a lot and had an extremely interesting life with ongoing ambitions. I think the word ambition scared me. But I didn't explain to him my opinion on it. the things that make me, my opinions and priorities. I felt like all I am is an abusive childhood and relationship survivor, a mom. I obviously didn't want to mention these. So I talked about my studies. But that's not me. About the webcam. He asked me about my hobbies and I got frozen. hmmm... reading, writing, watching things...

-do you go out sometimes?
-No not really…
-nature?
-I used to when I was little....

Many awkward silences filled with my worst memories of my past. I do feel like I have nothing to give. And I don't understand why he doesn't want my body. I feel hurt because he texted me right after saying how good he felt on the date and I tried to give hints about how good I felt. I didn't dare to tell I will stop dating, I thought it would be too obvious I liked him. He didn't go skiing, texted me trying to figure out how my (canceled) date went. I didn't see the message because we were getting the flat ready for the party. I answered much later. Still just giving hints. And when I was drunk I tried to call him, but his phone was turned off. I sent him a clear (?) message about me thinking the date went well, I would be up for a third one.

Oh, I forgot to say he came to LiveJasmine, that was the first one. We had a private show. We've seen each other naked. I cum twice or three times. closing my eyes. He was ok but I wasn't impressed. the communication wasn't great but later he mentioned he was embarrassed, he said it in a cute but confident way.

Actually after the private I was thinking about how to turn him down. But once I did his reaction was so amazing that I changed my mind and we ended up meeting each other.

He actually called me on the phone while I was going to the train to go home. He might come to the lake to speak. It was sweet that he called and also that he didn't ask me to go back or stay longer but automatically offered to come. I liked the fact that he was very busy the day we met and still squeezed me in his agenda and didn't make a big deal out of it. He asked on the phone about my other dates, I said there were none. He said I should have some to be able to compare. I think I like him. Did I tell you he has a psychologist? He mentioned on the phone that he'll tell me about "his package" next time we meet. I mean emotional baggage or what.

He scares me with the "you should meet other people ". He is "other people". I can't manage several at the same time. I think he looks like a good practice, harmless, I hope so. He is the first one

I want to cautiously discover and spend time with while it feels good and analyze everything with the psy. A rebound guy.

My sister told me to tell him this. I'll try to be transparent. The honest message I sent him drunk worked. I just have to be able to beleive that I can be enough even if it's "just" sex and dating, not taking care of him and being his 24/24.

I can beleive a guy wanting to fuck me one time and that's it. I feel like most of them want that. I can also believe a guy wanting me to be his everything. Somehow this happens just as often and makes me wanna run away just as quickly. But I don't really know why someone would want to have sex with me repeatedly, or walk with or drink tee, be my lover.

It feels so good to have your stories in my head when I go to sleep. There is nothing complicated about us and I can just rest and feel safe. I fall asleep smiling.

I'm going to take a nap. This week-end was too much and I want to work tonight.

hug

Elle

*

March 12, 2017

Calvin,

I laugh every time I see FMNC. It sounds like a political party.

Yes I read every word.

I don't know what I want. I don't even know who I am. I know. I know what you think of me. Although it feels warm to hear that I also know I want to rely on myself when I think about who I am and what I want.

I didn't feel like working yesterday, I practiced trying to think about how I see myself right now. I'm still not really here in the present. I practiced telling my past as a true story but something that made me stronger and who I am. I figured I needed to learn how to tell my story without breaking down while telling it.

I think I'll go for a walk. I want to see the lake.

I know.

Elle

*

March, 12, 2017

Elle,

A walk is good. You have a lot of energy inside you building up stress. Peaceful nature walks always work for me. They allow me to think.

I enjoy that you hear what I don't write and that I understand your sentences.

"I know"

You might not know who you are but I like you and you should like you too.

You didn't change. If you did, you got stronger, more in tune with yourself, more honest with yourself and more independent. You are better. You are still a good mom. I think in some ways you can be a better mom now. A mother who is more in touch with yourself. A mother without baggage. A mother who still loves Lily full time.

You are not your job.

I was proud to be a math major in college. I am proud to be a professor. I was proud when I worked on rockets and when I started my own company. But that impresses people I don't know and who don't care about me. I am weak and I need the approval of others. But I also get that it is a weakness. The people who love me and do for me, the people who give and don't ask for anything in reply…Those people love me, not my job. I am not my job to them.

I am not a wrestler to you am I?
To you, I am not someone who used to work at a place that made weapons, am I?

If I lost my job would your view of me change?

If a stranger looks at you over a table and asks what you do, he is probably being friendly and trying to get to know you. It is the start of the conversation, not the end.

-I am a math teacher...
-So why do you like math?...

You are a mom, but she is with her dad a lot.

You are settling in a new place getting to know people after being away for a long time. You love talking about Hungary. It shows your spirit and what is important to you. That is what is important.

Don't get stuck at question number 1.

Who are you?... I think you are going to the psychologist to figure out that answer instead of saying.

"I was told I am this so that is who I am. I am what someone wants me to be."

You have your languages, you have your art, you have your interests.

Yes you are overwhelmed on a date because your art is deep and universal and big. I don't mean your drawings, I mean your expression of your feelings; writing, thinking, exploring. Your sexuality.

Everything is an expression of you.

It is confusing. It is multi-faceted. It takes many viewings to try to understand. It is intriguing. Like all good art should be.

Do you want to have "who you are" be a drawing that people look at and say, "Oh yeah I recognize that," and walk on? Or do you want to be a painting people return to and sit and study each day and get a new feeling from it and notice new things and be touched by it. You are not a bowl of fruit.

You are a landscape with clouds and mountains and places in the trees where you can see animals live and a trail where people walk to a lake and a small cabin in the background barely visible. Is the cabin abandoned? Is it used for fishing trips? Does someone live in it? Hey there's a bird in the sky I never saw before! The color of the sky is dark and yet warm. I think it is evening.

You are an interesting piece of art that can't be summed up in a couple words. Fruit in a bowl. banana apple and pear.

You are Elle.

Do you expect for yourself to be settled? I don't expect you to be comfortable in your new bed yet. You expect to be able to describe your new life over dinner? You have a new life. A better life but new. Remember what I said about normal not feeling normal. You want to feel afraid. That feels normal to you. You want to be confused and not know if you will be greeted by comfortable and asleep or angry and hurtful. That is normal to you. Of course you don't feel like yourself. This is supposed to be. But feeling loved and strong and independent is what Lily needs you to be. I think it is healthy.

I feel like I should share about myself. I touched on the two boys racing. I don't mind talking about that but I don't want to bring it up just because I feel guilty for focusing on you and not sharing about myself.

Ok we are going to leave the whales in Fort Bragg and drive through Mendocino through the trees and timberland to Burney Falls and the volcanic subway caves where the lava traveled so quickly it left tubes underground. We will go camping and “sleep" in a tent. Our lunch can be vegan sandwiches. Then climb XY and have sex at the top. Just so you have a place to visit in your head when you get overwhelmed.

FMN

Calvin

*

March 13, 2017

Calvin,

You are not a wrestler for me, not a math teacher, not someone who worked at a place that makes weapons. You are someone who took the decision to leave that place because it didn't fit your life philosophy. You are someone who is passionate about math and knows how to transmit your passion to others. You are someone who has physical strength and agility and uses it to play with a willing other.

You talk a lot!

Your awkwardness is funny and sexy. You love your place. You end up finding yourself at people's place working on their things all the time! You stay up late at night to check whether I am online and write me long letters that go way behind three words that are used so much to express all kinds of affection toward someone but what they really do is to simplify, banalize a unique connection between two hearts. Cover up and hide the meaning.

If you think about it, saying those words could mean so many different things and saying them makes one get overwhelmed by those words and not be able to dig deeper and face what's behind. Ok. I don't know what I am speaking about. I am glad to have you on my mind. I am grateful to see behind it because it is clear and beautiful.

You can share your two boys racing story. If you feel comfortable sharing it.

I feel guilty that we are focusing so much on me. (It also makes me feel like I am the more problematic one.)Ok, it's silly. I know you wouldn't spend time writing as much about me for me if you wouldn't want to. I can enjoy it without feeling guilty.

Of course I like when you unzip your skin and let me have a look. I feel trusted and special.

You mentioned you had a tendency to take risks. I am glad you don't do it anymore. I will be scared a little bit in my heart when I read stories about you in danger, confused if I read something that doesn't fit with the kind person I know. But your past is part of you, what you did, what happened to you gave you the lessons. What counts to me is what you took from those lessons and experiences.

The painting part left me speechless. No not really! It left me crying.

I think the stress is coming out, bursting out of me in the form of tears and it's getting more intense every time. Last time it felt the most intense I ever cried, like my whole body was moved by all the emotions I had to keep down in control and be strong, not show. My chest still feels heavy and full of things I cannot express.

I want to write so much. It is consuming me. But the moment I open a blank page or grab the pen I feel the anxiety coming. I don't even know what I am so scared to face.

I had a big revelation during my walk. I was so much in my head I don't even know what streets I was walking on. I stepped in the lake! They cut the reed every winter (if the lake freezes enough to go over with the machine). It looked steady, like it was only reed and no water under it. My feet went in the water and they got wet.

I thought:

"Well, that's me"
"Of course I had to try to step on it and wasn't even afraid or counting on it being risky"

I continued my walk. I changed! When something unexpected happens I'm more focused on problem solving than hating myself for creating the problem!

"I have this problem, let's see how to solve it. I will try this first. Not working. Think. Let's try this."

I just keep trying, feeling stimulated by the challenge and proud of myself for trying.

The other day the electricity went off. It was night time. I realized everybody was gone. I don't know where they were. Strangely I felt so safe in this dark house, where I don't even know where the bow is to switch things back on. I don't even know whether we have candles or lights that work on batteries.

I was almost excited and happy about having a challenge, something I had to do all by myself! I ended up finding a bicycle light and used that to get myself out on a sidedoor that was locked from inside and found the electricity box on an outside wall of the house. It was fun!

I remember times where soaked wet shoes were enough of a reason to want to give up everything.

What's the name of your home town? It doesn't matter! I believe I saw it on your google account.

You'd be so much fun to camp with!

Good night Calvin

FMNC

Elle

*

March 13, 2017

Elle,

I liked the way you worded your last email.

If you like a flower you pick it and enjoy it. If you love a flower you water it everyday and keep it healthy.

Ok. I am going to stick a little to facts and probably not be overly personal about the racing boys. I suspect I avoided this topic. If I shared already then ignore this.

I also am trying to be honest and share that I felt a little uncomfortable about your reply to my camping story.

My wife worked down in the city. I loved that she never felt she had to give up her life to be part of mine. I did things without her and she did things without me. She had female friends and would have lunch at work with them or whatever. We wanted to be with each other but we weren't needy.

She drove home along a road out in the fields that wasn't ever busy and she enjoyed the lack of traffic to fight with. Two boys, under 20 but over 18, thought it was flat and they could see a long way and no one was ever on the road so it was a good place for them to have fun. They were young and dumb and were racing side by side. They tried to slow down and miss her but one hit her head on.

The other came back and they both got out and got her out of the car. I believe in my heart she died in his arms right there. They called for an ambulance and they had to do all they could to keep her alive.

The doctors put her on machines but I think the body that arrived at the emergency room didn't have my wife in it. They turned off the machines without my having to make the decision to. I am glad about that.

I believe the boys were being reckless but sending them to jail won't change anything. I said I wasn't going to press charges but when someone is killed the police have to do what they do no matter what I say. I said I didn't want any money because they would just never work because they knew I would get whatever money they made. I didn't want this to ruin another life.

I honestly have forgiven them. They didn't want to hurt anyone. They weren't drunk. They were young.

Having a woman die in your arms I want to believe made them careful and matured them up before their time.

When I was 18 I drove too fast and played with my friends. I don't think there was a new lesson for them to learn that they didn't learn already after that night.

Putting them in with criminals for years would just ruin lives and not make anything better. I never saw their faces. I was overwhelmed by everything and they were not something I wanted to waste time dealing with.

So that's how it happened. I am at peace with it. I wish it didn't happen. She didn't suffer, I didn't suffer watching her have some disease that slowly changed her. I honestly have nothing but fond memories attached to her. It has been years now and I feel you are ahead of me in some ways moving on.

You don't want Lily's dad. You can see how life can be better, or you can find happiness just as good. You are free to pursue a new life or not. That's not true. We both have a new life. Everyday life changes. But our life will never be the same and we can't change that. You have changed and if you decide you still love him and want to live with him and be his wife, Life will still be different.

Your lives will be different, Your relationship will be different. We can't stop life from changing. We have to just go on and live life.

My life is great. I am so blessed. it is like I was showered in diamonds every day and now when I am just sprinkled in gold dust everyday I am upset.

Life is good today.

People search for happiness in drugs and money and parties. I like me. I like helping people in pain. I like helping widows and people who are struggling because of no fault of their own. I like being there for people I care about. This gives me such a better life and pride and happiness. "The greatest thing you'll ever learn; is just to love and be loved in return." I am loved. I like my life. If I had my own kids and they grew to be young adults I wouldn't care about my kids in my classes as much. I have gotten joy and love and pride because I never was able to have kids. If my life was different I would be someone different.

I am not going to use those three words. But you like who I am. People think I am someone special. I think I am pretty darned great. My life is pretty darned great. I have grown deeper and more sensitive and wiser and searched out my faults more. I like who I have become and I would never have become who I am if I had a life without struggles or self doubt or had to overcome wanting to stop living. I never considered killing myself. I just wanted to stay in bed and stop being a part of the world. Let life go on outside without me.

I just want to be alone. But each time I force myself to change and to be who I want to be I win and I grow and I like myself better. I like who I have become and I am glad my life has made me this way. If I could change things, stop my mistakes, not hurt the people I have hurt, make different decisions, invest and get rich, sure I would change things in my past.

But it happened for a reason and life goes forward not backwards.

Ok. I talk a lot. But you like it.

Calvin

*

March 13, 2017

Oh my god, I wasn't ready for this.

Elle

*

March 14, 2017

Calvin,

I have no words but I have a video.

Or two.

Elle

*

March 14, 2017

Calvin,

Of course I am ahead of you in letting go. I am letting go of something bad. I had months while how I pictured my future gradually changed without him being in it. It wasn't a shock. It wasn't sudden. It started way before the wedding. It was so slow at the beginning, almost unnoticeable.

The first time I felt something was not ok was at my internship.

The difference between how I was treated at work (although an intern so not really equal) and at home was huge. One day I was crying in the bus, it wasn't rare. I was always scared of him when going home, when I said it to myself for the first time "I am verbally abused at home".

I was so lucky to experience not being abused, that work environment was the healthiest environment of my entire life. I was treated as human, as useful, thanked after I've done something, appreciated for following orders and having ideas, for being there and doing my work. That was my first eye opening experience. But I loved him so much and I felt like I owed him so much and tried to accept him with his defaults. Plus I was 100% sure it was my fault because I let him take that role from the beginning and still had the wrong attitude that attracted his aggressive response.

I asked him to marry me about that time. Our relationship wasn't at its best, we were a very bad parenting team, I felt like I could fix things, apologize for the baby blues. I knew how disappointed he was with me. He expected me to heal from Borderline, to be a great mom, to learn his rules and stop upsetting him all the time. I thought showing him my affection and loyalty and offering him my life would be enough to calm him down and make us happy.

He was so happy when he said yes.

The second eye opening moment was during the wedding organization. He forced me to write threatening messages to the people who worked for us. We had so many fights. I refused to write those kinds of messages and wanted to get to the point in a kind way, staying polite and avoiding confrontation. He was mad at me for not doing what he told me to do.

Many many fights, every time we had to write an email. He needed me for them because everything was in Hungarian. I remember feeling ashamed of him. Being ashamed that I am marrying a jerk. I was constantly worrying about people questioning why the hell I am with him. But I thought they don't know him, he has many qualities, he suffered a lot, it made him be like this... He deserves love. It is all true. But I didn't realize that he likes to be this way, he chose to react this way.

Third: the way I felt after the wedding ceremony. I was too nervous and excited too many people to sit down and feel. But at midnight, Hungarian tradition, I went to the bathroom to change into my red dress. I felt... hopeless. Disappointed. Sad. so sad. So lonely. I didn't see him for the whole evening. He spent the wedding day smoking with his friends.

Everything went perfectly, on time, the way we planned. He played his role. But it was like a spectacle. I felt so empty. I kept asking myself "So that's it?" We were the perfect entertainment, the guests had so much fun, we tried to spoil them. I felt like an accessory. I wanted to feel like a teammate. I wanted to feel loved and cared for. But I felt like my life was over.

Even when we were together he wasn't part of my plans. I never noticed. But he did. He asked me once: "Ok, so you speak about doing your masters, and writing and moving here and there...where am I in all of this?"

He never had plans. He was like a puppy who followed me everywhere. I was upset sometimes that he had absolutely no ambition. He dropped out of university, although he didn't need much to finish his degree and become a history teacher. He never did.

The first week we met I told him I want a career and he said he will stay home with the children. He was serious. But then when we got to that point and I had to do my internship and he stayed at home he got all mad at me for doing so. That's what we agreed on. I am not made to be a stay at home mom.

I expected having a child together to be so different. Supporting each other, lifting up each other and working in a team. I just assumed he would be there for me.

I won't go back to him. He said if I take Lily with me he will burn down my parent's house, he will find us and kill everyone. In the bathroom he said he wants to smash my head against the wall and make it explode, blood running down the walls.

I don't know how to say this correctly in English. I should not know how to say this correctly in french. But I do. Some words stick.

When I look at my father I am cautious, it's someone I love but also he is the person to whom I was:

"not smart enough, not working hard enough, had a big butt from sitting on it and just reading all the time".

I was never his princess.

Lily's dad called me Princess... It is different with my dad. He will always be my dad. I will always be scared of him but I will always be glad when he makes a step more toward me. That he does, by the way. He changed. My brain knows. But Some words stick.The feelings those words generated stuck.

I could never take compliments from Lily's dad and believe he meant them, after that he repeated so many times that he tolerated me and nobody could ever love me because I am annoying and very very hard to live with. He made me believe that. For years. He loved me but still made me believe that.

I could not let him touch me, after he admitted when I asked him:

-Please could you take me in your arms sometimes and maybe gently stroke me?
-Why would I do that if I don't feel like doing so?

He touched me more when we were in public, I was so happy, I felt like he was proud to have me and have everyone see.

You know what sex was like? Kisses on the neck, he knew that turns me on, kisses on the side, same, than he got me wet, I cum, I could feel he was like "oh finally, let's get to business", he fucked me. He took forever to cum. I pressed my lips together because it was painful but I didn't dare to say so. He rolled down from me. Cleaned up. Left because he didn't have the patience to wait for me to be done with my many orgasms.

Sometimes he let me put my head on his chest for a few minutes. It calmed me down and helped me to fall asleep. His heart was pounding so slow, mine went crazy all the time.

I miss being able to relax. I miss having a man in my bed. I miss sharing tv shows and food and laughs. I miss regular sex. But I don't miss him. What he gave to me, I could get from any random lonely man who is a tiny bit into me.

You know how I select whom I am dating? I reject them and wait for their reaction. This relationship ended so badly, was so different and unexpected for me from the fairy tail like start. I want to know first how they handle rejection. Do they have enough self esteem? Do they get frustrated, aggressive, threatening? A lot of them did, by the way.

Gergö, the guy I had a date with, will probably come on Thursday. Probably fuck me. I know. I'll be safe.

I am sorry about my reaction to the camping story. I tried not to stalk you until now, but the other day I wanted to reread our first messages to check your star sign. I remembered you mentioned your birthday. And I ended up clicking on your google account and saw you had that information. See? I was so good, so I didn't look for it, I didn't find it until now.

Don't worry I won't appear in your hometown and start to ask people where Calvin and his 22 folded lives.

Why are you still feeling uncomfortable? About this and skype? It feels too early for me too. It is not supposed to happen yet. Relax. We can fantasize about it but it will only happen when and if it is supposed to. Not now.

Don't compare your letting go to mine. I have it so much easier.

You loved and were loved in return. You had plans together. An ongoing diamond shower with the promise of having nothing that could stop it. No hints or warning, or things getting slowly worse or fading. The worst is that it feels like if the accident doesn't happen, your days would still feel like that diamond shower you described.

I didn't know what I was missing, so I wasn't missing it. My eyes were used to the dark because I grew up in it and I enjoyed the fire light even though it was burning me. I didn't know how the sun looked and felt. I couldn't be missing it. I am letting go of the fire or the burning water or whatever. You are letting go of diamonds. Not the same.

I am not missing diamonds because I never had them. I am lucky.

You had them. You know what it feels like to have them. Of course you miss them.
By the way, your amazing heart got you those diamonds, she trusted you and thought you deserve them and wanted to give them to you. It wasn't random luck that you should feel ashamed of missing once it's gone. You treated her well, she was happy.

Those diamonds weren't falling on you from the sky, it was something you both made together as a team. Of course you miss that.

Ohh. I have more videos to trick you into liking me! I was a tiny bit horny yesterday night. If you could read my mind you could read FMNC. Believe me or not I felt too embarrassed to say it outloud. I don't look embarrassed, right? Ok, well enjoy. No pantyhouse, just naked.

Hug

Elle

*

March 15, 2017

Elle,

I don't have any clones but there are good men in this world. Don't judge us by LiveJasmin. Sometimes men who are comfortable with themselves and confident aren't as easy to find because we aren't out looking. So you need to search the places no women look.

You like nerds, where do shy nerds who aren't looking for women go? I think you search out ways to meet men who are not what you want. Find the opposite place and you'll find the opposite men.

Instead of the greedy rich guy who brags and tries to impress you at an expensive restaurant, go to the poorest place were all the men are needy, be patient and keep your eye out for a good person quietly trying to help people, caring, understanding and doing it because that is who he is not for credit.

I like that you met me somewhere I was not proud about. You met me. You saw my flaws and still liked me. I can be open and not try to make you think better of me than I am. I was not angry or accusing you of stalking me, I was being honest and sharing my discomfort. I wasn't really focusing outward onto you.

I was sharing my feelings.

Busy weekend hopefully things will slow down and I will write longer.

Calvin

*

March 16, 2017

Calvin,

Discomfort? When you share a feeling that hurts me, could you please explain to me why you feel that?

Don't give me dating advice.

Elle

*

March 16, 2017

Elle,

You explained that I had listed information on my profile I forgot I gave out. I guess I am a very private person.

I wasn't attacking you or thinking you had done something wrong, I don't tell my students where I live. I was surprised you had information I tend to keep private. Even if I meet people at the grocery store I tend to say I live in the countryside.

Sorry if my comments on what you are sharing about your dating and your feelings about your dates and what you want different and what you are looking for on a date upset you. I won't.

Today was a little less stressful for me.
I hope you are well and smiling.

God bless

Calvin

I'll save my sex joke for another email.

*

March 16, 2017

Calvin,

I want to be angry at you. But I can't. I know you have my best interest at heart.
What sex joke?

Elle

*

March 17, 2017

Calvin,

I'm sorry. The advice was good but right now I need what I am doing right now. I understand that it is not easy to watch me do this. But I feel that if I get myself into something it is for a reason, it has to happen, I need that experience to grow.

It made me so angry that you tried to make me move on, instead of replacing you. I don't want to move on. I know I should. I will try. Just don't push me. It is like you reject me. Again.

The psychologist appointment was good. My homework is to observe my emotional reactions and practice how to stand up for myself and be me. We went through the last week and it was overall positive, I improved at almost everything. She did my diagnosis. I have Borderline Personality Disorder. I have all the "symptoms" (you have to have 5 out of 9) except the impulsive behavior like reckless driving, unsafe sex, too much shopping,...

My relationship with sex is special but somehow still safe. I had 7 sex partners and used condom with all of them, only stopped with husband when we decided a baby would be welcome. My husband was very strict about it too. We always made sure he used one when not with me.

It's funny how I am so good with this one but how the other symptoms fully show, all of them, to a crazy extent. I wish there would be an explanation. It doesn't make sense to me. My sister does have a crazy unsafe sex life. Why not me?

The psychologist had one Borderline patient, told me that it is exhausting for a psychologist and many don't know what to do with it. She didn't send me away so I guess she does. I knew. I remembered from the first time I started to do therapy, they were all scared and didn't know what to do with me. It was awful to feel like I am too much, too complicated to handle even for professionals.

She asked me to not kill myself while we are working together. Is it me or is this the funniest thing anyone ever told me? Whaaat? That was weird. I have a child. I know it is not about me anymore. I believe Lily deserves to have me around, possibly close to her and being a good mom, but at least alive somewhere. .... I know. I just realized what I just said.

The psychologist knew I liked spicy food!!

She said people who feel empty often like spicy food. And chase extreme, intense experiences. Ahh... Calvin, if you'd know how bad it is. It's never enough. I always feel like I want more shocking things. Something new, something bigger, something that scares me.

I start to plan crazy things and then drop it at the last minute because I can feel myself going wild and crazy.

The psychologist told me it might stop if I find what I really want. She is very good at giving hope.

Something positive... I started to write again a bit. About my dating experience. That's only mildly frustrating, so manageable and not overwhelming. If I think about Lily or you, I go blank. I cannot write because I cannot even handle thinking about it.

Oh! I cooked a new recipe! It was a success. Split peas, Indian style. It was very tasty. I wish it would be enough to make my day better.

That guy has no time for me. He called me today and said he will be very busy on Friday, maybe we could meet between his meeting and ski holiday if he can squeeze me in. And what did I say?

Instead of saying:
"Ok, you clearly have no time for me. No problem but I won't be waiting for you. Bye"

I said:
" I feel worthy when you squeeze me in on your agenda."

WTF?!?!

I wanted to bang my head against the wall. What's wrong with me? How can I value myself as little as this?

I know how. Because he is still the kindest guy I ever met (in person). Because my dad had time for me and I wished he wouldn't have. Because my husband came to Hungary as fast as he could and was always available for me and it still wasn't what I was really looking for.

So yes, I guess someone not finding time for me for a whole week makes me thank him for wanting to. I know abuse, this is nothing.

Still. I feel rejected and unimportant and just fed up. I want sex! I have this monster inside me, it just wants any kind of safe relationship where I can have the illusion that I am loved and I can project things and feel like I can breathe.

Why do I need sex to feel loved?

In addition to all of this I have problems with LiveJasmin. They took back my good video quality rating. And don't want to give it back. They are so strict. The guy insisted that there are still shadows to see on me, which is unacceptable. I think what I have now is a much better quality from what I had in France. I was so upset. They made me change the background because it was too plain for them. And not average enough I guess. Argh. They asked me to have a nice bed and nightstands like every other girl.

Why do I have to have a room like every other girl???

Anyways, I got some pretty stuff, I really like the result. But the tech guy still keeps telling me to buy freaking umbrella lights. They are so expensive to ship to Hungary! I don't even have the money for. Normally they have other low budget advised set ups. Mine fits into one. But no he unfortunately cannot give me a good rating because it's not good enough.

What did I say? "Thank you. For your help. Very professional"

Why do I thank someone who is an asshole with me???? Now I have almost no visitors, they probably listed me at the bottom of the performers because of that bad rating.

I bought plane tickets to visit Lily from the 15th april until the 1st may. I cannot wait. I am also scared. The boss is still trying to bring me down. He hasn't let me see Lily since Monday. He is writing horrible things to me.

I am being brave and strong and explaining to him why those things are not true and why it doesn't matter what he thinks about me. But it feels like the harassment will never stop.

I feel ugly. I feel unloved. I feel like a mess. Like a work in progress. "Don't look at me!!! It's not ready yet! Everything is upside down and it looks more messy than before...."

I cannot get over the skype thing. Is it because you are afraid it will make things more real, less perfect? Because you are afraid that it will be too good? That we will miss each other afterwards? That it will be more difficult to live far away from each other? Am I projecting my fears onto you?

I don't understand. You saw me all the time in free chat. It would be the same. I saw you in ridiculous outfits and I saw you naked and I know your voice.

I don't understand this rejection, because you seem to enjoy conversation with me and I know you would enjoy a private show with me. Isn't Skype private?

I don't understand because you took me private. And you said that you want skype but you are being clever. Whaaat?

That you would take me on dates. But no skype. Skype is what… dangerous?

Just give me something, anything that makes me feel like it's not because you are fed up and you hate me and you don't know how to get rid of me.

(easy just say: Elle, you are average)

Shoot me. Does this count as a sexual joke?

Elle

*

March 17, 2017

Elle,

You are so not average.

I want skype. But you have told me it is a crutch for you. When you are feeling things you said you would look for me to make you stop. I am seldom on skype, but would try more for you. You made it clear you would (past tense) look to talk to me to make everything better when you are about to explode. If I am not there it will only make things more hopeless. I get that you are better now.

You also turn me on. Your videos stop me from being thoughtful and wanting to do best by you. You wanting to please me on skype, and I am getting hard right now writing this, makes me know I can be selfish and seductive even if that's not what you want. Our videos are a conscious decision. Very recently you asked me not to say romantic things or send close ups of my smile.

Part of my ego is fed that someone as good as you thinks so highly of me. You do not want to let go, the things you wote in this last message are very complimentary.

I love it, yet we both agree I am not the answer. I am not selfish enough to want you to be in love with me and pine away in another country never looking at other men because I am what you can not have.

That's evil. But if I see you on skype I am going to have difficulty. I can lie or at least give the impression that would make that moment wow, but after I would feel guilty. I don't want to play with your emotions or mine.

I think we are going to skype, but we keep deciding we want to be intimate but it is confusing and fantasy and reality are great to conflate but not healthy. I am weak and I have issues. This isn't all about you. I need to move on from my past and you are helping. But I tend to become satisfied with you teasing me and not go outside.

Both of us are happy with each other as an outlet and friend. But it's too easy for me to allow you to fill my needs and make me feel loved and admired. But we both need to leave the house. The happier I am with just you, and just you does and could make me very happy and satisfied, the less open I am to the rest of the world. I want to skype with you. But we were just saying we need to avoid saying certain words or being too personal or fantasizing about a future together.

Elle I have deleted emails I enjoyed writing but realized sharing with you would not help either of us. I would enjoy skype but if a conversation got too intense or I got a text from someone or had to go, I could see you feeling rejected. I could see myself coming online horny and not being an emotional support.

We have fun on LiveJasmin and I think we could enjoy skype. Joking and being playful and keeping up on each other's lives. By the way you look fine in lj and I liked the way your new room looked. He was being an ass and your ass is much better.

I hear you not giving yourself the respect and value you deserve, but then saying, "Wait that's not right! I'm the bomb! I am awesome and have way more value than that. I see my value. I deserve more ." That's progress.

Clever was in response to my giving you my skype name without you knowing... then checking and seeing I spelled it wrong anyway.

I shouldn't comment on things I know nothing about but I think you hear rejection at the slightest thing. You are pretty great doesn't mean you aren't completely great. Did you just read me criticizing you and saying you are too thin skinned? Because I was pointing out a perceived flaw but also saying you are loved and admired and not rejected.

You are not as bad as you tell me you see yourself. Others see you as much more a treasure than you recognise. I am writing to you because you are not average.

You are someone I want to keep in my life. I am not in love with you Elle. But I might be closer to it than anyone else right now.

Joke: I tried Viagra but I chipped a girl's tooth. She thought I was a Don Juan, but I needed the Viagra or I'd be one and done. (Don Juan, Juan Don)

Calvin who talks too much

*

March 18, 2017

Calvin,

Enjoying each other is healthy. (I can only speak for myself but I know that whatever I feel for you is healthy. It has a good influence on me and on my life. No, it doesn't need anything in return. It is just a nice feeling of fulfillment, peace, certitude... I like it.)

I think fantasizing about a future together is not. Because it is unrealistic and turns things frustrating... for me. It is not constructive, not something that would uplift and bring something good in my life. The "I cannot have this" feeling. I am letting it go, or maybe already did.
What I am now at is to allow myself the feelings that come and embrace them and enjoy but stay realistic. We won't wait decades for each other, longing. Duh. I will try to move on and live and experience things.

Ok. I fantasize about being old together. But it feels realistic and healthy. Like really old. 40 is not old. You will make fun of me....

I have this fantasy of us being old (I would still seem to be pretty young compared to you), no more responsibilities and no more attachments and we would just sit and look at nature and knowingly smile at each other. You would still talk a lot and I would sometimes forget to listen and get lost in my thoughts.

We would just enjoy each other's company when you are not busy helping out someone and I am not busy creating something. And we would go out and do old people stuff. My grandparents go in an old people group to play card games and dance. I see myself working in a garden. If it's not gonna happen, then life probably has something else for us. But I like to imagine that it could.

Elle

*

March 18, 2017

Elle,

I love that we talk about deep conversations but still joke and laugh. I fear I might talk even more when I get old. I understand what you mean.

About my life. The daffodils bloomed a while back and everything is green. Today was St.Patric's Day and everyone is supposed to wear green. I am going to try to remember to take some pictures while the flowers are still out and the creek is full. I was going to put a pipe under the driveway so it won't keep washing out but I was told it would probably be crushed if a heavy truck dives over it. Hopefully I can do a french drain of gravel and sand and rocks. If I can direct the water hopefully it will run under the drive instead of down it.

I know this is boring but the pipe under the road looks good. I take pride in simple things. My dad was a carpenter. At the end of each day he could look at what he had built that day. I give a test the first week of classes. My students are encouraged to write notes to themselves. They comment that they have seen it before but have no idea what it means.

Last week I gave the test back and let them retake it and see what they wrote themselves.. They laugh because it is such an easy test and they all know they got each answer right this time. It is good for their confidence before they take my final exam. But it also reminds me of what I have done. Putting in the culvert or digging a ditch is more of an instant gratification. Sometimes it is hard to remind myself I am making progress. I like being able to see results and progress at the end of a day

I was invited to a drive-in movie tonight. Do you have those? A.giant screen the movie is projected onto and everyone watches from their cars. Some kids like to go on dates and no one sees them make out in the dark. I always went with guys. We had fun. They charged more money for a full car than for just two people. My buddy had a truck with a board in the back because the bed of the truck got hot. You could sit in the back of the truck with your feet on the board or raise the board up so it was flat across above the tires.

My friend and I would ride in the cab of the truck and get as many friends as possible to cram into the back under the board and sneak in for free to the movie. We would always tell the person at the drive-in that we had a bunch of guys hiding in the back and the two of us would pay the extra full price for them. But it was worth it to us to make them suffer. We would go over bumps and drive around and let them get all sweaty crowded together. We would laugh and have a great time knowing they thought they were sneaking in for free.

Teenage boys are cruel to each other. I will share more another time.

Old Calvin who doesn't feel old.

*

March 19, 2017

Calvin,

my highschool sweetheart came to visit me today. Well, it was awkward. After catching up about life events, he started to act "you need protection from a strong man" . I felt tiny and weird, retrospectively he is very similar to Lily's dad. Of course.

He said very nice things to me but somehow it didn't feel good. Ok, I think I'm done attracting that type of man. I don't want any more "I will save you" kind of partner. It was a good reminder of how I don't want to feel with someone.

We don't have a drive to the movie theater. In my small town we have a movie theater without walls, but with seats and a roof. But to my knowledge that's about the only one in the country. I loved the story. Wow I am a less honest citizen :D I sneaked in food and drink multiple times in the movies and took buses without having a ticket.

The pipe is not boring. I love to know how things are made. It fascinates me.

You are a funny and creative math teacher. I wrote the most and downgraded it a bit. If I get too excited and exaggerate you won't take the compliment. And I mean it.

I think I'm having a date on Tuesday. My dates usually get canceled so who knows. But he adores me already and is a very kind guy who is not too impressed by himself. He planned everything, booked an apartment, and will come here and cook my favorite dish for me. The communication is easy and good, even about the practical details that need to be discussed.

This noon I'm going to see two high school friends. I have to go and get myself ready now.

Bye Calvin

My first ever boyfriend tried to hug me today and stroke my hands...ughhh. It was very uncomfortable.

Well, that's not like a warm fantasy hug with Calvin.

Elle

*

March 20, 2017

Calvin,

I had an awful day. No reason. Just my head messing with me. Everything seemed to be impossible to overcome.

Lily threw blocks on the screen I was on. I told her it's ok, it's ok to be angry, I understand, I love her, I'll be coming back and hug her. And I smiled. Although I felt dead inside. She is suffering, I can feel it.

I often have this urge now to go back to him. But then I imagine my future and I can't. It's a sad future, not worth living. Maybe spending every day with my child should be worth doing it. But it's not.

I just can't do it. I want to do it for Lily but I can't.

It is awful to be away from her. But when I think about my future I am happy. I see good things coming. I have hope. I feel excited about life.

I was having a writer's block. I didn't write much. I was panicking about how meaningless and uninteresting is what I write. I started again. I am currently writing about my sugar daddy dating experience. It is superficial and shitty. But this is the main thing I think about these days. I just need to have enough going on so that I don't miss Lily. Having emails to write and read and having to try to guess what they want and the sexual frustration and everything. I like to write about it.

I hope I'll manage to make something not so superficial out of it. Something funny, just an easy read. It is a new phenomenon in Hungary, so this topic might actually be interesting for the public. I am just so worried about getting into the "fifty shades of gray kind of book" category. I am terrified of cheesy, shallow... I feel like my writing tends to go that way and I hate it.

Elle

*

March 20, 2017

Elle,

I am sending you a warm fantasy hug.

Remember I have felt a warm fantasy Elle hug too.

I think I can feel it even if it isn't physical. It is comfortable and accepting. Probably the same quality that makes me talk so much and not filter myself when I should, is why I wouldn't stroke your hand but instead just feel comfortable hugging you, and probably just a little longer than most people are comfortable. But I know it would be well accepted.

I had a group of guys I ran around with but it was me and two friends and the others just tagged along. One I always teased was that he looked like Frankenstien's monster, but he always had the newest fashions and haircuts. The girls all liked him. The other guy wasn't as tall as us but he was big. I think he was insecure about his weight and so he was always joking.

We had a dress up day where every student was supposed to dress up as what they wanted to be when they were older. Most people dressed as a doctor or something. My friend came to school wearing sneakers on his feet and a big trench coat. He said when he grew up he wanted to be a flasher, someone who exposed himself to people in public. We were pretty sure he was naked under his coat all day. At a rally in front of the school he opened his coat to the whole school and had on very small purple speedos.

One day at school he opened his locker and it had a bag of flowers set up to drop all over his face and head. He knew only my friend and I had the combination to his locker so it began a series of pranks. Frankenstien had the truck and we filled his closet and all the clothes in it in his room with tiny balloons.

I lived closest to the school and one afternoon I came out and my car battery was stolen. After I walked home I found my battery wrapped up like a present sitting on my bed. Years later we found out he had put the bag of flowers in his own locker so he could blame us and get us to help him prank us as revenge.

I like the way you talk. You see clearly that you are attracted to certain guys and you can decide if you want to be with them or not. I know I haven't dated much in my life but I have gone out with pretty girls other guys liked and half way through the date asked myself, "Why would I want to be with someone like this?" Why did I go out with her?

Are you writing at all? Books, autobiographical stories…

I feel a little bad about some of my magic tricks. I always pretend they fail. Sometimes I pretend they caught me then surprise them. I feel bad because so many students try to console me or encourage me to keep going like they didn't see me mess up.

Sometimes I will have them pick a card and when I keep guessing the wrong card I get frustrated and throw the cards against the wall. Then one of the cards that splattered against the wall sticks to the wall and it was their card. It isn't fair because they all trust me. I'll say,"Is this your coin?" and they will look at me knowing it is not but wanting to lie to help me. I'm worried because their coin I have all set up on a sealed bag inside two sealed boxes that have been in plain sight this whole trick. But I can't reveal my real trick until they think I have failed and they think they saw me put it in my pocket.

Last week I had a little wind up toy I hid in my hand that made sparks. During a boring part of my lecture I dropped my pen on the floor by an electrical outlet. I asked if anyone knew what would happen if I stuck my pen inside the electrical socket. When I pretended to do it I made the sparks go off. It worked and the class woke up and paid attention after that.

Here's another hug

Calvin

*

March 18, 2017

Calvin,

Hi, I'm drunk!

Kiss kiss kiss!

My brain is gonna explode if I don't have sex, I just feel awful all the time and I know it is hormonal. I can feel the imbalance in my brain. Sex always sets back the hormonal balance.
Maybe I should get medication. I am seriously considering it.
My brother is having his birthday party tonight. I was mostly just

working in my room. Good session. A weird dude found me and we were happy to be both weird and different so that felt good.

I went to the lake today, laid down in the grass, watched the cloudless sky and airplanes and reed and water and sang along with my music. Heaven.

Ok I have to concentrate.

Skype. No, not a crutch. Not anymore? Wow, I don't even remember what I said. I wouldn't be looking for you. I know myself, for example I rarely check my emails, because I don't like to see there are none. So I try to only check once a day, when I am sure to find something. I know now about when you write so I avoid the disappointment, clever right? I wouldn't be checking if you are online. I didn't even remember the skype name you gave to me.

I thought it would be more of an appointment kind of thing, like we agree on when to have a "skype private" and would only go on skype then. Skype takes up a lot of speed or something from the pc, so I never keep it running. Plus I am clever so I would avoid checking it continuously for my own benefit.

Huh, my brain is kinda working.

Romantic things, close up smile? I actually do expect you to break the rules. Obviously. Rules are just bullshit, it's just a way to say "I really want that but I will act like I don't because I'm cool and detached".

Hahaaa. That's not obvious. "Avoid this" rules mean, this is what I want but don't dare to admit.

I won't pine away! I love you because it feels good, it feels healthy, it feels easy. Not loving you is really hard, keeping everything in check is painful and exhausting.

Ugh, lots of love.... hum I don't mean heavy just normal love, like caring and liking and connection.

I am concerned about being enough for you and you not going out and missing out on things.

I know myself, I know you won't be enough for me. I need physical contact, I need sex, real life sex, I need holding hands and rediscover kissing. And I know I will still go out and try to look for it and hope I find it. So as horrible as this sounds, for me you can only be a plus, something positive, someone who raises my standards and teaches me how to love and be loved and makes me feel real feelings and it is a life experience that I really enjoy.

You deleted emails???? Aww... I am pretty sure I am projecting now. And imagining the content and it's nothing like that.

I am not average? I know, right, I feel all the progress.

Your jokes are very bad but your improvised funniness based on ongoing conversation is epic.

Thank you. I know, I know I do often put you on a piedestal and you probably don't dare to mention a lot of your flaws and thoughts to not destroy that image. But, Calvin... what I see is you , it's just that I look at you from a flattering angle, by choice. Everyone deserves to be looked at from a flattering angle. I don't care how little facts I base my opinion of you on. Whatever you wrote to me is something that came from your brain and you worded it so it exists somewhere in you.

Maybe I will never have the chance to experience how to see you being at your worst and regretting the words you pronounce or your acts. I wish I'd have the chance to do so and learn to accept and forgive. But maybe that's something you are not supposed to teach me. I can already be very very grateful for everything I discovered with you and could practice on you.

Thanks.

Kiss

Elle

*

March 21, 2017

Elle,

Somehow I didn't read this one before.
I like you. You have a way of saying things very honestly but still making me smile and feel good about myself and about us.

I took some pictures before it rained. I will send them next time.

I understand and don't mind checking my inbox and it being empty but I also enjoy having you write. I sometimes write at different times. When I write late at night it is bad and good. I have no filter and I enjoy reliving my day or week and you make me feel better and it helps to get it all out and sleep softer.

But also I am tired and don't type well or always filter what might not be said right or what is better not said. I do feel comfortable with you. Also when I sit down to type I sometimes am just too tired and go to bed.

Better for you if I write in the afternoon. I seem to be busy in the afternoon.

Can I give you a look for being drunk?

So the rule is no sexy video and break the rule. Gotcha.

Calvin

Attached: daffodils, Calvin with dogs.

*

March 21, 2017

Calvin,

How did you miss this??

What do you think? The "you shouldn't be drunk" rule? My brother offered to make me a drink and put a bit too much vodka in my vodka orange. I sipped in it and got instantly drunk.

I wonder what that look looks like on your face.

I like you too. You probably got that from the drunk email, but just in case you think only drunk me likes you. I'm sober now and I like you very much.

Wish me luck, I'm going on my date. I'll tell you about it when I get back.

Sleep well Calvin!

Elle

*

March 21, 2017

Calvin,

I am back home. They say the first sex after divorce (I consider myself as divorced) is kind of like loosing your virginity again. Well, I got lucky again. It was a good first sex experience.

The guy warned me that he looks like Winnie The Pooh. He does.

But he is also as adorable as Winnie The Pooh. He called me "my little fairy". I thought that was cute, I always wanted to be one.

He spoiled me from the beginning and treated me with so much respect. He drove 2 hours to come here, picked me up and had a place booked for us. He gave me the money right away, which is so much better than at the end, which could have been awkward or humiliating. He put it in a nicely wrapped chocolate and handed it to me like that. How cute is that!

Honestly I wouldn't mind getting money in my bra or panties either. That would be funny and kind of exciting. But I liked how careful he was to show his respect.

The sex came kind of naturally. I was more than ready to get some action, finally. He was extremely well prepared for everything in terms of safety and hygiene.

I was my usual self in bed, he really made me feel like a desirable woman so that helped too. Let's face it, I was pretty good. I felt attracted to his personality, the way he spoke about his childhood and divorce I could see how kind he is. Sometimes he reminds me of you, when he says something. It's just that he wasn't funny, didn't have the confidence you have, or your body. Wow, your body. I mean I am not reproaching him to not be bigger and stronger. But all he had was kindness. It's not bad but how many men would I need to replace the greatness of Calvin? Shut up Elle. I know you will comment on this and make me regret that I opened my mouth.

He made my favorite dish, krumplis tészta, turned out awful but we joked about it, so I think he wasn't too disappointed or ashamed. I hope so.

We had one more hour. So we cuddled. Of course I was still horny so somehow I ended up cuming again. I pleased him. He was very pleased.

It was more than sex, he was all about cuddling and touching and stroking. Wow, thank god I left my husband, I can't believe I was going to miss out on this!

Ok, I am relieved, kind men exist. You know what? He wasn't as good as my husband. Or maybe he was, but he wasn't that equipped... I don't know. But it was way way better. He was gentle and enthusiastic and giving. I felt loved and adored and worshiped. I felt like a woman.

He is my lover now. Once a week. I like the steadiness of it. I like that I get my dose every week...wow. I just realized I sound like a drug addict. Now I am a little bit worried.

I was actually a little bit scared of how good I felt mentally afterward. I felt good. This is exactly what I wanted. Sex and tenderness. I could get used to this.

Anyways, I guess I have things to discuss with the psychologist tomorrow...

My sister wants to live with me. We agreed on always helping out each other financially and emotionally. She is a wonderful support and we accept each other's sex addictions. I am still sleeping with her. We chat every night. Yesterday she heard me crying in the bathroom and came to hug me and told me it's all awful now but things will get better and everything will seem easier another day, it is just a bad day. How perfectly worded that is!!!

I like that we agreed that the wealthiest will help the other one, now that we both are just doing ok financially. So it's not like one of us needs the other one's help right now. We actually have no idea who will need it first.

Elle

*

March 22, 2017

Elle,

I will write more later, just thought I'd send a couple pictures.

The daffodils are blooming and actually almost done. Rain is coming all week so we'll see.

A tree I climbed. just because I was outside and felt like doing something.
A recent picture of me and the dog I sat on. The same dog I used to go hiking with me but now we are both fatter.
My donkeys.
The waterfall with water in it.

hug

Calvin who can hug you and not make you mad.

*

March 22, 2017

Hum.... you sound like you already read this but I just wrote it and kept it as a draft to send later, so it's strange. I didn't change a word, read it.

Calvin,

Thank you!!!

I forgot to say, you made me smile with your magic tricks. You are too perfect to be true... You are the weirdest guy I've ever met. And that's the best compliment from me.

We have daffodils in our garden too!! And violets. Your grass is amazing.

I prefer you fatter, the way you look now. I am not sure I'd be into young Calvin. You can get more and more fat. I don't care, I'll love every bit of it. I'd love to say we can get old and fat and happy together. But I have my mom's body type and habits, I will probably just get skinnier and be self conscious about that. Now I'm skinny so I'm in luck but I really enjoy the beauty of rounder body types.

I enjoy watching artistic nudes of all kinds. I couldn't choose between one that shows a rounder body and one that shows a skinny one. It's just beauty in different forms. Impossible to compare, because they are so different, yet so amazingly done at the same time. It is not that difficult to step out from the usual conception and look at things from a different angle. Like in your book. Your life philosophy must be similar to this, right?

I can't remember if I was always thinking like this. I see beauty when I look at you. And not "just" because your lovely personality shines through, but also because I love your beautiful brown smiley eyes with that deepness and even at a first glance your eyes tell that there is something deep behind the joking smiley attitude.

People like you overcame unbearable things and chose happiness. I somehow feel attracted to this kind of "saying yes to life, and being stubborn and hoping even if there is no rational reason" kind of happy, when I see it in somebody's eyes. That's just my type of man I guess.

I love your thin, kissable lips, I can almost feel them on mine and how your beard would scratch on my skin. Ahhh... I love your nose, your face is really harmonious, it's pleasant to look at because the proportions are great. You have a friendly face. There must be some science behind this. Ah, yeah the golden ratio. Your neck makes me want to give you a massage.

I'm missing your body, I didn't see it in a while.

Oh damn, your pictures are dangerous!

Elle

*

March 22, 2017

Elle,

I am glad you are getting out. Here it is sunny part of the day and raining hard the rest. I am trying to get out and walk or just enjoy some sunshine. Life feels pretty good and even with the problems with electrical and such I don't feel stress or deadlines. There is nothing really all that wrong and once I find where the feedback is coming from I think I just have to tighten a connection and solve the problem. Sometimes I imagine a problem and forget that it really isn't a problem I can't live with and it's also a problem I can fix.

I am getting some perspective because unfortunately I have some friends dealing with real problems. It gives me perspective.

I have mentioned a family. I worked on his house and his sister's place. I stayed with him. Well this weekend his cheek went numb. They think it might be palsy or something that will go away. I talked to him and he says he thinks his mouth droops a little in the corner but it's not like his whole face is drooping on one side. The scary part is his father had a massive stroke at around this age. So he is scared he might be going to have something like his dad had and not be able to move.

Another friend is really doing good. I hate the word cancer and she was scared because her hand swelled and they found a lump in her shoulder by her lymph node. But they put in a pump to give her chemotherapy and the cancer is just a very small lump. It hasn't spread and the chemo will kill anything that is too small to see. Worst case scenario is they have to cut out a very small pea sized chunk. Best case is the chemo kills everything and she is fine in a few weeks. These things put life in perspective.

My life is pretty good. So there's. It could be so much worse.

Ok not much to say, I am just sharing my feelings. I am feeling very blessed tonight.
How are you? How will you be in a year? I have no doubt you will be getting better every month and more comfortable in your new life and more confident. By a year from now life will be so much better. And your life is pretty good right now.

I could use a neck massage though...

Happy Calvin

Do you still have an awesome body? Hint

Attached: Calvin climbing a tree.

*

March 23, 2017

Calvin,

Warning: overly excited Elle from seeing your close up smile.

Thank you for the flowers!! I love yellow, my favorite color.

How am I doing? I feel good. I feel better than ever. The following will make no sense but I'll explain.

I got my test results at the psy. I am severely depressed. Extremely anxious. At the maximum at perfectionism and at compulsion to conform. Strangely I am not desperate for love and attention it's the opposite actually, on a scale from -10 to +10 I am -2. It means I don't accept or even want love as much as "normal" people do. The rest was in a normal spectrum.

The results don't really change anything. I am the same. It is just a comparison of myself to the norm. I felt so happy hearing the results and finding out that the way I feel and perceive the world is considered as severely depressed. It tells me that the average human has it so much better. It is so amazing to imagine how better it can get for me. I didn't think I was depressed because I felt worse than before. I am convinced that I experience things with increasing comfort and happiness. My childhood felt really dark and it always got just a little bit better. Middle school felt better. Traveling was even better. University was even better. Founding a family was even better. I wasn't aware of still being in hell, because I wasn't that deep in it.

There is something I love about my life. Progression. It is getting better and since I come from so far away it feels like a huge difference. Every tiny step feels like a major improvement in my life. Because it is something new and unexpected I couldn't imagine existed. And enjoying it gives me a feeling of gratitude. I think I constantly feel lucky. Yes, that's it. I think I repeat myself multiple times on a daily basis "I am so lucky!" I just grew up expecting the worst so I am easily impressed by life.

I got close up smiling pictures from Calvin. I am sexually satisfied. I enjoy the distraction Hungarian men supply me with so that I can think about how to flirt back and whom to go on a date with instead of worrying about things I am doing my best at and cannot do more, like the situation with Lily.

There is this guy I went on a date with, you know the one who took me to the expensive restaurant. I cannot get him out of my mind. I am wise enough to understand it's because we felt sexually attracted to eachother but nothing happened. That's like the best way to create lust. Especially if you meet the guy again and get a chance to do it but still nothing happens. That happened to me once (I was about 18). I couldn't forget about him until we finally did it. Then I was over him.

We didn't meet again with this one but I got so confused because he was clear about wanting to and just kept promising to call and set a date and disappear. He called me one night and explained everything. I thought I would fall off my bed. I couldn't believe it.

He lied a bit about his situation. He is on and off with his girlfriend...who is Borderline. That was the point where I started to not like him and be scared of him. Because in my mind he instantly became the same as my ex, someone who attracts girls like me. Ughhh.

We spoke for an hour and I trusted him somehow. His girlfriend is playing the suicide card, therefore leaving him is a tricky situation. That made me feel good about myself and me being borderline. That's something I don't do. I am extremely cautious to even mention that subject because I am so scared of manipulation. It made me realize, again, that I am more than a borderline. Not all the borderlines are the same. Also it seems like not all of them are sex maniac like me.

We spoke honestly about our recent past, me too. I could open up about my worries. He told me being lovers could be a good idea, because he has experience with borderline. That reassured me and made me remember that he cared enough to go to therapy to handle things better. My ex would never do that.

I am still concerned about him disappearing. He said he wouldn't but I am waiting for him to prove it. It was 1 a.m. and he really wanted to drive to come and have sex. I turned him down saying he has to be the one who contacts me (I wrote him something about being confused, and only then he offered to call me and explain everything) and that he'd better come back to me offering something not at the last minute.

I had the feeling that he mistook sexual attraction for love. He seemed confused so I explained him that from what he says to me and how he treats me, it is evident that it's sexual attraction. I think he was relieved. It's funny how people in a relationship get confused when they feel lust toward a stranger and feel all guilty and think they are in trouble. So I reassured him that it has nothing to do with his relationship that he should give himself time to sort out.

We keep flirting, it's nice. I feel like he is in my life on purpose. The initial mistrust and inability to communicate is gone. I feel more comfortable communicating with him and being myself. Things that I couldn't do because trying to impress him I blocked everything I wanted to say. So, it's good. He is less of a stranger to me and that initial magic that made me forget to breathe around him is gone.

It must also be due to the fact that he sent me a dick pick and a video that night. I thought that was a bit inappropriate so early. Anyways. He kind of makes me think about how I should just have kept Lily's dad as a lover instead of a boyfriend and husband. He would have been OK as a lover. This one is promising because he seems as open minded and wild as my ex but maybe more caring and ready to reflect on himself. I don't know. I want to figure it out.

Life is good. I'm having fun. And according to the psychologistI im so low right now that I will be very very happy in the near future because every little step will feel like a huge improvement. Sounds good.

Yesterday at yoga I could relax, it was working. The psychologist taught me a technique, it's getting my body as tense as I can, everywhere and holding it as long as I can. After this I can actually numb myself enough to relax. So today whenever I felt upset during yoga I stopped doing the exercises and did this.

Elle

*

March 23, 2017

Elle,

You complimented me because I am weird. I am going to prove it and you know I am telling the truth. My favorite part of your demonstration video was.... the end when you didn't know what to say but in not saying anything you said everything you didn't say. I know that's a weird thing for me to say, but I also know you get that I enjoyed that part. Compliment me on my penis and what it would feel like then.... awkward silence!

I loved it.

I am getting more comfortable with your hyperbola. I hope you can accept my compliments also. I know you mean them even if they seem like compliments someone else would just say to be kind. I know you mean them and hope you accept that I mean my compliments also.

I have a friend, she was like a sister to me growing up, but she did me wrong and we haven't been close since. She didn't do anything very wrong, she just asked me to do a lot for her and her family, expecting me to take care of everything when she was in trouble and when I was in trouble she disappeared. I see what type of person she is now. She has kids and I don't blame her for focusing on them and trying to do all she can for them.

I just felt used and like I was just someone there when she needed something but didn't exist when I wasn't useful to her. I mention this because she might be coming out to California for the summer. I love her kids but I don't really feel like doing a lot for her and I know she expects it.

I will tell you more and complain about it more if it happens. I am trying to not get upset and waste time worrying about things that might never happen. I like information and trying to logically solve what the best solution is. But when you write a mathematical proof you always state the variables. You can't solve the problem without knowing the facts.

On an aside, when I was in college I had a study group. Even the geniuses wanted to be in my study group because we were such a good group. But to remember to introduce our variable to start a proof and help memorize our proofs we would tell them as a joke.

"Epsilon the Real walks into a bar greater than zero, For all women named Delta from the naturals who are greater than zero but less than Epsilon there exists a Limit to the number of drinks. If the bartender x is an element of the zeta function...."

I am not going to use any energy thinking about what might happen until I have all the information and know what I am dealing with and what all the variables are.

I sometimes wonder how I am seen by others. I have had people check me out. Clerks and just random people, men and women, married and single, compliment my smile and say I am friendly.

You know how I like to talk and I do think I take people as they come. If you are homeless or a millionaire, I'm interested in you the same. I know good people who are pretty rich, some who are pretty famous, some with political power, some with very little, some with poor health. some old some young some shunned by others some who have been to jail some who are preachers. I think I just talk to people who seem friendly or want to talk.

You mentioned the guy on the train you talked to. I think I see my life as very blessed. I don't regret my life and I wouldn't avoid the good to escape reliving the pain. But I have had people tell me they see my pain. They know I am hiding my suffering. I don't feel that is me. But I can't see myself through other's eyes.

I will try to give you a description of Elle through my eyes. No, not just how I like the way your nipples stick out and your ass in pantyhose. I mean the you I see. That will have to wait. Sleepy time.

Sleepy Calvin

*

March 24, 2017

Calvin

,
I am dreaming about your chest… falling asleep on it.... I am so tired. I would probably feel instantly awake as my body touches yours... Shut up Elle and go to sleep.

The blowjob demonstration was so embarrassing to film I couldn't even watch it back, just sent it without checking. I hope I'll never have to see my sucking face.

I feel bad. No, I'm probably just tired. Or maybe it's because my child said to me today "I am Lily "family name"... mom is not "family name". Ouch. That hurt. Her dad is swearing he didn't tell her to say that. Maybe.

I don't know why it hurts so much. I just feel like it is so unfair. I wanted to stay or take her with me but he put pressure on me to not to. I guess I feel guilty that I was too weak and broke under his pressure and left my daughter behind to save myself.

I am so cold. The heating is off because it's warmer outside but not warm enough for me to not be freezing. I am so cold.

Tomorrow I am going to visit my grandparents, my cousins will be there too. I have to explain things to my aunt and then I am done.

The guy I slept with, we will call him my lover...so my lover keeps sending me good morning and good night messages. So cute. He just sent me one saying "I am going to sleep now. Good night and sweet dreams! Your Winnie The Pooh". He wrote me a nice feedback email too.

I just can't believe my luck. This is exactly what I wanted to experience. Somehow I always get what I want.

Life is good.

The other one doesn't text me back , of course. It made me think about that funny picture I saw on facebook one day. Titled "when you are waiting for him to text back", written on the picture "If I send you a text message you are supposed to answer within an hour, otherwise I would have sent af...ing pigeon!" Hahaaa. I wish I would already be over with this crush. It is so ridiculously meaningless. All I am getting out of it is frustration and distraction. Ahh, I take it. I would take anything to keep my mind busy.

kiss

Elle

*

March 24, 2017

Elle,

Technically those are stockings. Pantyhose cover your ass also but thank you. I am sorry you are cold and I am not there to snuggle with and keep you warm.. and distract you. You can fall asleep on my chest anytime.

Speaking of your ass. I love what you do. Thank you. You know I don't want a close up and you always let me see your face, even when you orgasm. One of these times though, I can see you have both hands down there but I have never really seen what all you are doing. I also got a little harder when I saw you were wearing those heels.

You are Lily's mom. You are both of Lily's grandmother's granddaughter still.

At that age they repeat words but understand feelings. She knows and I know you love her like no one else. She also senses your attitude about her dad. I think the hardest thing for a kid when their parents split is not having the security of love in the home anymore. Even if it wasn't there strongly before she imagined the perfect marriage.

Now hearing her dad be hateful to her mom feels wrong. Hearing you be soft and kind and caring about him resonates in her. She sees you as the mother and him as making you go. Being mean to you makes her mad at him for taking away what she thought she had.

You are still what she had and misses. He is showing her how things have changed and she doesn't like it. Don't worry about words. Just keep loving her and letting her know how important and loved she is to you.

You said you liked getting a dick picture after the first date?

Ok. I will try to make you a dick video next time. This is just me saying "hello"

Hug and chest to sleep on

Calvin

*

March 24, 2017

Elle,

I forgot something... Pictures of my pipe.. and video.
Have a great day!

Calvin

Attached: video and photos of building the pipes.

*

March 25, 2017

Calvin,

Just a quick message to say I'm doing great.

I enjoy spending time with my mom, cousins, aunt, uncle, and grandparents. Lily's dad suddenly became very nice. It's strange. Yesterday he responded to my text message. Not only did he react to it but he said "oh, that's too late for skype. I'm sorry for you. Say hi to your family from me" Something like this.

I instantly pictured ourselves living all in Hungary happily separated in two different flats, having a nice "business partners" -like relationship. I shouldn't get my hopes up but I was so happy he didn't say anything mean. Today he is still very normal. I am secretly hoping he found peace with this situation, maybe met someone who made him feel good about himself. I am really really hoping it's not because I told him about my diagnosys and he is hoping for me to get better and get back to him.

Are you really climbing trees? Of course, you are!

Your "szia" pronunciation is perfect! You made me laugh, thank you, I couldn't stop laughing. I saw them so many times and it still is so funny. You seem more relaxed, more comfortable talking to me. I like it. You are so much fun. You make me go from happy laughing to surprised horny.

Thanks for your words about Lily, it helped.

You did a good job with the pipe. I mean I have no idea how to do it. But the result is very pretty, to my ignorant eyes that's the only thing that matters. It looks good.

Your penis is the best. I've seen some... :D but nothing like yours. Wow. Elle shut up.

FMNC

Elle

*

March 26, 2017

Calvin,

I hope everything is ok for you. How are you? Busy?

My mood is in the extremes. I felt down yesterday, although we played board games with the family and it was really nice. It is painful not having Lily here with me. I can almost feel her and see her. I miss waking up to her voice and cuddling her while she slowly wakes up, watching her run around and make a mess. I am so fed up hugging the air and kissing the camera. She is standing there watching the screen, looking so lost and sad and shy. 3 more weeks.

I love being in Hungary, I love to play with my family and chat about boys with my cousins, and be best friends with my sister. I am very grateful for the dates and messages.

But everything feels wrong. I could do all that with her being here. The days are going by so slowly. I only have stuff to do for a few hours that I could easily get done while she'd be asleep. I miss her so much. The only thing that keeps me going is that I know she is healthy and taken care of and hugged and kissed and I know when exactly I can hug and kiss her. I miss tickling her. Hearing her giggling would make my day.

I sleep with my younger cousin, she loves to hug and kiss and cuddle. It feels nice but is extremely painful at the same time. Those early mornings when I took Lily with me on the couch and we fell asleep in each other's arms were the best.

It is so hard to eat without her and go out without her. There is no point doing things just by myself.

My family is very caring and they don't mention her, it helps but I still see her everywhere.

My uncle is 9 years older than my aunt. He was his math teacher at university. They are cute. My grandparents are cute. We celebrated a bunch of wedding anniversaries and birthdays this weekend.

I am so happy and unhappy at the same time.

The disappearing guy reappeared and invited me to a date for Tuesday. Crap. It makes me feel loved and wanted. I wish my self esteem could realize that I was just as lovable an hour ago when I didn't see his message yet.

I filled out a 600 questions test for the psy. It was very interesting. It made me realize that I have many many physical symptoms I wasn't aware of. I am dizzy all the time, I 'm nauseous, I have no appetite at all, I have headaches almost constantly, I feel weak. My heart beats very fast sometimes and sometimes I cannot swallow. Or my breathing gets difficult. I pee way too much but drink too little. I sleep badly.

I'm curious what all this means. I felt like the questions were looking for schizophrenia and paranoia and aggressivity too.

My older cousin is 16 and she is dating a 28 years old guy. I liked chatting with her about love.

Ok, I have to go and cook myself something vegan, I miss being excited about eating.

KMNC
Kiss me Now Calvin.

Elle

*

March 26, 2017

Elle,

KMNE

I don't know if this will help but I had someone tell me something comforting. You miss Lily and it hurts and affects your whole life. But that is reassuring.

Someone said they thought my wife and I had the perfect love affair and we were so in love. If I had gotten over it quickly and gone on with my life like nothing had changed they would have doubted what they believed. For them it was a little bit of a comfort for my pain to reinforce their thoughts about how much I love her.

Maybe Lily hears that you love her and you try to love her, but now she knows and you have no doubts how important you have made her in your heart and your love is undeniable. Not just that you love her, but how deeply and how much a part of you loves her is.

Nice for you to be assured you are a good mom but good for her to know she is loved. People love candy and flowers and seeing Santa. But it doesn't hurt like this unless you miss them this much and love them on a different plane than the way you love others.

Ok. I will write to you later tonight.

I am good, went out with friends for lunch, then again with family for dinner. I ate way too much yesterday. I just want to sleep but I have things to do. I had 3 cousins and my uncle met me for lunch with another family but we went to a restaurant and they put us at 2 separate tables.

I really like two of my cousins but didn't get to talk to them much because they were at the other table. It kind of felt like we both went to all that trouble and didn't get to see each other. But we know we tried and love each other. Family is precious.

Easter break is coming soon but I might be watching my friend's 4 daughters a couple nights. Actually a break from what I am doing is nice even if it physically wears me out.

Kiss

Calvin

*

March 27, 2017

Elle,

Not much news about my life. I am doing well. Mom is healthy but someday I need to encourage her to write a trust. I guess everything goes through the courts if it is a legal document like a will but a trust just gives me title and is only a problem if someone challenges it. Mom doesn't have much but what she has I don't want to worry about. My dad's old car was in his name and I couldn't do much because I had to get it into her name first. I found out instead of putting everything in both their names if he would have spent $50 and made a trust it would have made my life easier. I hate bringing up the idea that I think she is going to die soon and I want all her money. She will understand and he is the one who brought it up before, a couple times. The stuff she and dad wanted to leave for me she wants to make sure I get. I just hate to bring it up. awkward.

As I say, nothing she has is worth upsetting her. I just want to honor their wishes. There are also some tax issues. If we put her house in my name the taxes go up. If it transfers in a trust it goes up a little. If I inherit the house the property taxes go up $600 a month. They have a law here that they can't just keep raising taxes because the value of houses goes up. But once you sell the house they tax it for what it is worth. If I inherit it they treat it like I bought it.

So what did you say to the 16 year old dating the older guy?

Ok here is something; You always give me good advice. Even more importantly, I think your advice is true to yourself. You give advice you truly think is best. I know it is hard to give yourself advice because you know what you want and in this moment you know why you are doing what you are doing. Your advice is based on decisions and motives you are living.

I wonder if you could give yourself advice like you would that 16 year old. Not judgemental or puritan, but honest advice for what you think is best and right. I wonder what advice you would give if you could write yourself at 16. If you had a magic mailbox you could send letters through time with, (I know this is not original with me) what advice would you give yourself years ago, and what advice do you think your future self would give you now. I suspect it would be to keep living. Don't change. You are glad you have Lily even if it was a lot of hardship that came with it.

Maybe you wouldn't change your past. Maybe you would just encourage yourself. Tell yourself you survive and are stronger and happy in the future. I think you are doing good. I hope my future self would look back on today and smile and be proud of these years.

boring Calvin

*

March 29, 2017

Elle,

I played junior detective today. There was a children's book series called, "Encyclopedia Brown". It was about a kid who would solve crimes like who stole the pencil from the school, or who put the frog in the teacher's desk. Today I was able to put into practice my skills of solving those riddles.

My friend called me at lunch time. She has two locks on her front door. One has a door knob and you can turn the latch on the knob while inside and just close the door and it will be locked. The other lock is a dead bolt and you must close the door first then you can turn the knob inside to lock it or use a key to lock it. She seldom locks her deadbolt lock and this morning she remembered having her daughter just close the door. Since her daughter doesn't have a key to the door she was expecting only the door knob to be locked. When she came home at lunch because she had forgotten to feed her cat she found the dead bolt locked also. She was afraid someone had broken in but nothing was stolen or moved she could see.

No one was hiding inside. Then she realized that the bar was in the other door so the only way they could have left was out that front door, and they would have needed a key to lock the deadbolt. She called me because I am one of the few people who have a key to her house and the only solution she could think of was someone with a key had come over. Can you solve the mystery?

I did. Her cat likes to play with the door knob and make it turn because it makes noise. He also has learned to scratch at the knob of the deadbolt and now can lock the door from the inside. Her cat had locked the door. Later she saw him trying to do it again.

I hope you are staying busy and having fun. You can be distracted because you are deep and you know being distracted from your deep thoughts does not make them go away. You are solving your problems and making life better and better. I don't mind you safely allowing yourself to forget and relax and be distracted, because I know you are not running away from them, just taking a break.

Some people do drugs or party or adrenaline acts or even work out to ignore their problems but they don't think the problem will still be there when they sober up. You just need and deserve a break.

Life is good but a bit overwhelming when you study it as deeply as you do. I am not your doctor but you don't sound depressed to me, you sound like you have some depressing things happening right now, but you are excited that they are getting better.

Sorry I can't do anything to help you with your horniness. I would enjoy it.

Happy Calvin

*

March 29, 2017

Calvin,

I couldn't solve the mystery! Good job!

It was ... weird chatting with you this morning.

I biked to the next town and bought a smartphone. I was the one who never wanted one, the living proof that life is possible without it. Well, it is possible but it became really frustrating and difficult. I don't like it yet. It doesn't feel like mine. It's pretty but I have no idea how to use it. Anyways, I was proud of myself. I was well prepared when I arrived at the shop, I studied their website, it's really complicated. When I got there I knew what I needed and actually could explain it better than the guy who worked there. I got the internet cable thing. I'll test it tomorrow. Phone with a package that fits my needs the best.

I'm happy with myself. It was a big deal for me. I hate spending money so if I do I research and sleep on it and think about it like a million times before taking the decision. I felt like a responsible adult. It also represents a lot for me. The contract is for two years. Meaning I just signed a Hungarian phone and internet contract for two years. This is how much I want to stay in this country. It looks like I have already made my decision.

I went there with my sister. She had her birthday today, 24. I invited her for lunch and we went to yoga together and then the whole family and some other random young people went to a bar to drink. I felt uncomfortable, had a vodka orange and went super drunk. I am still struggling with it. I don't feel well.

My private show was great. You turned me on so much, I didn't need anything. He didn't talk much and the things he said were sweet and I basically had a nice Calvin fantasy sex. I cum four times. And it was absolutely crazy. I like when you have a request, I am happy to do that on camera for you. Next time I will be horny. That private show was enough for today.

I feel like I should shut up because if I say something negative about this morning you won't come to chat anymore and that will make me sad. But you like when I am being honest with you. Chatting with you this morning upset me.

I was happy, tearing up happy when I read this:

"Tell your past self not to ignore the funny math guy who will talk to you at work. Tell your past self the "cowboy enigma" is him trying to give you his email address and not to give up. He is not that clever. But he cares about you very much and you are going to make his life much better for many years. Thank you for the happiness you have brought to my life"

But today's chat was just a lot and very intense. I am not in a good state of mind to start to analyze what and why I feel and think about it.

I am angry tonight and I started to type why but it's so stupide.

You know what, this has to wait. I am feeling too drunk. I regret that vodka enormously. God, I hate to be drunk. I cannot think.

I am going to the psychologist and then to Budapest tomorrow. I have a "date", I am spending the whole night in a hotel, dinner, night and breakfast. He seems to be fine, I'll tell you more about it afterward.

I miss you

Elle

*

March 31, 2017

Elle,

I hope you enjoyed your date and were safe. Let me know you are still alive.

Wednesday was sunny and so after work I tried to get in a couple hours of work. I cut brush and grass. I wore myself out and afterwards I was tired and aching. I had to stop a couple times because I got so tired. Also because it rained so much and is now sunny all the trees and everything are blooming. Wednesday night it rained. I don't know what happened but I got really sick. I had a fever and my throat hurt. I had a headache and was sore all over. I also was coughing up phlegm.

Thursday morning I still felt bad but I felt better than at night and it was late to cancel classes so I went. I felt worse and wished I had canceled classes. I had trouble speaking. Yes, I'm having trouble speaking!! It was very windy and maybe this is just allergies. I went to sleep as soon as I got home and I am feeling much better now. I am still a little hot and I will take medicine if needed. I am glad it is almost the weekend.

I hope you are well. it is pretty at your place. I am going to bed now. Wish you were here to keep me warm and take care of me.

Calvin

Magic trick another day.

*

March 31, 2017

Calvin,

I'd love to take care of you. Wow that sounds dirty :P I'd also love to get medicine for you and bring it in your room with a cup of tea, orange juice... and candy. And wrap you in the blanket. And reassure you somehow like this " Don't worry, even the worst sickness gets better after 7 days. Unless it's fatal...like getting a cold"

You made me laugh with the "yes me trouble speaking!!" :D Lol.

Yeah, definitely don't do magic tricks if you feel bad. Even at your best you are dangerous with them. :P

I survived my date.

I started the day at the psy. We discussed how I don't feel absolutely anything since last time. She told me it's probably because a week ago Lily was playing with figurines while we were on skype.

The figurines had a discussion:

-You should go to sleep. It's time.
-No I don't want to!
-But you have to!
-No, I can't, mom left...

I feel dead since.

I am going out a lot, I am constantly surrounded by people. I still don't feel anything but it helps keep my mind busy. I hurt less. It's weird. I know what I am supposed to feel but there is only a void.

I had some time before my date and I sat down in a bookshop. And cried. I have no idea how to handle this emotionally. Until now I could reassure myself that maybe she is not really missing me, she had her dad, maybe he is right and they don't need or miss me at all. I still wanted to get back into her life but that thought,as horrible as it felt for me, reassured me somewhat that she might not suffer that much.

The date was interesting. I liked that we got normal food. Not pretentious little bites but normal food for hungry people. I got a pizza.

He was a better kisser than the other one. He was very good at teasing; stroking and kisses and whispering stuff. When we entered the room I thought we would just drop our stuff and change. But he kind of just threw me on the bed. I was like "Ok, well then I guess we will have sex right away" But he didn't let me do anything in the room, than took me to the jacuzzi so I had to hold myself back for hours. Of course by the time I was allowed to be in charge I was electric. ;) The sex itself was lame. I felt like it was thanks to me if we had any pleasure. He was quite bad. He seemed to not notice but I know how I usually am and I wasn't enjoying it as much as I could. I still enjoyed because it is still so much more and better than sex with myself.

I had a little problem with my body being exhausted from yesterday's private and biking and yoga and drink. I thought I would get sick, I had similar symptoms to yours but fortunately no fever and I ended up not getting sick. I caught it on time so lemon juice and lots of water and candy was enough for me not to get sick. It seems like you are already deep in it. I really regret not being there.
So..I had a hard time to cum hard, the "closed eyes, repeating FMNC" (FuckMe Now Calvin) trick helped me though and he never saw me cum before so he had no idea it's much spectacular usually. I was very happy with my performance, I pushed my body so hard these last 2 days, I will give it a break now before it breaks.

He was the kind of guy I've never met before. The cumming and getting hard again...and again...and again kind of. God, it was exhausting. He let me sleep 3 hours, but before and after he used me as much as he could. And since he wasn't the most sportive guy ever, I did all the work. I think I left past 11. My body needs to rest.

He was very gentle with me. I didn't have to speak about my past at all. He spoke quite a lot and didn't really let me place a word, but I was glad with that.

Weirdly enough he found it out anyway. He asked me several times if everything is ok, because he said I looked like a frightened animal, so he wanted to check. He asked me why I was shaking when he touched me. I didn't explain but he found out by himself. I let him think it was physical abuse. I didn't want to speak about it. He said it's ok, he just has to get used to it.

Not the sex but the rest was really nice, very addictive. Somehow I felt like I was healing while he was just enjoying stroking my cheeks and lips... I discovered probably all of my body is an erogenous zone, all of it. It was fun. I couldn't have imagined something like this before. He was very playful. I thought " wow, so what Calvin spoke about is something like this" I cannot even imagine how crazy it could get if you actually like your "playmate".

Sleeping with him was what I was the most excited about beforehand. But I ended up not liking it. It didn't feel comfortable. It just made me miss you more. I would have even preferred to sleep with my sister instead. Or even alone. That was definitely too intimate to do with a stranger.

The psychologist was worried that I am not worried about my safety at all. I can't help myself. I just can't bother to worry about being raped or hurt. I feel like I wouldn't care.

God, this sounds horrible. I thought I am not having unsafe sex since there is always condoms involved but I do realize now that meeting a stranger might count as unsafe.

Everything is blooming here too.

Can I do something for you, to make you feel better? Let me know! ;)

Wait, are you working today? I hope you canceled your classes

Question: What name would you choose for yourself if you couldn't be called? It's kind of needed for my project... I was thinking of Theodore or Matthew. Would you like something else?

How to formulate this without making you freak out. Let's suppose, hypothetically, one day I'd take you on a date, like in a year or two. Would you let me?

kiss

Elle

keeping you warm from far away

*

April 1, 2017

Elle,

I woke up feeling better so I went to work. I was fine, just tired after. I took a nap when I got home. I am about 65%.

I love the idea of having someone care for me and bring me vegetable soup and juice. But honestly you would just watch me sleep. It is nice to wake up and have someone watching you and caring. I am fine and going out to a birthday party Sunday night. I just need rest and lots of water. I didn't know chocolate helped.

You are reminding me of when I went through this feeling of loss. I didn't want to but you are doing the right thing by going out in public and staying busy. My friends made me. It is good for you. Talk to people, feel a part of something again, recognize you can be distracted and smile and it is ok. I also get a numb feeling. "Void, Feeling nothing". Maybe because you felt hurt. I don't know, I just completely get it. I am good at logic not emotions. I don't understand it to this day. But I didn't lay in bed and cry or feel sad, but remembering happy thoughts or reading a sweet story or video and I would cry at the drop of a hat.

I cry at movies easily. But movies like Rocky, or anything and I would notice myself crying. I get mad when my emotions don't make sense. I just am trying to accept that emotions are not logical and can't always be turned on and off. It is ok to have fun.

You already recognized what you said, but Calvin says "Bad girl!" Don't get raped or hurt. Be safe. I won't get mad because you recognize that is wrong stinking thinking. You matter. If you are hurt I am hurt. Don't hurt me by getting hurt or raped. Please.

I will think of a good name for myself. Are we talking about my visit to Hungary? I guess I like the idea of being in control. I know you aren't going to just show up at my front door and say "Surprise!!" That would not elicit a good response. The idea of meeting somewhere other than my house, my bedroom, my bed just would be much more comfortable.

That's a compliment. If I just wanted to cum it wouldn't be as big a thing. I am uncomfortable because of my feelings for you. I guess in two years IF I decided I wanted to go out on a date with you. AND IF I came to Hungary or France or wherever, AND IF I felt it was a vacation and not us trying to start a relationship...Then maybe we should discuss it in two years and let me answer then.

I am not ready now.

I'd like a mysterious name. Something not ordinary. Jonas Salk saved millions of lives by discovering a vaccine for Polio. Almost everyone knew someone with Polio before him. I don't like the name Jonas. I love etymology. The meaning of names and words and where they come from.

Adva means "small ripple or wave on still water". Eyal means "Might or strong".

Elle is Scandinavian for "bright one" or "shining one".. It is from the Greek "Helios" meaning sun. You are bright and stand out.

Keeping me warm. Thank you. be safe. You never commented on why my visiting you at LiveJasmin was overwhelming and upset you. I understand that might be on purpose and I don't need to know. I just don't want to cause you discomfort.

Big long soft warm hug. holding you.

Calvin

*

April 1, 2017

Calvin,

I'm glad you are feeling better! 65% sounds bad though.. I remember you mentioned that it feels more lonely to be alone in that house when you are ill. I don't like that you are alone when you are ill.

Chocolate doesn't help but hard candy you can suck on might help your throat.

I cry at movies. I cried when at the neighbors a child was shouting "mommy". I cried at the movie "Me before you", well that actually doesn't mean anything, it's a romantic drama...made for crying. I cried when I got off the train and saw the trees blooming. Too beautiful. She'd enjoy that. I stopped at the empty playground, cried some more. I cried in Budapest because I enjoyed being there and felt guilty for enjoying something she couldn't be part of. I cried in private that day you were in free chat. That was awkward.

Chatting with you was amazing. I just couldn't bear my

excitement. Nope, you don't need to know. I'll be smart and I'll shut up and won't dig a whole for myself.

I had a date with Winnie The Pooh today. You probably are sick of my dating stories but I'll tell you anyway. He is the sweet one who is coming to the next big town to see me. He is very excited and cute. Sending me over the top messages. I like it. He is so into me that he even likes to listen to me rambling about anything and everything and just cuddle without sex. He still hides the money in the chocolate. We had pizza. I know... pizza :D

The sun was shining and we ate it outside on the balcony. He brought me fruit juices. He is always very well prepared and has everything I might or might not need. :D I was so happy he did, I didn't have any breakfast today. He came at 9 and left at 15. We'll go to a wellness hotel on the 10-11 april. Ok...the sex is not good with him. I mean... he makes me feel good about myself and I feel safe so I am good. And he is happy with everything. But he is not funny. And sex feels average and not exciting. Again, I felt like we weren't having sex. I was having sex and used him to make it better. Oh, Elle shut up, stop complaining. For the record I am not complaining. Your fault if my expectations are impossible to meet.

Oh, I got a Swarovski... analplug from him for my birthday ... :D It's the 5th april. I am turning 26. You were right on New year's eve, it is gonna be a great year for me. I love to be single! There are so many men interested in me, all so different. There is this "A whole new world!" disney song, this is how I feel about being single. :D

I don't want to hurt you. Ok.

I guess I like the idea of being in control too. Do you picture us having sex? I am not sure we could decide who is in control. :P

No, we are not speaking about you coming here. I was thinking about going on a vacation or something. I will find some other reason to go there, if not for you :P We already are in a relationship... We communicate intensely and on a regular basis. Friendship. We send sexy pictures and videos. Lovers. See? That's a relationship. Calvin, friend, lover. Yep. I don't blame the Greeks. You are an awesome friend and lover. Thank you.

I didn't mean a romantic date actually. Although I'd love to go on a normal romantic date one day, where I can be normal and offer to split the bill instead of awkwardly staring away from the money and thanking the man for paying. No bedroom? So no sex date either. :(

Ok, I won't try to convince you that it's not what I was thinking about... Although I did want to smartly seduce you first, somewhere public, you wouldn't expect anything...just small hints that could be taken for flirting or not... and push you on a bed. Yeah... Let's cross this plan out for now. Ok, I get that it is risky because of the feelings. I am a little bit disappointed you don't want to "just cum" but yes, it is enormously flattering. Thank you.

We can have a friend date. We could say Hi and hug and walk somewhere. I won't go if you'll be seriously dating someone. I would want to give you a chance to live your life and not drop myself from the sky and confuse you and leave.

I am not ready. Just a bad bad girl... who is pushing your limits. I'm sorry. I want to set up my life and divorce. Not to be able to "start a relationship". But because I want to know myself better. I like you and I want to know you better too. Also I like adventure. You seem to be fun to hang out with.

That's it. Actually. No matter how good of a friend and lover you are through emails. I feel like I am cautious and curious about you. I do feel interested in you but the point is not to start something but just continue discovering you because you intrigue me.

Wow. I can't wipe off the goofy smile of my face since I saw this:

Big long soft warm hug. holding you.

Get well soon!

Elle

Germs...like everyone else, find you irresistible. Get well soon!

*

April 2, 2017

Elle,

DUH!

I like the answer I gave. So accept that as my answer. But DUH, I want to hug you. I want to touch you. I want to spend time with you. I want to be turned on. I want sex with you. I want you to fall asleep in my arms. I want to be sore the next day from cuming so many times and having sex with you so much. Yes I want to hear you when you are turned on and orgasm. Ok I have done that one. But I want to be the reason and see the results of what I do right or wrong. But…

Elle, what we have is pretty special. You can orgasm with a lot of men. If I wanted sex there are women here available and I am not that much of a loser. I am sure I could go out and find a woman for sex. I am a bit charming and desirable, I have been told. I admit I haven't had many sex partners. But I don't want to endanger what we have, whatever it is. Partially fantasy, partially friendship, part deep emotional connections. I don't think I would be disappointed or even worried about disappointing you. I just feel like you being in my life is a positive but doesn't feel like I am forced to make a decision.

The whole "Tell me you love me or don't" thing was hard on me. I don't want the "Is this something, are you going to advance, does this have a future or should I stop wasting my time with a guy in America and forget him". If you fall in love I hope he understands and allows us to still be friends. Hopefully he encourages you to send videos of yourself in stockings and heels using that butt plug and telling me you wish I was in your other hole while you did that. But you said something about if I was in a relationship in two years you would not want to complicate my life. I don't mind you being happy and having a pleasant future. DUH I want to enjoy you. I just don't want it to change us. I like us.

I went shopping and did a little cleaning today. But mostly I slept. Tomorrow night I am going out to dinner with a 13 year old and her family to celebrate her birthday. I love that she wanted me there. To her I'm family. or maybe it is just another birthday present. Hopefully I will feel back to normal. I slept all day and am feeling better now. Still a little weak but the bad stuff is past.

When I am back to full health I think my story had us by the waterfall and camping. I was thinking you on your back and me under one leg kind of sideways. That way I can play with your hard nipples while pulling on your leg to get leverage inside you. I am not talking about rough or hard or even how deep. I mean nice long strokes and maybe being able to finger your clit while I am in you. using my finger between us so I can feel how wet you are and how hard I am as I slide past my finger in you. Also I love your legs and having one on me... I am feeling better. I found the cure.

Curl up next to me and be concerned whenever I cough in my sleep or moan. Caress my shoulders and whisper "It's ok Calvin", as I sleep restlessly. Then fall asleep and let me wake up with you content and completely comfortable in my arms.

Calvin.

*

April 3, 2017

Calvin,

Good that I didn't really react to your last messages.

Guess what, I find myself at "your place". It happens to me often in life. Good way to learn.

I met the 58 years old this afternoon. It was an instant connection and crush. We walked by the lake and talked for hours.

I should explain what I mean by finding myself at your place. I understand your not being ready a little bit better.

He was great. So great. I loved his life philosophy. I didn't say anything about myself, I didn't want him to try to impress me by saying things I might like or want to hear. I loved the way he treated me and I didn't see time flying by. But I couldn't stop but feel extremely cautious and scared of what this could lead us to. I got so upset when he didn't understand that I just ended a relationship where everything I said was used to hurt me later on. We only know each other for like 24 hours. It is just way too fast.

We exchanged long messages and he decided to come to see me. And now he is already planning to come back on Thursday. This is scary because I really like him and whatever he says I don't know him yet. I need time to see his actions. I cannot just trust him.

Anyways I could feel a little bit how it feels to not be ready and be pushed into something serious. He called me back like 4 times since he left, he doesn't stop reassuring me that what we have is special and that he would never hurt me blabla. I don't know what to say. I wish he wouldn't be so excited about "us". He told me not to speak about what happened because it is precious and better to keep to myself....

My first instinct upon arriving home was to tell you all about it.

Oh, by the way. I didn't see his dick. Yet. There goes one point to him for not being explicit on the first date.
I cannot tell him, dude I like you but I have someone else on my mind. Because it's none of his business. You are my business.

I feel like he doesn't respect my feelings, yes I do understand how pointless it is to be afraid of feelings, I do understand that I should just give myself to it and see what happens. But hey, I have the right to feel whatever I feel. I cannot just turn off my feelings and throw my heart at a stranger whom I feel good with.

Time spent with you is not wasted time. Ever.

I love our fantasy. I don't want to analyze my feelings or my stupid and selfish move of mentioning the date in 2 years just to distract myself from the bad things coming (My travel to France, people try to prepare me but I don't want to. I will have to be strong and go through hell staying kind and proud of myself. I have to be smarter than ever.Lily's future depends on how I handle things so it is a big deal)

On a side note, consider yourself lucky I didn't ask you to marry me. That's the kind of thing I do to show my affection. Sorry. Not funny. I didn't know that the "love me or don't " was so hard on you. We didn't talk about it much. I get now how bad it feels to be pushed into something and not to have the gift of time and patience and options.

I love what we have. I love to have you in my life. It's simple. I cannot not have you in my life. I tried but believe me you never disappeared from my life, not even for the month we weren't communicating. I tried to "get over" and "forget" you but it was unbearable, when I went running I had to crouch down and my whole body was tense and crying and I felt dead like I lost someone. I never lost anyone I felt close to. It crushed me. I thought my body would tear apart from the inside.

That's why I told you when we started to communicate again that

I accepted my feelings and I am content having them and it doesn't need anything in return. Feelings cannot be turned off. You said. I try to remain relaxed about it. And let myself feel and not name the feelings just enjoy them.
So I don't care, you choose what is comfortable for you. If you are happy I am happy. I will satisfy my needs and distract myself with people who are willing to be used and "thrown away". You are not someone I want to use. You have time. As much as you need. And options, many, yours.

I want to be held by you. And kissed by you. And touched by you. And let you slobber on me in your sleep :D No matter how good of a sex I had and how satisfied I am. I am always dying to make love with you.

I had a good kiss, good kisses today, the most meaningful and enjoyable ones of my life. I will still fall asleep fantasizing about your lips and about making a mess together and being exhausted from having too much fun.

"It's okCalvin"

I'm here

("here" with you in fantasy but "here" far away to give you the space you need:P)

Elle

attached: photo of me wearing a blue bikini on the balcony

*

April 3, 2017

Elle,

You are too perfect.

Thank you,

You understand me so well. And yes it scares me a little when you imply you think I am your business and it will interfere with other relationships in your life.

I trust you. You will continue to live and meet people and enjoy life and whatever happens or doesn't happen won't change your life. If I meet a woman here and I fall in love and get married. I will explain to her who you are and continue to write to you. Any woman great enough for me to love that much will understand me and understand I love her and not be intimidated or worried. She will understand I can care about someone. That if I finally commit to a woman, writing to someone else won't tempt me. Obviously the sexy stuff will stop but I don't plan on anything happening in my life any year soon.

My point is Elle, I don't plan on stopping and disappearing. Unless you tell me it is bad for you. I am open to keeping in touch and somehow being in each other's lives even if you remarry. Three things: You say goodbye and stop reading even if I keep writing. then I might stop. If you ask me to stop writing to you. Second, you scare me too much. Track me down and show up or be the opposite of that last email. Thank you for that last email and understanding me. Or third.

I wouldn't just disappear but If I/we decided I am bad for you. Having me as a crutch or someone who keeps you from moving on. I am still scared you will make me too much and I am too important to you. But I feel much better. I care. I enjoy writing and sharing and having you in my life.. like this.

Ok. Commenting on last night's email, I just wanted to thank you for understanding and not being hurt by my not feeling ready for more.

I am going to keep writing this: "I am not in love with you." But we are very close and you are very important.

Thank you for being there for me

Calvin

*

April 3, 2017

Calvin,

My skype is my real name. You must be really really horny to not be bothered to know my real name.

Elle

*

April 4, 2017

Elle,

If I went too far the other night I am sorry. I spent the afternoon feeling loved and accepted with the little girls. Maybe I enjoyed feeling loved too much and allowed myself to feel loved by you. Yes you did turn me on. But that is not unusual. Yes, you always break the rules but I didn't want to and don't want to mess with your emotions.

I love that you understand me better than I understand myself. At that moment I really wanted to Skype and the idea was great. I was not playing you or anything. I was being honest... at that moment. I am not that scared as I was.
Before the answer was "NO never". Now it is "wait and someday".. maybe even soon. I really like the idea. We say a lot

of things in emails that if we said in Skype it would just be more intense. I also think you are stronger and don't NEED me as much, just want to enjoy having someone to talk to.

I want to talk to you about France. I don't want you to think you need my help. You don't, but I don't mind listening and that helps. To me that's a big difference. If you don't need to talk to anyone and you have already decided. You can have me listen and talk it through. You are too good and this is too big for you to listen to me or anyone else.

I am just here to call you out when you doubt yourself or think bad thoughts. I do it too. I get down and don't always see things straight. It helps to have someone say, "It's not that bad and the horrible thing you are worrying about can't happen. You made it up."

I am not sorry for what I was doing just for telling you.

You asked me to stop and I continued to mess with you. It was playful but also selfish on my part. The whole night I was a little beyond our rules. I don't mind asking about your shaving and assuming our relationship is intimate enough for me to ask personal questions. No that wasn't sexual at all. Just funny and where my thinking went.

I mean I was "loving" and the switched to sexual. both against the rules. Sexual we break that rule. but both were a bit unfair and you asked me to stop.

I will make sure you are comfortable and I understand.

Your video didn't load. But I did hear you say, "Do it now Calvin" that night. I wanted to feel loved and I hadn't relieved the build up in too long. I am sorry if I was thinking of me and not you.

On the other hand... Thank you and you were amazing and wow.

We will work this out. I want to stay true to myself. I want you to stay with me. I don't want us to pretend you are less to me and I am just a dick. We have to be careful about emotions. It's all good, but we are careful. We both know what the other person wants to hear.

You are great for my ego but I don't want to be " dude I like you but I have someone else on my mind." You said, "mind" and still spent the time with him. I am not stopping you or preventing your heart.

It is ok if the guy who makes you forget me hasn't shown up yet. I will try not to say the things you want to hear or allow us to fantasize too real where we forget.

My stories are you and me. I can change the names, But they are imagining how you and I would spend the day camping and sleeping and everything. It sounds a lot like plans instead of fantasy. Sometimes that is unfair. Sometimes I get caught up because I like this fantasy so much.

Ok SUC (Shut Up Clavin)

Now I am doing it.

I love that we don't have a filter on our feelings or words. You shave your ass from the front. I will remember that if I ever decide to shave my ass. not going to happen. But we also recognize just too late, "That didn't need to be said." about emotions.

I will try to be better. Sorry if I messed with your emotions or your head or got you all steamed up and left you alone all day.

To make up for it I will pull a Van Gogh and cut off a finger. Or do a magic trick.

I am feeling better.

Calvin

Interesting fact. Van Gogh had a friend buy one painting from him. A landscape of a field. That is the only painting of his he was ever able to sell and it was a mercy purchase because his friend felt sorry for him. Vincent Van Gogh died a failure as an artist and couldn't sell his paintings. They weren't popular until after his death.

*

April 5, 2017

Calvin,

I already made my decision about the divorce and living in Hungary. You seem to doubt it. He got his chance; many chances. I offered him to take your place... become my confidant, someone I trust and share my thoughts with and become friends with. He rejected it.

That's it. I am good at compromises and pleasing. I try hard and long and don't like to give up. But when I suffer long enough and realize it feels like failure for a long time now, I kick people out of my class. ;) I don't let go easy, but when I do it's definitive. I am very stubborn and when I change plans I stick to the new plans. I have new plans now. He has very little place in them.

It was my birthday today. I don't like to over celebrate it. My mom came into the room with pizza flavored pastry and a candle on top. I blew it and made a wish. I went shopping with my sister (I found high waisted jeans, my only jeans are super old and it wasn't in to wear high waisted yet. And a beautiful green plaid shirt.), ate chinese and went home to work out but ended up not doing anything. Just laying around and chatting with men.

I saw Lily!!!!! She was adorable. I saw her playing on the couch, reading books and building a slide out of blankets and making funny memes about how much she loves chocolate. Oh my god. I felt like superwoman. When I got pregnant I had this overwhelming mighty feeling, like I could lift a car and move mountains and do just about anything for her.

I watched a movie with my whole family. Cure for wellness.

It was quite bad. I liked that we were all together and I love criticizing films and books and food... If the movie is bad I get excited to explain why.

I don't have on facebook my birthday date, it always upsets me to have all the messages. I felt like it was fake and made me feel bad about being sad, because I was supposed to be happy. So it felt like spending the day pretending to pretend happiness when all I do on my birthday is reflecting on my life.

I found a business idea today. I love personalized surprises. When I left my internship I arrived early on my last day and left a post-it at everyone's desk with a personalized message about why I appreciate that person. It's just an idea but I'd love to have a business that offers to surprise men's girlfriends (birthday, anniversary, ..). Or friends or colleagues with funny cakes (bite me) or teasing cards. So it would be a funny romantic business. :)

My books are not really progressing... :/

Tomorrow I have a psychologist appointment and I'll meet the old guy right after. I am kind of falling in love with him. The only thing that bothers me a tiny bit is that the age gap is super obvious and people stare. But I do like to upset people so... It is so weird to be with him. I feel like we are both kids. I get really excited and confused thinking about him and embarrassed. He is so unpredictable.

I started to open up myself a bit in emails. But his reactions are never what I expected. He seems to be something reassuring, he always answers and he is just really present all the time but still not nosy.

Maybe he is what I need. He seems to give me the freedom I need and the steady caring too. The emotional stability. He studied psychology amongst other things and said he knows Borderline well and what it needs. He is so great. I don't want to repeat the things he spoke about but .. it was fascinating. He is different, with a very broad vision of the universe. He is a very confident man too. I liked how confident he was about showing me off in public.

He put his arm around my waist right away even though children were biking there and kissed me by the lake, where some men were fishing. I don't know what to expect for tomorrow. I tried to step back and act like it was just an exchange. But he didn't let me.

I am very excited. Cautious but excited.

At some point in our mailing today I got scared he cannot or doesn't want to have sex. Did you know men can have sex even at 80?? Wow.

Ok. I feel silly. This is weird.

I don't want your ear or finger. Calvin, you have to stop speaking about how I flatter your ego and how you are not in love. It makes me really hurt and angry and run into the first man's arms no matter who he is and not care about him hurting me because I hurt already anyway.

Get it? Please stop.

I am living my life but I love you and I am ok having a space in my heart for you. You know how easily I get excited about people and fall in love. I have a very rich emotional life. I can adore you and want to date someone else who fits my needs better.

You leave me frustrated all the time, and this lets me go out and find someone who doesn't. I don't speak about sex. I want to love and be loved. I want to be called and receive short messages throughout the day. I want to feel cared for and adored and trusted.

I often feel like our "relationship" is unequal. Because you feel satisfied and tell me that I can fill your needs with an email every now and then and sexy pictures and videos. But my needs are different.

I am letting us go.

It is masochistic to hope for your feelings to change. It's a rollercoaster of hope and disappointment. I am so stubborn. You keep repeating that you don't want me like I want you.

I want to give myself a chance to love someone who loves me back.

Yes, we can stay friends and you know me teasing and sexy talk is definitely ok even if only friends.

Elle

*

April 6, 2017

Elle,

I just got home. I am going out now but I will write more later.

I am glad you lived another year and made this last year better for me.

Happy Birthday!

Calvin

*

April 6, 2017

Elle,

The fact the earth has revolved one complete trip around the sun is a reason to commemorate all the things that have happened this year and all the years you have been alive. I am especially glad you have been here this last year. Thank you.

My view has been that it has been a good year for you. Much of the pain was recognizing pain you have lived with and ignored. Some pain is curable. When we suffer we become stronger and immune to that sickness. When we are around people who give off their diseases we are immune to their sickness. Their hate, their unkind words, their manipulation. You have grown much more healthy and strong from where I stand.

You have also healed me and made me smile and made me cum. Thank you for everything you did this year. You made me feel young and lovable and good. This is a gift you have given I cannot match. I can just thank you for giving me so much joy and strength and confidence this year.

You are a good person.

Have a great Day, I didn't say birthday because that was yesterday I think. But I celebrate you being alive and in my life last year and now.

Calvin

soft long hug

*

April 7, 2017

Calvin,

I need shoulders to cry on…

Elle

*

April 7, 2017

Elle,

As it happens I have two shoulders. You can use them anytime you wish. I will gladly hold you. I won't lie to you, but if you need assurance that everything is ok and life is good and this is a temporary thing… I will gladly say soft words of encouragement.

You are strong. Lily loves you and is going to be in your life and you in hers. You are better than you give yourself credit for. You are lovable even if you don't always pick loving men... what am I missing?

Hold you and let you cry even if you don't want to talk about anything. Feel my caring and my long distance hug. Think hard and you can actually feel the warmth and yourself being hugged.

I am trying very hard to send them.

Calvin

*

April 7, 2017

Calvin,

It was awful yesterday night. I feel used. :'(

Thank you. I know. We don't lie. I don't need to hear fake I love you-s. He was such a fake person. Completely different from the first time. I should have noticed earlier and not put myself through this. I want to speak about it. Don't wait for my message, it might take a while. Thank you for holding me and not forcing me to speak. :'(

Elle

*

April 7, 2017

Elle,

Aren't you glad you are you and you are not him. Each person has an integrity that can only be harmed by the actions of that person. You got hurt, but you are still you. You are still strong and know you have overcome a lot. You also know I am still hugging you.

You never have to speak about anything.

It's raining here. Enough wetness here so when you lay down and imagine yourself here don't cry. Dry eyes. warm arms. Life is good even when it doesn't feel good.

Spring is coming and sunshine and flowers and happy thoughts. Sunsets on the lake and sunrises when it is still cool out. Walking hand in hand with me in your mind as you stroll around the lake. Occasionally leaning in and putting your head against my shoulder to prompt me to put my arm around you. just quiet walks, nothing needed said. just enjoy nature's beauty. Yes when I am in awe of the light broken up into one millions sparkles on the ripples of the lake or the overpowering mix of colors and yet the color and beauty on each leaf and flower and tree.

When I am in awe of nature I actually shut up. Yes. Calvin shuts up! I even listen when it is peaceful and there is no sound at all. People say they love my place because you can walk my trails. The trails I have cut, that go under the shade of the trees lining both sides and it is so quiet. They are overwhelmed by the quiet and peacefulness after living in the city and all its noise and business.

You are welcome to imagine yourself here with a very quiet Calvin.

Quiet Calvin...NAWWWW Not a good name for me.

You don't have to smile. Just try not to hurt. it hurts me when you hurt.
Certain wetness is still allowed here.

*

April 7, 2017

Calvin,

You are so perfect.

Elle

*

April 7, 2017

Elle,

I am not perfect, You are just very important to me. Also I know you well enough to understand you.

Calvin

*

April 8, 2017

Elle,

If this story ends in great sex... I will wait until tomorrow to finish that part.

Quiet Walking

(because I care and want to do whatever I can do for you.. Unfortunately this is all I can do.)

We are walking quietly by your lake hand in hand. You are wearing your new high jeans and the air is still cool but the sun shines against your cheek and feels warm. The lake is a nice place because all the smells from all around blow across and hit you at different times. The mud and the water, the flowers, the trees are just now finding spring. You can also smell me when I hold you close. I am wearing English Leather deodorant but there is also a hint of me. I don't smell bad but I smell like a man and not just perfume.

It is a warm day but the sun is only rising. I am wearing a thin coat, almost like a flannel shirt over my blue T-shirt and jeans. Also I am wearing my hiking boots so I can go exploring. I have never seen your lake and I am somewhat like a child. Every animal or animal track or new flower or view of the lake I must stop and explore like a child. Sometimes I look at the same tree and the same lake just from a little different perspective as we have walked a ways since I last smiled at it. Sometimes you catch me just smiling at you.

We are holding hands but it is almost unnoticed. It is not passionate or intense, just comfortable. It is my way of saying "I am here" or to squeeze your hand to say "I like you" or to give a hug. Oh I stop and give you hugs too. DUH. Of course I am going to hug you. but it is a quiet walk meant to enjoy the peace and beauty and enjoy each other's company and we both individually enjoy the same sites and experiences..

The birds are new there and uncommon to me. The sky is always beautiful. I love the clouds, I love the blue when there are no clouds to enjoy. I love peacefully enjoying the colors of the sky slowly, subtly changing as the sun rises higher above the horizon.

Sometimes we make eye contact and recognize we are enjoying the same thing, sometimes I am simply sitting with my arm around you enjoying everything and enjoying being with you. Without a word I can go from holding you tightly to wandering off by myself following a rabbit's tracks into the woods. But it is not random; you are consciously and unconsciously controlling me.

When you feel small you lean against me and my giant arms encircle your little body and you are small yet strong and safe. When you feel big again you focus on something and like a big dog I go chasing after it with my tongue wagging. Sometimes you even send me away just because you enjoy my reaching out for you to take your hand again.

The town is asleep and quiet except perhaps a few fishermen who are still to not scare the fish. The sun sparkles on the lake and I love to stop and look at it every few minutes. As if life was irreplaceable and those moments are never going to be exactly like that again. Every few meters the moment is different and I am completely in that moment. Also when I stop and sit ,you crawl under my shirt and cuddle close to me. I like the signals you send when you want to be held. It is not cold at all but you still pretend a little, not really trying to fool me, just giving me the signal to place my arms around you.

Nothing happening in public so we will complete our walk hand in hand and maybe go inside next time I write...

Calm happy peaceful Calvin

I feel better. Quiet walking hand in hand helps. :)

Thank you for caring. Please don't hurt, I don't hurt anymore. I feel cared for.

*

April 9, 2017

Elle,

I don't need a reply, I just want you to know I care and I hope you are alright. I believe you can overcome whatever bothered you. If you are busy being happy that's great. I am not sure LiveJasmin or a dating website is the best place to look for honesty. I think men look for fantasy there.

It has rained here and snow just up the hill. Spring is trying to peak out.

Soft hug.

Calvin

*

April 9, 2017

Calvin,

I'm floating in nothingness.

I am losing it. I am so tired of fighting. I didn't notice how it's all decreasing. It was so subtle. Just feeling a bit unmotivated to "work" so I did it less and less, but thought it's ok I always had some excuse. I couldn't write but tried not to freak out about it.

My homeworks for the psychologist has less and less content. I spend more time in bed. A bit more dark thoughts. But it grew almost unnoticeable inside me.

At this point I don't cook anymore, if I eat it's bread. But I don't feel hungry and nothing tastes good. I don't want to be spoken to. I get so upset when my parents or siblings speak to me, I don't understand my reaction, so without making eye contact I just turn away and go somewhere I can be alone. I feel invisible. I feel like it's the decor around me and not real and my senses betray me.

What's the point pretending it exists? I woke up this noon to the sound of someone taking a shower; And it upset me because it was so loud and it made me realize I haven't taken one since the psychologist appointment. And I didn't wash off my makeup. I feel like I am falling. In this deep whole with no bottom. Just an infinite deep darkness and I gravitate downwards at a speed that feels like floating but everything around me is passing so fast that it is all blurry.

Ok, let's think. I probably feel overwhelmed by what is happening, and especially what is ahead of me to handle. And subconsciously gave up. Also I was just faced with the particularity of my personality disorder. Not all the borderlines are the same. I just had to listen for an hour to the psychologist analyzing from my test results how much psychopath, schizophren (a lot), and paranoiac and other symptoms show in my way of functioning. It was probably overwhelming. It probably scared me that she expressed her worries about me being in pre psychosis. Said something like it can easily gravitate to psychosis and asked me to not stay alone when I feel things getting worse.

She asked me to consider seeking a psychotherapist and taking medication. Going to the hospital for a neurological examination. I can't express how much of a monster I felt. She asked me questions about sounds and shadows and things I see and hear and think. And just... when you think it's all normal because it was always like that since you can remember and somebody acting like you are on a trial for being a freak.

Oh, no. My brother is calling me, my grandparents are here. I can't do this. I can't even speak. And I look like crap. I look like someone who is empty. I am so fed up with panicking about

"What would a human say?"

"Come on ...Elle what would a normal human being say now. How would she hold her arms, smile"

Ok. Not going would be more suspicious than apologizing for being half asleep or something.

Quick kiss on your cheek.
Thank you for yesterday.
Have a beautiful weekend!

Elle

*

April 9, 2017

Calvin,

I feel the same but I know my brain is messing with me. My feelings are fake and they lie. Tomorrow is sunday. If I feel the same I can just lay in bed. I hope I can do something. It will feel like an accomplishment.

In a week I ll have lily to take care of. Soon I'll start working as a receptionist. Did I mention I found a job for summer? A real one! :) It all seems scary and impossible to do. Today no matter how amazing I couldn't have enjoyed or even just do what I have to. I am afraid I couldn't even properly take care of her now. It is not just the mood. My brain feels so sleepy I can barely hold my head

up and my eyes open. I can't communicate with my family. I am glad she is not with me. I would be a useless mom today, using all my strenght to feed her and keep her safe. I am supposed to do so much more for her.
I hope having a purpose will help keep my head out of the water.

Ok room spinning and darkening and getting nauseous again.

This cannot get worse. It has to improve. My brain feels sick. Broken. Defective.

Elle

*

April 9, 2017

Calvin,

When I blew the candles I wished for staying as lucky as I am. Because I felt like I have everything and things are evolving anyway and I am working toward what I want to achieve. So I don't really need anything I could wish for.

I just came across a video that made me reconsider what I want for this next year in my life to come. At new year's eve I wished for getting more comfortable with my personality disorder and being overall more balanced, less in the extremes.

I found this idea of falling in love with my situation and myself very beautiful. This is what I want.
I remember that moment when I started to come up from the depression hole. I was standing outside of the mental hospital, it was a cool spring night... or morning. I looked down the valley, it was a beautiful place. I wondered at the blinking yellow and orange lights from the next hill. And I felt overwhelming "in love". It was so sudden. An emotional background music in my brain and very intense greens and blues and violets and grays in

the darkness. Flickering lights over heavily moving shadows. My skin felt highly sensitive, like tiny needles were getting in it. And I loved being overwhelmed and stabbed in my heart by the greatness of it.

I fell in love with the world, this place I used to feel like an alien at became so special to me. I felt honored to be part of it and stopped fighting against it.

What I wish to feel now is being in love with the beautiful chaos of my mind. No it is not a genius mind. No it is not a "normal" one. If I could fall in love with the world and life in general in whatever form it takes... I can also apprehend that I am a form of life. A channel for emotions to go through. A chaotic, intense pack of half finished projects. The way I live, everything is an adventure.

Yesterday was bad. But still it was huge, mind blowing and very special. It's Sunday evening , I'm still in my pajamas. But today was a life changing adventure too. I wonder whether I have boring days. I don't think I can be bored. Every day is special to me. Every day is like a very intense ballet performance, or a moving movie or a life changing book.

At night before I go to sleep I am still searching for words to describe what I just went through. I struggle so much that I can't share my experience. It is behind words. Very frustrating that whatever I write down is not close enough to my perception. I feel like I'd need a line of paintings hanging from the ceiling and ballet dancers spirling and bowing and music, loud and then soft and emotional and the lights changing accordingly but sometimes all of it going crazy and creating a chaos, somehow still enjoyable although hard to take in.

I really think I am experiencing in a not human way sometimes, trapped in this human body, in this limited shell and frequencies that are just not enough for me.
Wouah, I let my crazy come out. I feel dizzy, breath, breath, ok.

I'm good. I need to get down to the earth though, or my head will swell up like a balloon and pop and my bits will fly in circles. But eventually they will hit the floor.

Elle

*

April 10, 2017

Elle,

Porn sites and dating sites are not the best places to meet good men.

You understand love. You know how someone in love with you should treat you.. the way you would treat someone you loved. You would bring me soup and sit at my bedside and wipe my forehead with a wet towel if I was sick. You are a great wife, great girlfriend and a great date. You are a lousy chooser of men to marry, as boyfriends and for dates.

One of the little girls I tutor had pneumonia a few weeks ago. I hurt seeing her so miserable and not being able to do anything. I told her if I could I would reach in and grab two hands full of pain and take them for myself. She looked up at me and said, "Could you take 5 handfuls?" But you understand. You know what love is. You know how good people should act and treat each other.

The problem is not you. You even tend to see good in others you want to be there even if it isn't. When you needed help, you curled into your husband's arms. When you needed or felt you needed to be used for sex, he gave you what you wanted and thought you needed. When you needed to feel appreciated, protected, secure, whatever you gave him credit for, he was the one you saw as giving you what you needed. Of course you miss that. The idea that you can't do better I am not sure I agree with, but I honestly have never met him so I should not judge. I am just saying you want to be in love. You feel your life is less secure and you miss a lot about being married and having a man in your life. That is normal.

You know what is normal because you are normal. You are loving. You are giving. You try to make others happy. You care about others and not just yourself. You carry on a conversation and don't just brag. You are normal. You just don't seem to be with a lot of normal men of your caliber of person. You wonder why they don't act the way you would? Because you are a pretty great person. You are above average. There is nothing wrong with you. I mean listen to the psych. But as far as how people who care act, you are spot on and just not finding men on dating sites and porn sites who think of others.

I hear your pain and your darkness.but I think you are down, but life just has darkness in rooms still you can see the light. You aren't going into a room where it is black, you are just wandering down halls that are not well lit or bright or sunny filled with happy colors. You are down but you are looking at the light trying to follow it out to the garden, You just have some dark halls to go through. Don't lose track of the light. You are ok.

I am not in great health but will get over it soon. I keep feeling like I have turned the corner and am 100%.

I went to a funeral today and was tired and a bit aching from a cold. I had two thoughts. One was the man lived his life rebelliously and did his own thing and made his own rules and enjoyed being wild. He was homeless and drunk and had hepatitis. Seeing his lifetime of pictures his actions caught up with him and he was never happy. He was all about himself and never got the pleasure and happiness he thought drugs and drinking and being a free spirit and not working would get him. I had trouble feeling sorry for him. He was sober for a few years and then got drunk so bad he died. He was selfish and caused pain. He made mistakes others had to pay for.

I knew his wife. She was very large from a family of obese people, her brothers had gotten into drugs and troubles and she loved them. I was having trouble feeling compassion for this man but I realized he was a person. She didn't throw him away. When he was homeless and drunk she saw the beauty and humanity. She took him in and got him sober and made him the man he could be.

He was still selfish but he was a human. He was lovable. He had something that made him who he was. Something special that no one else had. He was loyal and loving and caring. He was selfish but he loved her. He saw the person inside her body. Her sweetness. She didn't think anyone would ever marry her but he saw what we all loved in her. She saw what I didn't inside him. I learned a lesson today. I tend to be too judgmental and write people off as good or bad. But bad people have beauty in them. You can't just see the bad. You can love the beauty they have inside.

He always chose drinking over his family. He always chose the easy way and was never responsible. But he did love. He did feel. He did try to bring joy and be friendly. His intentions were good, he just hurt people by his actions. But he was a human and good and not "bad people".

You complimented me by recognizing what I mean and feeling what I feel when I say it.

For me being called "good people" is a big compliment. it means trustworthy and honest and gracious and fair. But I need to see people as people first no matter my view of their life. I need to love the way his wife did and see what is there to love not focus on his shortcomings and failures.

Ok. I will shut up now. I was just embarrassed that I was judging the man and his friends at his funeral. I am not a good person.

Calvin

*

April 13, 2017

Calvin,

How are you, Calvin? 100%?

You are a good person. You are kind and loving and you try to see the good in people. You are very strict to yourself. You notice when you judge someone too strictly but you don't notice when you judge yourself too strictly…

I feel like you didn't quite manage to see him better but...it's ok. You are allowed to have an opinion. I am sure you would have treated him just as you would treat anyone else. You don't have to be perfect. Your actions matter but even with your actions you have the right to mess up. We are human. I didn't know him. But I know you. You are beautiful. You are a good person. The proof is that you doubt yourself. It feels good to live in a world where you exist.

My mini vacation was amazing. He downloaded everything from Twenty One Pilots, Tessa Violet, Dodie Clark and Milky Chance and let me sing along in the car. He was well prepared again! A bag full of fruits and juices. Pear, strawberries, grapes, oranges, bananas... And he had chips and chocolate for me. The hotel was very nice. Beautiful room. I loved the food and there was a pool that went outside. I swam underneath the stars in the dark. Wow.

I was alone in the pool, the air was cool but my body was covered in hot water. Wow.

Out of this world special.

There were multiple saunas. There was one not too hot, tiny, only for one. I sat there and named it my "thinking spot". His eyes were sensitive so he sent me down to the spa area alone the second day.

He brought movies, I think we watched 5. I cried quite a lot. I tried to be discreet about it. He was very loving. I slept well. He was caring and loving and he mostly wanted to just spend time with me and feel comfortable. I catched him dreamingly staring at me a few times. He seems to adore me. Everything I do is fantastic and everything I say is cute.

He did a very serious and deep research on me. Kind of creepy but quite sweet of him. He found everything. My blog, my youtube channel, my facebook, every website I ever signed up for... Yep, he knows everything about me. If it wasn't him I'd be upset and worried. But he was amazing to me. He encouraged me to rest and not have sex. He wasn't pushing me into something at any point and didn't even ask or hint anything. He just wanted to love me.

Apparently he loved everything he read about me/from me and thought I am kind and lovable. It was weird. The only awkward moments were (about every 5 min) when he said he adores me and I smiled awkwardly but really gratefully just not knowing what to say. It's crazy he seems to remember everything about me. He brought vodka too, he found written somewhere that it was my favorite. And he admitted that he almost made me deliver flowers for my birthday but couldn't find my address.

I felt safe with him, I felt like myself and I liked myself. I could be silly and serious and sexy and just resting or sad and deep.

I cried about Lily, there are too many freaking movies that play with your emotions.

"It's your child. You don't need her consent to love her. You just love her. Go ahead and find her. You are her dad"

Keira Knightly gave advice to a dad who cheated on his wife and his daughter was very angry at him about the divorce and didn't want to see him anymore.

"My daughter's name was Olivia. She was very ill. She died at 6 years old"

Will Smith whom it took 2 years to be able to pronounce her daughters name after losing her.

"Take care of our daughter"

Boom she killed herself because she was a secret agent for the Germans and Brad Pitt was left alone with the baby.

I crie after each orgasm too, unnoticeable, I don't know what's happening.

My sexdrive shifted. First I was fed up with the webcam because it wasn't enough. I wanted to be touched. But now I kind of feel fed up with bare sex. To a point where I would rather not have any. I want to be adored. I don't want to be used. Oh, no. I'm broken. What will I do if I am not a sex maniac anymore?

Thinking back we did make a lot of sex, it just doesn't feel like it because he honestly aboslutely didn't care whether there is any. That's probably my biggest turn on. Weird, right?

The guy is very silent, but not awkwardly silent. We were quite a lot but it had a married couple feeling to it. Comfortable silence. I really really enjoyed this vacation. We both lived with someone who reproached us that nothing we do is good enough. I enjoyed being spoiled and adored and just being and feeling like whatever I do is good enough. I am good enough. It feels strange being with someone who is not looking for flaws or mistakes.

He adores the way I walk, he adores the way I eat, my outfit, watching me put my makeup on, listening to me sing along to "Make me a robot", he keeps pushing "repeat". He watched me with so much tenderness. When I came back my crush asked me to send him pictures. He sucks at flirting. Honestly I was upset about his requests but didn't know how to communicate it.

So many men want to know if I love butt stuff. I cannot blame them. But I am upset that they want something and not someone. If you find someone you feel attracted to and it is returned then you can discover things together and push limits. Ok, maybe you are right about dating and porn sites. It's good that I feel like this, right? I am getting closer to a normal date one day.

Don't shut up. I love listening to you. I am listening.

You are pretty amazing...even to your own standards ;)

Elle

*

April 13, 2017

Elle,

I love that you are adored. Even more, I love that you feel adored. You are lovable and everything you do is so you and unique. I think he is taking the time to see the real you and the real you is beautiful. Maybe this was also good because you were missing having Lily's father taking care of you and this guy showed you how a real man takes care of a woman. I don't mean the money and vodka. I mean the caring to want to please and the attention. They respect and value you. It is easy to take care of physical needs. Emotional support and caring takes risk and involvement and sacrificing your safe armor. You can't connect and still keep your own weaknesses hidden.

I am happy for you. I liked when you said you felt like an old couple.. but be safe, you aren't an old couple yet. Feel like an old couple but don't expect him to know the right thing every time or that you know him completely just because it feels that way. My only caution. Otherwise I enjoyed hearing your happy words.

I am on Easter vacation from work this week. But I haven't written because the 4 girls are out of school too and their parents work. So I got them this week. I stayed at their house the first two nights and right now they are about to wake up so I need to make this note quickly. Just say I am loving it. We do simple things and they are so happy and love my time. I went out to the barn and found "robot parts" .They got to crush rocks with hammers, I found an old costume from the 1700. They get to make breakfast themselves and to make Rice Crispy treats and decorated cookies and go for walks.

The best part is they love to cuddle. I always have one on my lap. The oldest went away to volunteer at a food bank to feed the homeless so I just have the younger three. I am in heaven. Worn out, but in heaven.

I will write to you soon when I have a break. It is nice to be needed 24/7 but new to me.

Calvin

*

April 14, 2017

Calvin,

I should go to sleep. I am leaving tmr morning very early. But I want to speak with you before I leave. I'll take my pc with me, I want to use it at night and also send emails to you. For the next 2 weeks I'll be good, no webcam, no sex, nothing. I won't let him find anything that he can use against me. I protected all my stuff with passwords. I will be kind and calm and caring. But I'll keep a safe distance from him and won't answer when he'll try to get me into a fight or bring me down.

Well, that's the plan.

The last few days were crazy. I helped interview a second receptionist. I met the interior designer of the hotel too. My boss gave me a research project in French to work on. I was running around to find gifts for Lily and cigarettes for his dad. I had to pack. Winnie started to really invest in my personal life and worry about me going back to France. He was a lot. He is already envisioning a future or actually many different options for us, one being us raising Lily together. I don't love him. And I don't think I ever could. I feel like such an emotional zero, I am trying to calm him down and try not to use him but he is ok. I like him and I am ok having a loose lover relationship. He is probably just being too excited. Anyways, this situation is really not comfortable for me.

I had a psychologist appointment too. We spoke about you. Not only. She added something to my diagnosis: borderline personality disorder with schizotypal traits. And I told her what I learned from my experience with the old guy and told her about my new job and winnie and the spa. But she really wants me to move on. It is nice to have someone worry more about my love life than myself :I agree that it is silly to be waiting for years. She used the word "wasting months' ' but I don't think there is such a thing as wasting time. If I take years to learn something, then I need years to learn it. I don't feel stuck, I am changing and evolving and advancing. At my speed. It doesn't feel like I am wasting my time. She was like:

-How much time will you wait for him? 2 more months? 3 more months?

I didn't even dare to say that we are speaking about years not months.

I have plenty of time. I do whatever I want. If letting my heart wait feels good I will do that. If a fantasy is making me more happy than anything, I am choosing happiness. If not I will still choose happiness. I will try to move on and eventually it will happen. I don't think there is anything to worry about. This kind of problem solves itself. If I am supposed to meet someone who does want a future with me, who I love... then I know it will happen.

I am not leaving with closed eyes and a closed heart. I won't let it go unnoticed or turn an offer down. If someone as great as you steps into my life, plus he is ready for a relationship of course that fits what I want better and I will take it. I do see myself growing old with you, ok I admit that this is not helping to commit with someone else. It will pass. Maybe if you could tell me you don't see us crossing roads when we are old. That would help. But I think you do. Or you are unsure and think it might be possible. I know you will tell me when you figured it out even if it is not good news.

Maybe you hope for me. You represent the caring loving partner and you are the proof it exists. And that's why I can't and don't want to let you go.

I know you are not in love. I know you love me. It doesn't need to be said to be felt.

I am happy you are busy and cuddled. I enjoy my own happiness more knowing that you are happy too.

I am very happy. I will see my child tomorrow. Nothing could bring me down. I can only think of how happy and reassured she will feel when she sees I came back. She'll be asleep by the time I actually get there. But she will feel my presence and she will know I'll be there when she wakes up.

She is so happy since I told him she only has to sleep 3 nights and I am there. She took her car and said:

-I'm coming by car, sitting and speaking with mommy!

She sat down in front of the screen I was on. And she told me she can count, she stood up, looked at me and very proudly said:

-I can count. 1...2...3...6!

and she ran away. Oh my god. She is so cute. She mentions mom and dad a lot in the same sentence. I don't quite understand what she is saying but I know she'll be super happy to have both of us with her. She already looks more relaxed and happy.

My heart breaks thinking about how she must have felt thinking I might not come back.

Thank you for being here.

Soft long hug

Elle

*

April 15, 2017

Elle,

I am here.

Life is good. I will say whatever I feel needs said about the whole growing old together when you get home or when it needs said. For now enjoy Lily. I do love you and I am happy for you and happy for me.

I think she will do things you can never expect or imagine. Kids can be adorable in their own way unique to only them. Please don't expect too much or plan everything to happen a certain way when the way it just happens can be so much more wonderful. Advice I need to take for myself and my own life.

The story about the girl holding two apples and the mom asking for one. The girl quickly bit a chunk out of each and the mom feeling hurt her daughter was selfish and would bite each to keep her mom from getting any. Then the girl walked up and said, " I tasted both, This one is sweeter so it's the apple for you." Just let her love you her own way.

I am now so tired and school starts again Monday..

If you feel like writing I will be looking for it. If it is difficult or you are too busy taking care of Lily or need rest to be your best with her. I totally understand and would prefer you to be your best with her. I can wait to hear all about it after you are dipped in joy and covered in love. I will also pray for you being with him and being immune and stronger than to have anything bother or hurt you. You have grown and gotten stronger. Now you get to overcome your doubts and see just how strong you have become.

No matter what, life is good and after this week it will be better. Don't let him try to convince you otherwise. It is a chance for her to be with you and you with her. Believe me nothing can make things worse, only better. Enjoy.

Tired Calvin

... to be continued

Books available on AMAZON:

Rea Doren: WEBCAM GIRL

Rea Doren: TOO LATE FOR LOVE

Rea Doren: TO BE CONTINUED

Rea Doren : J'AI ENVIE DE TOI

Rea Doren: VACANCES AVEC MON SUGAR DADDY

Rea Doren: THE END

Rea Doren: POUR PAS QUE J'OUBLIE

Rea Doren : DE LA LUMIERE NAIT L'OBSCURITE

Books available soon :

Rea Doren: JOURNAL INTIME D'UNE SUGAR BABY

Rea Doren: FALLING IN LOVE

TikTok : rea_doren

Instagram : rea__doren

YouTube : rea doren

Printed by Amazon Italia Logistica S.r.l.
Torrazza Piemonte (TO), Italy

41638312R00223